The Hiawatha Man

THE HIAWATHA MAN

The Life and Work of Samuel Coleridge–Taylor

Geoffrey Self

SCOLAR
PRESS

Published by
SCOLAR PRESS
Gower House
Croft Road
Aldershot
Hants GU11 3HR
England

Ashgate Publishing Company
Old Post Road
Brookfield
Vermont 05036
U. S. A.

British Library Cataloguing in Publication data:
Self, Geoffrey
  Hiawatha Man: Life and Music of Samuel Coleridge–Taylor
  I. Title
  780.92

Library of Congress Cataloging–in–Publication data:
Self, Geoffrey.
      The 'Hiawatha' Man / Geoffrey Self.
          p.   cm.
      Includes bibliographical references, discography, and index.
      'List of works': p.
      ISBN 0–85967–983–7
1. Coleridge–Taylor, Samuel, 1875–1912. Composers — England — Biography.
I. Title.
ML410.C74S45   1995
780'. 92—dc20   94–45001
                                                                      CIP
                                                                      MN

ISBN 0–85967–983–7

Designed and set in 11 pt Dutch by Jonathan Foxwood

Printed in Great Britain by the University Press, Cambridge

CONTENTS

for Richard, Jennie, Alexander, Abaigael and Lewys

PREFACE and ACKNOWLEDGEMENTS

My earliest conscious memory of the music of Samuel Coleridge–Taylor is being set by my piano teacher to learn *Demande et Réponse* from the *Petite Suite de Concert*. To my delight, I found that its tune had long been familiar to me; although the performances usually had an anonymity, it was to be heard everywhere. It was my first 'grown–up' music. Then before this, I am told, there was a further, if slender, link. My parents, with me as a babe–in–arms, lived in a house overlooking the Bandon Hill Cemetery, Wallington, where Coleridge–Taylor is buried.

It would thus be fitting to say that my interest in him developed from an early age, but nothing so neat actually happened. I did not come across his music again, in any practical way, for many years — long after I had left Surrey and those haunts where he had once been a familiar figure. The Croydon that I knew, as a child in the 1930s, was probably not that much different from his Croydon of three decades before; certainly the fields on its outskirts had filled with semi–detached houses but, in the town itself, much was still as it would have been at the beginning of the century.

My interest was at first kindled by an amateur performance of *Hiawatha's Wedding Feast* and then fired when I subsequently conducted the same work. The music struck me then, as it does now, as astonishingly accomplished, fresh in its choral writing and masterly in its orchestration. This was in the early 1960s, when his reputation was at its lowest. Little of his considerable output was heard then, and only the *Wedding Feast* still received an occasional performance. It continued thus for many years — so that, all but forgotten, he seemed to be little more than a casualty in the history of English music. If he was mentioned at all, the question most frequently asked was: 'Isn't he the man who wrote 'Hiawatha'?' It was this question that suggested both his epitaph and the title for this book, *The 'Hiawatha' Man*.

Or so it seemed when I started working on it seven years ago. Since then, there has been a stirring of interest in his music. New recordings have appeared, including a sumptuous one of the entire *Hiawatha* Trilogy. The *Clarinet Quintet, Symphonic Variations on an African Air* and the rhapsody *The Bamboula* have all been recorded and, at the time of writing, we are promised a first commercial recording of the *Violin Concerto*. I have nevertheless decided to keep the title, since it was *The Song of Hiawatha* which first brought him fame, and which is still the best introduction to his work.

But such a title for this book also raises fundamental questions. Was he, as has been suggested, a one–work–only composer who burned out after it? That doubt is fairly easy to banish. A much more difficult question — the contemplation of which underlies much of the book — arises from the spread of his music to the United States. Here, in the early years of the new century, he was soon accorded a place in the pantheon of admired Black figures. The further questions concern his response to what was expected of him: was he totally committed to the cause of his father's race? Or was the pull of his musical training and experience just too strong ever to run in harness with the aspirations of his Black brothers?

As no diaries have been located, a present–day biographer must perforce construct his chronology from correspondence and from public records — newspapers, concert programmes and publishers' documents, for example. Fortunately, four people who knew him have left their own accounts of him. Though his daughter Avril was but a child when he died, her book covers not only his life and work but also his musical legacy to her, on which she was to build her own distinguished career. For personal reminiscences, we have his wife Jessie's 'Memory Sketch', as well as the recollections of his half–sister Marjorie, recorded verbatim by Jeffrey Green. Avril, Jessie and Marjorie all either wrote or recorded their memories many years after the composer's death, but his first biographer Berwick Sayers set to work within a few months of it, publishing his book in 1915. Inevitably his work has the disadvantages of an 'official' biography, and it includes some inaccuracies. It remains, nevertheless, an incomparable portrait of his subject, drawn from life, and any subsequent biographer must be indebted to it.

It will not pass notice that one other composer joins Coleridge–Taylor in my story from time to time. It is not that Elgar was a major musical influence — although some musical influence is there for all to hear. Rather it is that Elgar touched his life, and at one point intervened decisively. For his part, Coleridge–Taylor's life and experiences seemed often to mirror those of his elder colleague.

A biographer can hardly avoid making value–judgements on the work of his subject. I am conscious that mine may on occasion appear harsh, and can only recommend that readers hear or play as much of Coleridge–Taylor's music as they can so that they can make up their own minds. For, whatever my or anyone else's appraisal might be, one fact remains: that, during the first decade of the twentieth century, perform–ances of his music exceeded those of his British contemporaries, Elgar, Delius, Parry and Stanford. Such a man deserves a new hearing.

*

Passages quoted from Michael Kennedy, *Portrait of Elgar* (O. U. P., 1968) are reproduced by permission of Oxford University Press. Those from Percy Young, *George Grove 1820–1900* (Macmillan, 1980) are reproduced by permission of Macmillan, London, Ltd.   In a few cases, all efforts to trace possible copyright owners have been unsuccessful; where necessary, due acknowledgement will be made in any later edition.

I would like to express my gratitude to the following, all of whom helped me in the production of this book:

Pamela Blevins, Christopher Bornet, Sidney Butterworth, Millicent Chappell, Charlotte Eva, the late Martin Fogell, Spencer Freeman, Vanessa Gates, Peter Gellhorn, Rhonda Hammond, Michael Kennedy, Beverly Knight, Linette Martin, Dr Doris McGinty, C. D. Paramor, Adrian Self, Wendy Toye, The National Sound Archive, Karen A. Shaffer and The Maud Powell Foundation, Deidre Tilley and *Opera Magazine*, The School of Oriental and African Studies, The Boston Symphony Orchestra, Clare Colvin and the English National Opera Archive, Oliver Davies and the Royal College of Music Portraits Department, The Library of Congress, Yale Music Library, Jacqui Dawber and the Hallé Concerts Society, M. A. Pearman and the Trustees of the Chatsworth Settlement, Sheffield Local Studies Library, The Dorset County Library, The Royal College of Music Library, The British Library, The Cornwall County Library and its Camborne branch.

The generous help of the British Academy is gratefully acknowledged.

I am deeply indebted to Stuart Upton who prepared the List of Recordings, to Pamela Eccles who prepared the music examples, and to Martin Renshaw for his expertise and advice at all times. I am indebted, too, to Jeffrey Green, who placed his profound knowledge of Coleridge–Taylor at my disposal.

Avril Coleridge–Taylor gave me much help in the early stages of my research, and her son Nigel Dashwood has supported and encouraged my efforts throughout. Charlotte Eva read the typescript and made many helpful suggestions.

Lastly, I thank my wife Beryl, whose patience and wisdom is proverbial.

Geoffrey Self, December 1994

ILLUSTRATIONS

1. Class photograph, the British School, Tamworth Road, Croydon
2. Samuel Coleridge–Taylor in maturity, studio portrait
3. The composer's mother, Alice Evans, in old age
   (No photograph of his father has been traced.)
4. Gwendolen (Avril) and Hiawatha Coleridge–Taylor with their
   father, 1905
5. Contemporary cartoon, dating from the early performances of the
   Hiawatha Trilogy: 'A distinguished composer escaping from
   the autograph fiends'
   (Reproduced by permission of the Royal College of Music.)
6. Jessie Coleridge–Taylor, studio portrait
7. The Croydon String–Players' Club, with their conductor
8. Samuel Coleridge–Taylor, writing music at his desk
9. 'Aldwick', St Leonard's Road, Croydon — Coleridge–Taylor's last
   home; the 'Music Shed' in which he worked can be seen to the
   right
10. A page from Coleridge–Taylor's letter to Maud Powell
11. Memorial Stone, Bandon Hill Cemetery, Wallington, Surrey; the
    verses are by Noyes
12. Cartoon, inscribed by members of the Beecham Orchestra, among
    them Albert Sammons and Eugène Goossens

1 PARENTAGE

The circumstances of Samuel Coleridge–Taylor's parentage were, for many years, obscure. It had long been thought he was the child of a secret marriage between Daniel Taylor, a coloured medical student from Sierra Leone, and a young white woman named Alice Hare who lived with a family called Holmans at 15 Theobalds Road, Red Lion Square, Holborn. The obscurity concerns the identity of the woman (was she really Alice Hare?) and whether or not there had been a marriage. But there is less confusion concerning his father, so we will start with him.

By the late eighteenth century, Sierra Leone had become a magnet for freed slaves. For a few years, it was administered by the Sierra Leone Company, but in 1808 it became a colony which grew with the setting up of a naval base for operations against the slave–trade. Slaves who were found on slave–ships were given their liberty in Freetown.

Because they had been captured, enslaved, and then recaptured by the British Navy before being finally freed, they were called 'recaptives' in the colony. These recaptives — there were over six thousand of them by 1815 — had come from all over West Africa, and they settled in and around Freetown. Increasingly, black recaptives and white settlers adopted a pseudo–British way of life, and the growing prosperity of the colony led, in its capital at least, to the emergence of a black bourgeoisie. Both black and white merged into a group called the Krios, who were for a while a dominant force in Sierra Leone. This prosperous group sought to emulate the white civil servants, not least in education, where it was usual to send children back to English boarding schools.

Sierra Leone was subject to considerable missionary activity; Methodists in particular sponsored a number of able young men for a finishing education, possibly to be followed by University, in England. Daniel Peter Hughes Taylor, thought to have been born in April 1849, was the son of John Taylor, a wealthy Nigerian–born Freetown merchant and himself most probably a Krio. After attending grammar school in Sierra Leone, Daniel arrived in England in 1869 and travelled to Taunton in Somerset, where in February 1870 he registered at Wesley College (now Queen's College) as one of a number of students sponsored by the Methodist church. Records at Queen's College show him to have been twenty–one years old on entry and that he had made a three year study

1

of Greek and Latin; however, he was not good at arithmetic and had neither mastered Book One of Euclid nor had much knowledge of English grammar. It must therefore have required great tenacity and hard work to achieve a university entry by 1873. He studied medicine at King's College Hospital, London, Medical School from 1873 to 1874 (the calendars in fact list him from 1873 to 1876) and he graduated as M.R.C.S. The time–scale necessary to achieve this degree is remarkably compressed; as the failure rate is high, it is evident that Daniel Taylor was a man of exceptional determination and brilliance.

Coleridge–Taylor's half–sister, Marjorie Evans, believed that Daniel Taylor first met Alice on a professional call to minister to illness in the Holmans family at Theobalds Road. She thought that he became a frequent visitor to the Holmans' home, where he and Alice formed a relationship. A child would have been conceived at some time in December 1874. That child, christened Samuel Coleridge, was born on 15 August 1875. Both the composer's first biographer (W. Berwick Sayers) and his daughter Avril (born Gwendolen) stated that Dr Taylor practised medicine for a while in South London, and that he and Alice lived together after the birth of Samuel. Avril believed that, although Dr Taylor was at first successful as an assistant in the practice, he encountered problems when his senior left, and that those patients who had cheerfully accepted him as an assistant were not prepared to be tended by him without his white principal. Berwick Sayers wrote:

> As an independent doctor he was mistrusted. The patients fell away rapidly, Taylor's means were soon exhausted and the young man realised he was on the verge of ruin.[1]

'Being coloured, no–one trusted him, because colonial people weren't competent then,' said Marjorie Evans many years later, probably echoing Sayers. Finding little prospect of making a living in England, he left Alice and their child to return to Sierra Leone. But there are problems with this scenario: the Sierra Leone colonial Blue Book shows that Dr Taylor took up an appointment there in mid–November 1875. Since he was certainly in the colony well before this, it would hardly have afforded sufficient time for such a course of events as is suggested above. And if it is remembered that Dr Taylor's father was a wealthy man of some consequence in Sierra Leone, we might conclude that there had been pressure from his own family for him to return. For the Sierra Leone fraternity in London would have monitored the progress of the young man and reported back to his family, who may well have been dismayed at their son's involvement with a white woman, not to mention their offspring. It may be that Alice was offered the chance to go with him but she perhaps regarded the South London environment that she knew, and the Holman family that she knew, as offering more security. It is unlikely that Dr Taylor ever saw his child.

Dr Taylor remained in West Africa for the rest of his life, holding various medical appointments until his death from dysentery at the age of fifty–seven. At the time of his death, 25 August 1904, he was living in Bathurst (now Banjul) and was employed by the Gambia Medical Service as a coroner.[2] He probably had little choice but to leave Sierra Leone; by the beginning of the twentieth century, Krio influence in that country had declined to the extent that African doctors were no more acceptable there than they had been in suburban England. Indeed, by 1902, the policy in what had by then become a protectorate was to exclude African doctors from all senior official positions there.

Avril never knew Dr Taylor, but she would have drawn on her grandmother's memories for this description of him:

> He was in person short, and neat almost to dandyness and was remarkably fastidious in his tastes and appearance and was the possessor of considerable charm of manner which won acceptance for him with his professors and amongst his fellow–students.[3]

Notable about him was:

> the joyousness of his disposition, in which he continued the tradition of his race, and his buoyant good nature.[4]

But he yearned to establish a private practice; finding no satisfaction in a succession of minor official appointments,

> he seems to have been overcome in later life by disappointment.[5]

Samuel's birth certificate names his mother not as Alice Hare, but as Alice Taylor, formerly Holmans, residing at the time at 15 Theobalds Road, Red Lion Square, Holborn. The certificate thus clearly suggested that Alice Taylor was married to the named father, Daniel Hugh Taylor,[6] and was related to Benjamin Holmans. There certainly was an Alice Holmans residing at 15 Theobalds Road at the time; the assumption to be made therefore must be that Alice Taylor and Alice Holmans were one and the same.

The house seems to have been a lodging establishment since a number of families lived there. Among them were a farrier, Benjamin Holmans and his two children. The immediately–previous census return was that of 1871, four years before; this shows the Holmans family to have come from Kent.

Benjamin Holmans was born at Sandwich, and his two children at Dover. In 1871, his son John was sixteen and his daughter Alice was fourteen. No mother to the family is mentioned, yet the census differentiates between 'married' and 'widower' status. On the form, Holmans is stated to be married. It is possible that he falsified his entry to establish the legitimacy of his child or children or that he was in fact a widower, and was genuinely confused between the widower and married states — or that he was married but his wife had left him.

Who, then, was the 'Alice Hare' mentioned at the beginning of this chapter? When he wrote Coleridge–Taylor's biography in 1915, Berwick Sayers was probably unaware of the wording of his subject's birth certificate, and it was he who wrote of 'Alice Hare', describing her as a 'ladies companion' who was seventeen years of age at the time of Coleridge–Taylor's birth. The suggestion of a 'secret marriage' had its origin, too, in Sayers's book; but no record of a marriage has been found. Sayers was writing at a time when illegitimacy provoked so much opprobrium that, because his subject had become a composer of almost universal distinction, it is easy to see why conjuring up a secret marriage might have been thought necessary; at least thereby the mother and wife of the great man could hope to spare his memory from social stigma. But there was a further problem: Alice, in due course, did marry — in the early 1880s she married George Evans, and they had three children, Alice, Victor and Marjorie.

Clearly, if she had contracted a secret marriage with Dr Daniel Taylor (who did not die until 1904), her marriage to Evans would have been bigamous and the three children by him illegitimate. Equally, if there was no marriage to Dr Taylor, then her elder son Samuel was illegitimate. Hence the delicacy of Sayers's treatment of the matter.

Was he far of the mark in writing of an Alice Hare? Was his 'Alice Hare' one and the same person as Alice Taylor, née Holmans? Their ages would support this possibility, for Alice Holmans too would have been about seventeen in 1875. Here we might consider an interesting piece of evidence:[7] that of Marjorie Evans, the second daughter of Alice and George Evans. Talking in 1984, when an old lady aged eighty–eight, she said that her mother was Alice Hare Martin, born at Dover in 1856. Her mother, she said, had four children, the first of whom was Samuel Coleridge–Taylor. Marjorie herself was born in 1896, by which time her half–brother was a young man of twenty. (The Evans family did not call him Samuel, but they called him Coleridge, as did his wife Jessie.)

How did the name 'Martin' figure in her mother's name, Alice Hare Martin? Her grandmother, she tells us, was Emily Martin, 'a rather stout lady who worked as a housekeeper in Croydon and visited us from time to time ... we liked Aunt Emma's visits because she always had the odd gift for us — gold sovereigns'.[8]

'Aunt' Emma? A doubt immediately flits across the mind. But we should not discount her relationship merely because she was known as an aunt. In London, the term was and is used in many a circumstance, and to cover many a sin. It was also a term of endearment, and there is no reason to doubt Marjorie's remembering her grandmother as 'Aunt' Emma. We have to pick up crumbs of evidence; one crumb concerning Aunt Emma was that 'she always had the odd gift for us ... gold sovereigns'.[9] A sovereign, at that time, was hardly the currency of poor families. This 'Aunt' or grandmother who appeared like a guardian angel when needed was plainly a woman of substance.

Another doubt is raised when Marjorie says (as Sayers had said of Alice Hare) that her mother 'lived as a lady's companion with Mrs Holmans' for, as we have seen, there was — at any rate not in 1871 — no Mrs Holmans living at 15 Theobalds Road. We must allow the possibility that Benjamin Holmans may have re–married by 1874–5; even so, it seems unlikely that a farrier of the time would have earnings sufficient for him to employ a lady's companion. In any case, other servants would have been found more immediately useful.

Perhaps Benjamin Holmans was also doing some covering up? For the conflict of evidence at this point may just be one of name. A workable explanation might run on the following lines:

1 That Alice Hare, Alice Hare Martin and Alice Holmans were one and the same person.
2 That they were really Alice Holmans, the daughter of Benjamin Holmans and *x*.
3 That *x* was Emily Martin, née Hare.
4 That Alice was herself illegitimate.

The final piece of evidence falls into place when we consider the birth registration of a child born to Emily Ann Martin at 43 Castle Place, Dover, on 17 September 1856. That child was named Alice Hare. No father is named on the certificate, nor is any separate maiden name for the mother indicated. The inference to be drawn from this must be that Alice Hare herself was in fact illegitimate, and that Berwick Sayers had come close to the truth.

It cannot be proved, but it seems likely that Alice Holmans was in fact Alice Hare Martin. At the time of Samuel's birth she would have been a month short of her nineteenth birthday. It is probable that Benjamin Holmans was her father, and it is certain that Emily Martin was her mother. Musical evidence is tenuous and circumstantial, but Holmans was a violinist. All Alice's children, whether by Dr Taylor or by her subsequent husband George Evans, were musical. Her elder daughter, Alice Evans, was a singer; Marjorie became a piano teacher (Samuel's grandson Nigel remembers being taught by her as a child[10]); and Victor Evans was sufficiently distinguished as a viola player to play in the London Symphony Orchestra. The musical abilities of Samuel and his three step–siblings seem to have been inherited through his mother and his maternal grandfather. Alice survived her most famous son by very many years; she died in 1953 at the age of ninety–five.

In conclusion, mention must be made of a suggestion that has had some currency: that Emily may have been a member of an incognito wealthy family — possibly even of the Coleridge family. The evidence for such a link is scanty indeed, but (such as it is) it will be considered in a later chapter.

2 CHILDHOOD IN CROYDON

If any questions remain over Samuel Coleridge–Taylor's ancestry, there is no doubt over who brought him up or over those *he* regarded as father, mother, grandfather and grandmother. Marjorie Evans thought, from what she had been told by her mother, that it was highly unlikely Dr Daniel Taylor ever actually saw his son, although Alice set the boy to write to his father when he was old enough.

In terms of ability, what was the legacy of Dr Taylor to Samuel? There does seem to be an innate feeling for rhythm and improvised harmony among West Africans, and this has been more obviously apparent in times of great emotion; that engendered, for example, during the periods of slavery and enforced migration to the southern United States. Those otherwise disparate musicians, Dvorak and Delius, were profoundly impressed by their experiences of the natural music–making of the uprooted African — Delius so much so that it is no exaggeration to say that he spent the rest of his life trying to capture in his own music the heart–breaking sounds of improvised harmony heard in the distance as he sat on the verandah of his Florida hut.

Yet it is difficult to accept that Samuel's innate musical genius was the legacy of his father, for there is no evidence that his father had any particular musical ability. Musical genius needs three factors: industry, the ability to think in sound, and pure intellectual capacity. Dr Taylor was an exceptionally brilliant man: 'He was gifted with an acute, rapidly–working mind and unusual powers of assimilation',[11] and it was his intellectual ability that was inherited by his son. Clearly, too, the doctor, on the evidence of his academic achievement in so short a period, had a capacity for industry that his son Samuel also possessed to a marked degree. But in the Holmans's household there certainly was much music–making. It was Benjamin Holmans — evidently a man of some culture — who gave the young Samuel his first violin, and it was he who taught the boy the rudiments of music. Although she herself did not play, Alice liked to sing, and her daughter Marjorie said that her mother

> told her that, on the night before Samuel's birth, she was playing
> the triangle at the Holmans, to accompany the violin and piano —

'But that isn't really music making, is it?'[12]

Among the many small shops in Theobalds Road in 1875, the block in which house number 15 stood included butchers, an oilman, tobacconists, a cooper, a confectioner, a shoemaker, and two fishmongers. There was also a Music Hall. The Holmans lived above a vet's surgery, and we can suppose some correspondence of work between the vet and the farrier. Marjorie remembers her mother once sketching the house for her: it had a separate front door, iron balconies on the first floor, and two further floors above that.

It is difficult to say precisely when the Holmans family moved out from Holborn to Croydon, but we can get fairly close. The 1877 census showed no Holmans at Theobalds Road, and by 1878 the premises were demolished.

Since there is usually a lapse of time between the decision to demolish and the fact of it, it is likely that the family were given notice of the impending demolition and set about finding a new home during 1876 and 1877. While the rapidly developing network of suburban railways and public transport would not at that time have made much impact on the work of a farrier, those same railways could point in which direction a family might go.

Along the line of the chalk foothills of the North Downs, villages had grown: Cheam, Sutton, Carshalton, Wallington and Croydon. Gradually, the area between Cheam and Croydon was 'developed' with housing estates and avenues that spread outwards from each newly–built railway station. But Croydon was pre–eminent: the Surrey Iron Railway, the first of its kind in the world, had been constructed in 1799 to carry limestone and it had run from Wandsworth via Croydon to Merstham. Although the 'Grand Surrey Canal' from Rotherhithe to Portsmouth was never completed, it was constructed as far south as Croydon. There it terminated in the large basin in which now stands West Croydon Station, built by the London and Croydon Railway Company to serve the south–eastern suburban safety–valves for the teeming population of London.[13]

Today, with its tower blocks, multi–storey car parks, under–passes and fly–overs, Croydon is among the most transformed towns in the country. But, despite its proximity to the capital, it has always striven to preserve its independence, and it has a rich cultural heritage, best symbolised by the Fairfield Concert Halls. The Croydon Symphony Orchestra, on which the youthful Colin Davis and Norman Del Mar first practised their art, had few superiors among amateur orchestras in the decade or so after the Second World War. In Alan Kirby, the Croydon

Philharmonic Society had one of the few great Elgar interpreters, and it was in the late and lamented Davis Theatre that in 1946 Sir Thomas Beecham chose to present his splendid new Royal Philharmonic Orchestra.

The Croydon of the last years of the nineteenth century was, however, somewhat more 'south–suburban' in character; its attractions not so obvious when the Holmans family moved there. Life cannot have looked rosy as seen from the lodging house in Elis David Road. The family's rooms there indicated accurately their financial and social low water.

As soon as circumstances permitted, they moved away to 67 Waddon New Road, very close to the town centre. They were certainly in residence there in 1878, and Holmans remained there until 1888. The census of 1881 showed Benjamin Holmans as head of the household at Waddon New Road and, by then, Alice 'Taylor' was shown as his daughter and the young Samuel as his grandson. Benjamin had also acquired a new wife, Sarah.

At this point, the trail goes cold. The next event that can be related with any certainty is the marriage of Alice to George Evans in the early 1880s, when Samuel would have been between six and eight years old. The new family, including Samuel, moved a short distance away — still in Waddon New Road, where they lived until 1894. Samuel's step–father was a railway worker, a storeman whose work included measuring out oil. In the late nineteenth century, a staff job on the railways was seen as offering almost limitless security, if little actual wealth. While they were undoubtedly poor, the Evans family were far from being destitute. There was a regular wage packet, and Alice was spared the need to go out to work.

They could afford at least one of the symbols of status: a piano. They could keep their heads above water, but would hardly be able to cope if one of the family attempted to rise above his situation and opt for an extended education.

Little is known of George Evans, and he remains a figure in the shadows. Yet it needs only a small measure of imagination to appreciate his courage in taking on a young woman with a coloured child. Perhaps here is the place to pay tribute to someone who unobtrusively brought stability to Samuel's childhood and youth — if for no other reason than that most of *Hiawatha's Wedding Feast* was eventually written in the Evans's home.

The young Samuel was sent to the British School, Tamworth Road, in the shadow of the parish church, just across what is now the busy

A236 road. The records of the school are incomplete, but he was certainly in attendance there on 16 December 1885 when a school log–book makes reference to him. The British School movement was a legacy of the British and Foreign School Society, created in 1814 to succeed the Royal Lancasterian Society, itself formed in 1808 to promote the educational ideas of the Quaker, Joseph Lancaster. The network of British or 'Lancasterian' Schools, which grew to be country–wide, had no religious denominational leanings (apart from an antipathy to the Anglicans, who in return thought that every parish which lacked one of their own National Schools was one abandoned to the enemy) but it did require its pupils to attend a place of worship. By the 1880s, the original Lancasterian principles would have been much diluted, but something of their punishment by ridicule and reward by tangible prizes remained, and would have played a part in the formation of Samuel's personality. Parents were expected to contribute what they could financially — probably a penny or tuppence a week — and there would have been an additional list of voluntary subscribers.

At that time, the headmaster at Tamworth Road was John Drage, who must have created some kind of record for long service as a teacher at one school: he had been appointed in 1850, and retired fifty years later in 1900. Samuel told Marjorie that 'his headmaster was very strict and if you didn't behave yourself you got a clap on the head'.[14] But the boy came under more influence from his form teacher, a certain Mr Forman.

With psychology as a discipline in its infancy, the no doubt well–meaning efforts of Mr Forman can have done little to strengthen the ego of his young charge. For the boy, in Marjorie's precise description, had a 'medium light coloured skin, which looked light compared to those Africans who were quite black'.[15] And which looked dark, she might have added, when compared with that of his school–mates. For this alone, he would have been at best an object of curiosity and at worst one to be tormented among his fellow pupils.

But he played the violin, and that further set him apart. He was made to play to school visitors; even worse, he was placed on a table to lead school singing with his violin. Mr Forman also set him to make a new arrangement of the National Anthem for the school's use — and he won the singing competition, in which he offered 'Cherry Ripe'.

Croydon school children were no more or less cruel than elsewhere — that is to say, very cruel. On one occasion, they set fire to his crinkly hair, to see if it would burn. Even apart from the intentional physical torture by the children and the unintentional mental torture by the teacher, such early exposure of a child already set apart by colour in an almost totally white environment must have contributed to the patho–logical shyness which was a primary characteristic of Coleridge–Taylor in early manhood. But Holmans had done his work thoroughly; the makings of a musician were established well before the end of the child's first decade.

Some years after Coleridge–Taylor's death, the composer Arthur Hatchard was interviewed for an article in *Radio Times* for 20 November 1925. It appeared that he also gave the boy some musical tuition, and he showed the interviewer (K. P. Hunt) the programme of a concert given in 1886 at the Croydon Y.M.C.A. at which the eleven–year–old Coleridge–Taylor played his violin: he contributed Sullivan's *The Lost Chord* and a melody which he had composed himself. His performance of the Sullivan piece received more applause than that for his own melody, with the result that he promptly tore up his own effort. It would seem that sensitivity to a luke–warm reception (a sensitivity that recurred in later life) was early in evidence. Nevertheless, those whom fortune favours are marked out from the start, and Coleridge–Taylor's prospects improved with the appearance of two men in his life who were to help to direct it purposefully along its creative path.

Berwick Sayers tells an attractive story to account for this develop–ment: in south–east London (or, more accurately, north–east Surrey, as it was then) each childhood pursuit and pastime still had its due season. There was, for example, the season for playing conkers, and another time for playing marbles. One day, while looking out from his window, Joseph Beckwith saw a coloured boy, probably on his way home from school, playing marbles in the gutter. There was nothing unusual about this, but what really attracted his attention was that this particular boy had a violin case tucked under his arm. Beckwith was a professional musician — a violin teacher who was also conductor of the orchestra at the Grand Theatre in south–east Croydon. He made the acquaintance of the boy, and from that chance encounter grew a teacher and pupil relationship which lasted some seven years. More than that, Coleridge–Taylor in due course repaid his teacher by teaching Beckwith's son in his turn. The story is neatly concluded: when Coleridge–Taylor some years later became conductor of the Handel Society, he appointed that son, A. R. C. Beckwith, as his orchestral leader. But it must be said that neither Marjorie nor her mother believed the story of the marbles.

From an early age, expression through music, whether by playing it or scribbling it down, was as natural to the boy as breathing. Another story, that 'whenever anyone gave him a penny, he would run to a (music) shop and buy a sheet of manuscript paper and write music',[16] may or may not be true, but it testifies that those who saw him perceived the intensity of the music within him.

One of those who certainly perceived his passion for music was Herbert A. Walters, the second major influence on Coleridge–Taylor at this time. Colonel Walters was formerly the commander of the 4th Battalion of The Queen's Royal West Surrey Regiment; he then went on to serve in the 'territorial army' of the day, and was in due course awarded a Volunteer's Decoration for his twenty years' service with them. Herbert Walters (1863–1934) was some twelve years older than Coleridge–Taylor, and was only in his early twenties when they first met in 1884 or 1885. A man of moderately wealthy means, who derived his income from his business as a London silk merchant, he illustrates all that was admirable in the Victorian tradition of service in voluntary and charitable causes. He was a governor of, and subscriber to, the Tamworth Road British School; and he was choirmaster of St George's Presbyterian Church (now the Freemasons' Hall). Within that phil–anthropic Victorian tradition, Walters's interest in his choir went well beyond music. His concern for the boys was paternalistic: he cared for them and, where he could, helped them to secure work. He certainly came across Coleridge–Taylor at the Tamworth Road School, although Avril suggests[17] he knew of the boy before this, and indeed may have had some acquaintance with Dr Taylor. Whatever the truth of this, all the privileged young soldier's charitable instincts were aroused by the seemingly impossible odds stacked against a coloured boy whose talent was, of all things in philistine England, only for music. Further, if Avril is right, then in all probability he would have known of the boy's illegitimacy.

Walters, says Avril, became *de facto*, if not *de jure*, guardian to the young Coleridge–Taylor. Probably it was Walters who arranged the violin lessons with Beckwith. Nor is there reason to doubt the gratitude and devotion of the young man to his patron: one of his earliest exercises in composition was a *Te Deum* dedicated to Walters, as was the anthem *Break Forth into Joy*, written in his sixteenth year. The *Te Deum* is lost; according to Sayers, it dated from 1890. Walters said that, although it contained some harmony mistakes, it was admirably conceived.

Coleridge–Taylor joined Walters first in St George's Choir; then, when Walters left for St Mary Magdalene, Addiscombe (where his brother was assistant organist), he took his star singer with him. The Colonel may perhaps be forgiven for the kidnapping; the perfect voice of a choirboy was as much a pearl as the skills of the family cook — and as liable to be enticed away.

Initially a treble, that voice settled into a pure alto. Coleridge–Taylor was the soloist in a choir of some repute, for it was in demand to perform over a wider area than would normally be expected of a church group. There is, for example, a report of the young alto singing Gounod's *There is a Green Hill Far Away* at a Presbyterian meeting in the Exeter Hall[18] for which 'the audience rose and cheered him'.[19] At the time of this event, Coleridge–Taylor was in his thirteenth year. As a violinist he was also Beckwith's protegé, and at the age of twelve was able to play brilliantly. He appeared in April 1888 at the Croydon Public Hall to play Dancla's *Air Varié*; and at Carshalton, according to the local paper, his performance was encored and 'fairly brought down the house'. It is clear that, whether in school or in choir, the boy was seen as exceptional, but there was an inevitable price to be paid. Apart from the incident of hair–burning, nothing in the way of hard evidence has survived of his relationships with his fellow scholars or choristers, save his nick–name. That nick–name was 'Coalie', one that seems to have been a simple diminutive rather than a reference to his colour: the family called him 'Coleridge', so 'Coly' or 'Colie', spelled thus, would carry no overtones of racism.

But colour was difficult to ignore when it came to deciding a career. There had been precedents of coloured men following successful performing careers in the music profession, but few if any instances of coloured music students at the colleges. Moreover, in Samuel Coleridge–Taylor the circumstances of colour, upbringing and education had conspired to create a shrinking, timid young man hardly suited to the robust conditions prevailing then, as now, in the music profession. The Evans family, itself growing, would not in any case have been able to support a student. The problem therefore fell into the hands of Colonel Walters; even he seems to have had some doubts, as he first thought of apprenticing the boy to the piano trade. Something seems to have con–vinced him that his charge deserved better; perhaps it was that *Te Deum*.

The Victorian ethic required the fortunate to extend a hand to those less well endowed socially. Even so, the colonel could hardly have conceived of stiffer challenges either to his own resources or (even greater) to the character of his protegé. Perhaps there was an element of Shaw's Pygmalion in his make–up; could a poor, illegitimate coloured boy be transformed by him to adorn the pinnacle of the art they shared? Having methodically visited and appraised the available London music colleges and conservatories, he approached the recently–established Royal College of Music. Here first he had to overcome the doubts of the director, Sir George Grove. Since the boy's talent was self–evident, his

doubts were concerned with how a coloured student would survive —
both at the College and onwards into the profession. One passage in
Sayers's book is revealing in this respect:

> Children of negro blood ... usually showed a brilliant early promise
> which always suffered absolute arrest before they reached
> manhood.[20]

But Grove was a remarkable man whose extensive interests already
encompassed a more than ordinary knowledge of and sympathy with
African coloured people. As a child, he had been a pupil at the African
Academy, founded by Zachary Macaulay, a former governor of Sierra
Leone. Nor was he unaware of the racial situation in the U.S.A. — his
nephew, Arthur Bradley, had given him an article in *Macmillan's
Magazine* entitled 'A Peep at the Southern Negro' which he found to be
'a horrifying exposition of the principles of Southern Society'.[21]

Coincidentally, but interestingly in view of the fact that Coleridge–
Taylor would set the work of both poets, Grove had in 1878 met
Longfellow and was well–read in the work of Samuel Taylor Coleridge.

Walters made the financial commitment, and Grove the social and
musical one. At the age of fifteen, Samuel Coleridge–Taylor was en–
rolled at the Royal College of Music for the Christmas term of 1890.

3 AT THE ROYAL COLLEGE OF MUSIC

London has been fortunate in the diversity of its music schools and academies, each of which has developed an individual tradition which marks and stamps its students. The Royal College of Music, set in the sober surroundings of South Kensington, reflected the influence of four men: Sullivan, Grove, Parry and Stanford. The R.C.M. started life as the National Training School for Music; its original premises — the ornate building which until quite recently housed the Royal College of Organists (to the right of the Royal Albert Hall as it is approached from the Albert Memorial) — formed a part of the pattern of museums, institutes and public buildings which today are the most tangible legacy, in its zeal for high moral and worthy purpose, of the Great Exhibition of 1851 and of Albert, the Prince Consort. Arthur Sullivan, the first Director of the Training School, brought to it his experience as a composer of oratorios, hymns and — perhaps less welcome to its founding fathers — his work in the 'tainted' world of operetta. Under his successor, Sir George Grove, the establishment took on its title of Royal College of Music in 1883.

As a civil engineer, Grove had designed lighthouses; as a music–ologist he had already published the great dictionary of music which still bears his name. Given his academic background, it was natural that he would recruit two of the most distinguished musicians of the time to his staff: Hubert Parry and Charles Stanford.

Parry and Stanford would in due course become Professors of Music at Oxford and at Cambridge respectively, and would thereby forge a formidable bond between Grove's fledgeling College and the two senior universities. Of these three figures, it was Stanford who was to have the most marked effect on British music of the first half of the twentieth century, if for no other reason than that a list of composers whom he taught reads like a roll–call of the most distinguished and best–known: Holst, Vaughan Williams, Howells, Bliss, Ireland, Gurney, and Goossens. All Stanford's pupils had memories of the irascible Irish–man's teaching methods — or lack of them. Most remember his phrase: 'It won't do, me boy'. A crude approach, perhaps, and yet it had the merit of making his charges constantly review and revise their work in search of perfection. Although he wrote 'Irish Rhapsodies' and used

Irish tunes, Stanford's own work was rooted in the European mainstream, especially as represented by Brahms. Somehow, the characteristics of that mainstream — a secure technique, harnessed to a high aesthetic purpose — were passed on, so that there is a family likeness, however faint, which binds the R.C.M. composers together; one which is perhaps more apparent if it is compared with the Royal Academy's composers.

But the young Coleridge–Taylor was not immediately to be admitted to the presence of Stanford; he was not, in 1890, a pianist. Despite such examples as Berlioz, it would not have been thought possible — as far as Stanford was concerned, at any rate — to be a composer without keyboard skills. Fifteen, too, was a rather earlier age than usual for a new student. We may picture him turning up at the College that autumn, clutching his violin: an under–sized young man with somewhat over–long arms, very thin, with a large head covered in profuse short curly hair. Also arriving for the first time but unknown to him was Ralph Vaughan Williams, rather older at eighteen.

Grove had allocated him to Henry Holmes for violin, to Algernon Ashton for the all–important piano, to Charles Wood for harmony and to Walter Parratt for 'music class'. Henry Holmes (1839–1905), a violinist who aspired also to composition, was later to leave the College under a cloud of scandal. Grove at first objected to him lecturing 'his girl pupils not only on Atheism and Socialism — but on other matters which no man ought to talk to any woman about ...',[22] but worse was to follow: when Holmes was accused of 'enticing to commit the grossest immorality with his female pupils', Grove had to forbid him from enter-ing the College.[23]

The Irishman Charles Wood (1866–1926) succeeded Stanford in 1924 as Professor at Cambridge, but survived him by only two years. He is remembered today for a handful of fine anthems which may still be heard gracing cathedral services. Walter Parratt (1841–1924), himself the son of an organist, was one of the most distinguished organists of his day. In addition to his teaching at the R.C.M., he was the organist of St George's Chapel, Windsor Castle, from 1882 until his death, and was the Professor of Music at Oxford from 1908 until 1918. Algernon Ashton (1859–1937) was one of the great characters of the R.C.M. A composer, pianist, and letter–writer of near–professional stature, his boast was that he had, in a period of twenty–five months, succeeded in getting 656 different letters published in the press. Nor did his achievement end there. In 1932, he announced that he had completed 'twenty–four string quartets in all major and minor keys ... without the slightest hope or prospect of having one of them performed, let alone published'. Sadly, these are now lost. There can be few more disgracefully neglected composers than Ashton, from whose huge output discerning critics including Harold Truscott and Gerald Abraham have singled out eight piano sonatas and certain of his chamber music for particular commendation.

Coleridge–Taylor showed an antipathy towards Parratt's music class and was constantly reprimanded for missing it. In December 1891, for example, Parratt reported his attendance as being 'very irregular', in response to which Sir George Grove fired a shot across the bows: 'Why this irregularity at music class? Please let me never have to complain again'.

Why would the young man, so zealous in every other respect, risk displeasure by missing this class? Probably because, possessed of an acutely sensitive ear, he saw no need for it. But it may also have been because it was a *class* which necessitated a contact with fellow students from which, at this stage, he shrank. There can be little question that the two factors of colour and social class, accompanied by the stigma of poverty, were largely responsible for this. Prejudice for reasons of colour had not, in the 1890s, grown to the extent it is present today; covert anti–semitic sentiments were probably then more common. Although frequently to be met with in sea ports, dark–coloured citizens were still comparatively few and were consequently perceived as objects of curiosity rather than of competition. But, from the point of view of such an 'object', the attentions of his fellow students would have been an ordeal.

In any case, the question of his 'class status' in society may well have been a much more serious problem for Coleridge–Taylor. The term 'working class' may be virtually redundant now but in the late nineteenth century it had real implications: for obvious economic reasons, working–class children rarely contemplated a musical career. Those that did would aspire no further than to secure work as executants in poorly rewarded orchestras. In the provinces, working–class music meant the works brass band or the choral society. For a child of such a background to go to a college to learn music was rare; for such a child to go to a college to learn composition was unheard–of. Elgar could not manage it, and the bitterness he felt at the consequential divisions between himself and the men of higher social station who could afford this education was never to leave him.

That other working–class composers of the period are so few and far between underlines the point. There were, for instance, Joseph Parry — sent to study by the collective efforts of a socially–responsible Welsh mining community — Havergal Brian, Henry Coward and Rutland

Boughton. Perhaps more than the other arts, musical composition in Britain was the preserve of the middle and upper classes until 1945. Class, poverty and colour; all these conspired to isolate Coleridge–Taylor in his new microcosm — the Royal College of Music.

All work other than in the music class was done on a one–to–one basis; he could cope with this and therefore his progress was certain. Particularly striking was his keyboard development. 'A mere beginner', remarked Ashton in his report of December 1890. But just two terms later, in July 1891, Ashton was commending him as 'one of my most satisfactory pupils'. Even so, in July 1892, Grove pointed out that his 'fingering on the piano seems to want attention', and a few months later he wrote to Colonel Walters that his protegé needed to work harder at the piano: 'piano is all–important for a composer'. The remarkable thing is how proficient Coleridge–Taylor actually became as a pianist. While he himself deprecated his keyboard skill, he was considered a good accompanist and — most remarkable for one coming so late to the instrument — it is on record that he managed to play much of so taxing a work as Schumann's *Carnaval*.[24] William J. Read heard him play it, and said that the florid bits did not seem to trouble him: 'It was the manner in which a great composer would play, directing one's attention to the beauty of the tones he was producing'.

Attendance at the music class went from bad to worse and, by 1892, Grove was admitting defeat. Coleridge–Taylor was allowed to drop this and his violin study, Grove nevertheless urging him to 'attend to scales in violin'.

Grove knew of his charge's aspiration to compose; hence his comment on the importance of keyboard skills for a composer. But the publication by Novello in 1891 of an anthem, *In Thee, O Lord*, must have struck him as a remarkable achievement for a sixteen–year old, and must have been a key factor in the change of course now sanctioned.

The anthem (for S.A.T.B. and organ) does not attempt a great deal, but it is well–shaped. It is evidence of the choral diet with which Coleridge–Taylor had been long familiar during his continuing singing career with Colonel Walters: a diet in which Mendelssohn and S. S. Wesley represented the very best quality, but which tailed off through the lesser Victorian favourites. Already present in his music is a sweet harmonic chromaticism: a characteristic which, at its worst corrosively weakening, he would eventually contain but never entirely banish.

In Thee, O Lord was followed in the next year by four more anthems. Of these, it seems likely that the Christmas piece *Break Forth Into Joy* pleased its composer the most, since this is the only one to bear a dedication — an expression of gratitude to Herbert Walters. The music has a robust, rugged quality, and within a small space it achieves much variety of texture: a tenor solo, separate passages for men and boys, and a concluding chorale. *O Ye That Love the Lord* makes no attempt to escape from Mendelssohn's influence, but it is well-structured and the writing for voices, even at this early stage, is exemplary. *The Lord is My Strength* covers much the same ground as *Break Forth*, but is inferior to it because of a weaker chorale. But all of these, and the fifth anthem *Lift Up Your Heads*, are well above the average offerings of other contemporary anthem-mongers.

Publication of these pieces marked the beginning of Coleridge-Taylor's relationship with the house of Novello. This publisher had pioneered the production of cheap octavo editions of choral music, and had virtually cornered a huge market which ranged from small church choirs to large choral societies. Novello's ubiquitous brown-and-buff copies were produced in great quantities so that they facilitated the promotion of choral singing as a cheap and popular pastime. For a composer, therefore, to be taken up by Novello ensured publicity for him and easy access by his public to his music. By the standards of the time, Novello's business was not ungenerous; but if a work really 'took off', the composer would not necessarily share with his publisher in its success.

4 STANFORD'S TEACHING

Coleridge–Taylor was judged ready to join Stanford at the beginning of the 1892 Michaelmas term. The relationship which now began was to last until Coleridge–Taylor's death, and was one of the most important in his life. He trusted Stanford and his judgement totally — a trust which is the more noteworthy when it is remembered how many did not. He would not hesitate to destroy anything which found no favour with Stanford; no instance is recorded of his even attempting to defend such a work. Perhaps he did realise that, as a composer, Stanford was not of the first rank, but he would stoutly maintain that this was because Stanford had too many calls on his time for true concentration.

He recognised, too, the splendid craftsmanship which was the hallmark of Stanford's work. For his part, writing after Coleridge–Taylor's death, Stanford emphasised the remarkable flow and brilliance of the young man's ideas; 'but he seemed to lack the power of sustaining them, with the result that there was too much repetition in his work'. Stanford considered that the lack of sustaining power was a racial defect — a defect of the coloured races. Ironically enough, this was also to be a recurring criticism of *English* music in the early twentieth century, one which even Elgar did not escape.

But Stanford was no racialist. There seems no reason to doubt a story that he overheard the young Coleridge–Taylor suffering deroga–tory remarks on account of his colour, and that he thereupon reassured the victim that he had more music in his little finger than his tormentor had in his whole body. Stanford also noted a quick wit, a retentive memory and a sure dramatic sense. As with Elgar (and perhaps Stanford himself) it would be Coleridge–Taylor's misfortune to be working in England at a time when dramatic and operatic opportunities were still largely only to be found on the continent, with the result that those composers who lacked the time, energy and financial resource to storm European opera houses had to channel their dramatic inspirations into that sterile form, the cantata so vociferously demanded by choral societies, festivals and publishing houses.

Stanford's contention that his pupil worked best under supervision seems to suggest that Coleridge–Taylor lacked self–criticism and that Stanford believed that the best works were written under his personal direction. Indeed, a strong case for this can be made out if one takes into account student works such as the *Clarinet Quintet* and the *Symphony*. By 1892, when Stanford first met him, Coleridge–Taylor was still timid to the point of actual terror and was wanting in independence.

Gradually, he was to overcome these handicaps, but the struggle involved can only be guessed at. One factor in this struggle was his growing friendship with a fellow student William Yeates Hurlstone. A year younger than Coleridge–Taylor, Hurlstone suffered much ill–health and was destined for an even shorter life–span, dying at the age of thirty in 1906. Coleridge–Taylor and Hurlstone had much in common; they both spent most of their lives in the Croydon area, and travelled up to London from the stations at West Croydon and South Norwood respectively. Each had a patron — Hurlstone's was Captain A. S. Beaumont, at whose South Norwood Park home he would take part in the 'at home' chamber music parties that were a feature of so much of north–east Surrey's cultural life. Both students were poor, and they would attempt to relieve their condition by constant overwork: teaching, conducting, 'hack' arranging ... and yet more teaching.

Hurlstone was regarded as Stanford's best, and perhaps his favour–ite, pupil. He and Coleridge–Taylor together came to be considered by their peers as the two brightest young stars at the College. Their status acquires the more prestige when it is remembered that their con–temporaries included Gustav Holst and Ralph Vaughan Williams. Hurlstone's drudgery looked set to end when in 1905 he joined the staff of the R.C.M., but he lived to enjoy this small security for only a few months before chronic asthma finally overcame him. Sir Adrian Boult thought that his death deprived English music of one of its greatest hopes, but it must be said that stylistically his music is rooted in the dying 'European' tradition which Holst and Vaughan Williams would throw off.

The dominant influence in Hurlstone's work is that of Brahms, whose motivic construction techniques he thoroughly assimilated. This can be seen to best effect in such a work as his *Sonata in D* for 'cello and piano — a masterly piece for a young man to have written. While there is no evidence that Stanford consciously moulded his pupils in the image of his own idol, Brahms, the dreaded condemnation 'damned ugly' applied by him to Vaughan Williams's early efforts to break away from Austro–German influence do not seem to have been inflicted on either Hurlstone or Coleridge–Taylor, neither of whom was interested in change. Vaughan Williams's early attempts at assimilating English folk song into his music would have been meaningless to the urban and suburban Coleridge–Taylor.

'Brahms for Hurlstone' and 'Dvorak for Coleridge–Taylor'; the two young men would endlessly discuss their mentors' respective merits on the trains to Victoria Station. Fritz Hart (1874–1949) would be with them and, as is usually the case, they probably learned more from each other than from their tutors. But, for Coleridge–Taylor, there was a more crucial benefit; it was Hurlstone and Hart who enabled him to break out of his social isolation. Much as he loved his mother and her growing family, and much as he respected his step–father, there could be little real understanding at the family hearth of what he aspired to do and of the awesome problems facing him. Through Hurlstone and Hart, and under the baleful yet basically benevolent eye of Stanford, he would painfully but steadily acquire confidence and poise.

During the winter of 1892–3, he worked on quietly and was rewarded in the early spring with an R.C.M. scholarship in composition and so was given a little financial relief. Did the extra money enable him to attend any concerts or operas? Did he go across the road to the Royal Albert Hall to hear the Royal Choral Society, or to the Sunday afternoon organ recitals which you could attend for only threepence? August Manns's Saturday afternoon concerts at the Crystal Palace would have been conveniently close to home; Edward and Caroline Alice Elgar went there quite often in 1889–90 when they were living in Norwood. The 'Proms' started in 1895 at The Queen's Hall in central London, but this would be out of the way for a student from south–east London. The 1890s were rich years for continental visitors to London, among them Saint–Säens and Tschaikowsky (Stanford being instrumental in inviting them) and Puccini, who came to his *Manon Lescaut* at Covent Garden. Dvorak came on a number of occasions, and it is possible that Coleridge–Taylor was present at some of his concerts.

But poverty would have constrained him, and in any case his musical world was still Croydon rather than London. There, on 9 October 1893, the small Public Hall was taken for a concert probably intended to display the achievements of his first year's work as a composition student. It is not clear if this was done on his own initiative or if he was prompted by Colonel Walters; the Walters family certainly had a part in it, for the songs in the programme were accompanied by the Colonel's brother, E. Stanley Walters. The concert would have been a daunting prospect for any eighteen year old, but it must have marked an important point in the continuing struggle of a timid youth towards gaining social confidence. For this concert, the services of Somerset–born clarinettist Charles Draper (1869–1952), just then starting out upon what was to become a distinguished career, were enlisted, together with a string quartet led by Jessie Grimson, who herself achieved distinction as one of the first woman violinist members of Henry Wood's Queen's Hall orchestra. Ethel Winn sang a group of songs which included settings of *The Broken Oar* and *The Arrow and the Song* (both by Longfellow) and *Solitude* (by Byron). The Byron song was published posthumously in 1918 by Augener; *The Arrow and the Song* was assigned to Augener as one of a group of six songs which remain in manuscript.[25] *The Broken Oar* has not been traced.

Since *The Arrow and the Song* dates back at least to 1893, it is possible that the others in this group do also. Together with *Solitude*, they would be Coleridge–Taylor's earliest extant songs. Musical evidence is inconclusive, but it may be taken into account here: while the influence of Schubert is evident in places, that of Dvorak is not. The effect of his introduction to Dvorak's work becomes marked in the later music of 1893; that it is not present in these songs suggests that they belong to the earlier months of that year.

It is puzzling that, once having purchased them, Augener did not print these songs. They are an interesting group, in some ways superior to much of his later song–writing, abounding as they do in pregnant accompaniment figures and striking melody. It is in their freshness of inspiration and deft accompaniments that their quality lies: such lines as those of Longfellow in *The Arrow and the Song*, hackneyed even then, prompt a joyous response:

Ex. 1: The Arrow and the Song

Even now it might be worth the while of the assignees (now Stainer and Bell) to look again at these manuscript songs and to print them.

The concert in Croydon was to have included the first performance of a *Sonata in F minor* for clarinet and piano, but in the event the first and last movements were omitted. To make weight, a minuet and trio from a *Sonata in C minor* for piano were substituted. Sadly, both sonatas are lost, although it is not altogether beyond possibility that they may be found — other works thought until very recently to have been lost have re–appeared. One of these is the *Piano Quintet in G minor* — the major work in the concert.

Whether or not Colonel Walters intended to astonish his friends it is impossible to say, but the reviewer in the *Croydon Advertiser* (14 October 1893) was continually 'astonished' and, with the admirable etiquette of the times, he not once mentioned the composer's colour.

The movement from the *Clarinet Sonata in F minor* which was played 'astonished' the audience, 'being beautifully worked out from beginning to end'. They were again 'astonished' at the *Piano Quintet*:

> Mr Coleridge–Taylor seems quite original in his ideas, the work being full of beautiful characters. Indeed, one could not help being astonished at the work of a young man of but few years experience in the musical art, the minuet being full of beautiful melody. From a musical point of view, the concert was an entire success.

The composer counted this *Piano Quintet* as his opus 1. A big work in four movements, its ideas display a mastery of texture and a remarkable energy — and even the latent savagery that his reviewers claimed to see in much of his music of this time:

Ex. 2: Piano Quintet, allegro con moto

The second movement is an impassioned Larghetto with an ornate piano part — an eloquent testimony, since Coleridge–Taylor played it at the performance, of the progress he had made towards mastering the instrument. He loved the music of Schubert and from it he had learned how to evolve interesting accompanimental figures. But now the music of Dvorak was beginning to bite. We might be forgiven for thinking that there is an obvious debt to the *'New World' Symphony*, were it not for the fact that the *Symphony* was not heard here until June 1894:

Ex. 3: Piano Quintet, Larghetto

The third movement is a scherzo; if it has an ancestry, this is to be found in Dvorak's music, perhaps in the corresponding movement of the *Symphony no. 8 in G* which he was to arrange for violin and piano a short while after, for Novello to publish in 1896.

Ex. 4: Piano Quintet, scherzo

Its Trio provides a melody of contrasting innocence and simplicity:

Ex. 5: Piano Quintet, Trio

which in the last movement is recycled, to provide a fugue subject:

Ex. 6: Quintet, Vivace from Finale

Despite the occasional miscalculation, and some imperfections of technique, the *Quintet* is a very considerable first opus. Well may it have caused astonishment.

Three other works appear to date from 1893; in that year Coleridge–Taylor sold a *Suite de Pièces* for violin and piano (or organ) to the firm of Schott. Nothing could be more marked than the distinction he made between the serious chamber music written for the College and the light salon music he now began to manufacture for commercial purposes. The composition of light music is an honourable calling; Edward German and Eric Coates achieved success time after time with sharply–characterised scores marked by instantly memorable melody. Elgar managed to suffuse even his light music with the melancholy tinge which is the hallmark of his greatest work; as a hearing of, say, his *Chanson de Matin* will confirm. Coleridge–Taylor's earliest light music is often bland and insipid; its melody does not always deliver the memorable phrase. But he was young (eighteen in 1893) and with experience his work was to acquire a point and incisiveness to rival both Eric Coates and Edward German.

Of the four movements of the *Suite de Pièces*, the opening Pastorale is the best, although its rhythm is impeded in the central section by a clumsy left–hand piano part. The Cavatina is of interest because it seems reminiscent of Dvorak's *'Cello concerto*:

Ex. 7: Suite de Pièces, Cavatina

Just as with the Larghetto of the *Quintet*, it is another instance of empathy with Dvorak's idiom, for the suite was written some months before the first performance in Britain of Dvorak's *Concerto*.

Also dating from 1893 are the *Nonet in F minor* and the *Trio in E Minor* for violin, cello and piano; the manuscripts of both of these works, long believed to have been lost, are in the library of the Royal College of Music. Most of Coleridge–Taylor's early chamber works received performances at the College, but no performance of the *Trio* has been traced. The *Trio*'s movements are marked 'moderato/allegro', 'allegro leggiero' (scherzo), and 'con furiant' (finale). 'Con furiant' is further evidence of the composer's love and admiration for Dvorak, but the first movement, *Allegro*, seems more reminiscent of Mendelssohn:

Ex. 8: Trio in E minor, allegro con moto

Further into the movement there are moments of real passion all too rare in the later music:

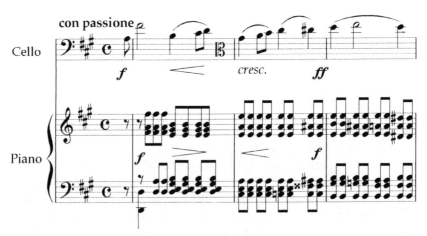

Ex. 9: Trio in E minor, con passione

The extant manuscript has no slow movement — nor, indeed, does it exhibit any evidence that one has been lost. The Scherzo seems rather like an Austrian Ländler; indeed, the contrasting central episode is curiously Mahler–like:

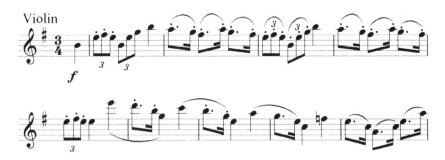

Ex. 10: Trio in E minor, scherzo

The 'Con Furiant' concludes a work of striking energy with an apparently inexhaustible flow of ideas.

The quality of the work accomplished in 1893 earned him a glowing report: 'one of my cleverest pupils', enthused Ashton. But overcoming the technical problems of playing the piano and writing idiomatically for it are two different things. As with Elgar, Coleridge–Taylor was never to achieve a full understanding of the nature of the piano, and his writing for it would often sound 'thick'. Stanford himself was no paragon in this matter, as can be heard in, for example, his piano *Preludes*. However, in every other respect Stanford was a master, who insisted on the importance of the craft of composing in the sense of the knitting together of musical textures. Holst had joined Stanford's class in May 1893 and had admired Stanford's capacity for never being at a loss for a musical example with which to illustrate his principles. Not that he taught composition as a matter of following rules; indeed, Holst was grateful to Stanford for having been taught to be self–critical. For his part, Coleridge–Taylor relied perhaps too much on Stanford's opinion. Stanford himself always thought his pupil insufficiently self–reliant in this respect.

In 1894, the Evans family moved house to Holmesdale Road, South Norwood, and they took Coleridge–Taylor with them. Their stay there was short and they soon moved again to Fernham Road. His position, as step–son and aspiring musician, could hardly have been easy. Because their neighbours objected to the piano, he could not play it in the evenings. In any case, as one of a growing family in a small house, he could have had little privacy. Of general irritation to everyone at Holmesdale Road, but a particular nuisance to a musician, was the noise from the building site as the north side of the road was 'developed'. It was an under–privileged domicile for, despite assistance from Colonel Walters, it was a hardship to keep a young man at college. Inevitably, too, a cultural gap was growing between the student and his step–father. George Evans would refer to him with obvious irony as 'my lord'; the piano, which in many modest homes would echo to hymn tunes but here produced no more than a composer's tinkerings and try–overs, was called 'the box of strings'.

There is no evidence that his mother and step–father attended his concerts; but some years after his death, his mother did go to see the staged *Hiawatha* at the Royal Albert Hall. He certainly valued his mother's opinion:

> Before he was married, Coleridge used to play ideas to mother on our piano. Mother often told me that she would be making lunch, and would have flour all over her hands when he would ask her to come to listen to his latest idea.[26]

Coleridge–Taylor unintentionally exacerbated the situation by the *persona* he attempted to project. Sporting a stick, he would move quickly and nervously. So too would he talk — quickly and nervously — but nevertheless with an authoritative manner. The scurrying dark figure, dressed invariably in black and capped with a broad–rimmed felt hat, was naturally conspicuous; but his patched trousers were eloquent of financial challenge.

By the end of the spring term, 1894, Stanford was beginning to realise that his pupil was out of the ordinary. The report he wrote in March that year speaks of 'infinite pains' and 'plenty of spontaneity'.

The summer term saw a performance of the other chamber work completed the previous year: the *Nonet in F minor*. The score bears the tag 'Gradus ad Parnassum'. The *Nonet* received its first and probably only performance at Alexandra House, in a concert on 5 July 1894 by College students. The composer found himself unable to face the warm reception which greeted the work, and he fled from the room. Sir George Grove, in his last few days as Director, retrieved him to even greater applause. The approval of the audience was reflected in *The Musical Times* for August 1894:

> Its themes are fresh and vigorous, and their treatment proves that the writer has learned to compose with freedom and to treat with skill. The *Scherzo* is unquestionably the most striking movement and few would guess it to be the work of one still a student ...

Coleridge–Taylor seems to have found the four–movement convention adequate for his needs; consequently his music at this time is rarely adventurous in form, but he could certainly be adventurous in his choice of instruments.

The *Nonet* is scored for oboe, clarinet, bassoon, horn, violin, viola, 'cello, bass and piano; in effect, an orchestra. With these forces he displays an almost inexhaustible resourcefulness in varying the musical textures. Even more remarkable, given the slender nature of so much of the later music by which he is chiefly known today, is the cornucopia of ideas he displays, not to speak of his skill in developing them. True, Dvorak is inescapable:

Ex. 11: Nonet in F minor, first movement

but from this opening is fashioned a sturdy sonata–form movement, even if the model's frequently–observed reluctance to come to a conclusion is also emulated.

Sometimes Coleridge–Taylor seems unable to identify and reject an inferior inspiration; but when the target is really hit, as it is in the second movement, his gift for melody is undeniable:

Ex. 12: Nonet in F minor, second movement

This harmonically–derived melody sustains itself by sequence, but the sequences are balanced with such subtlety that the listener is hardly aware of them. It was of this movement that Grove remarked, 'he will never write a good slow movement until he has been in love'. (Grove may have objected to the behaviour of Henry Holmes, but he was himself susceptible to the appeal of some of his female students.) The third movement is a scherzo, a goblinesque creation for which there is no obvious ancestry:

Ex. 13: Nonet in F minor, third movement

To conclude the work there is an Allegro Vivace, in the major home key, perhaps not on the same level as the earlier movements because its musical ideas are inferior. Taken as a whole, though, the *Nonet* maintains the standards of an 'astonishing' student.

In 1894, the Royal College of Music moved into its new premises in Prince Consort Road, and in the process it acquired a new Director, Hubert Parry, universally liked and admired as one of music's gentlemen. For a number of years after his death, Parry suffered from such neglect that hardly more than two hymn tunes (his setting of *Jerusalem* and the use of his music from *Judith* for Whittier's poem 'Dear Lord and Father') and his magnificent *At a Solemn Music* ('Blest Pair of Sirens') were heard with any frequency. Today, Parry's orchestral music is increasingly being recorded and is of such quality as to suggest that the time is right for a re–appraisal of his choral work.

Parry continued Grove's support for Coleridge–Taylor. He was now assigned to Walter Alcock to learn the organ, but this was not an instrument with which he felt any affinity; for him, it was 'mechanical and soul–less'. Works for organ were not to figure much in his catalogue of compositions, but he probably thought that proficiency at the organ console might be useful in earning a living.

He was reading widely. Longfellow attracted him — but then there was a vogue for Longfellow's poetry. J. G. Lockhart is little read now, but Coleridge–Taylor had a fondness for his work and set some of his lyrics. From his *Spanish Ballads* an attractive poem was taken and made into a kind of operatic Scena. The last months of 1894 were occupied with this work — the intriguingly-named *Zara's Ear-Rings*. This 'Moorish Ballad' is a rhapsodic setting for soprano and orchestra. The work received its first and, so far as is known, its only performance under Stanford at an R.C.M. concert on 6 February 1895, when the soloist was Clementine Pierpoint. By now, *The Musical Times* was quite familiar with Coleridge-Taylor's published compositions. Its critic noted:

> A decided talent, the orchestration especially being full of felicitous touches ...

But, although Miss Pierpoint sang well, the orchestra was found wanting:

> The orchestra was not in its best form; slips were not infrequent and we have often heard Professor Stanford's young people play with greater finish and refinement.

Zara's Ear-Rings remains in manuscript. Beyond its intrinsic interest, it is important because it is Coleridge-Taylor's earliest extant orchestral work, and as such is a remarkable piece of scoring for one so inexperienced. The instrumentation is confident, light in touch and transparent, with never a note too many. Apart from an occasional misjudgement of an instrument's best range, the woodwind writing is particularly attractive.

The poem's subject is a trifling incident in which a young girl laments the loss of her ear-rings down a deep well. How will she explain it to her lover who gave them to her? The piece is cast as an extended operatic aria and the manner is mock-dramatic. It has a nice sense of irony which yet makes room for fresh innocence. Formally, it is very secure: it is held together rondo-fashion by the intermittent falling seventh:

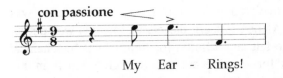

Ex. 14: Zara's Ear-Rings

and the symphonic use, as an accompaniment figure, of:

Ex. 15: Zara's Ear–Rings

Zara's Ear–Rings shows that all the composer's ease of technique, flow of ideas and richness of harmonic palette are already in place. No–one who heard it should have been very surprised at 'Onaway, Awake, Beloved', which came only a few years later.

Dating from about the same time, 1894–5, was the *Ballade in D minor* for violin and orchestra. It is a gloomily passionate work which lasts about twelve minutes in performance; Coleridge–Taylor subsequently arranged it for violin and piano. An effective concert piece, it is marked by violin writing which is thoroughly idiomatic and uses the whole range of the instrument in a virtuoso manner.

The early months of 1895 found Coleridge–Taylor teaching the violin in the evenings at the Croydon Conservatoire of Music. Only five years before, Elgar too had to accept that in England a living was not to be made from serious composition, and had to return defeated from London to Malvern, to teach the violin. But he was eighteen years older than Coleridge–Taylor, whose music, though he was still a student, was being performed an impressive number of times.

In addition to *Zara's Ear–Rings*, the first two terms of 1895 saw two other performances at the Royal College of Music. The first of these, his *Fantasiestücke*, was given on 13 March. (How the German titles underscore the direction of his thought!) They were soon published by Augener. The work, dedicated to Stanford, is for string quartet; it consists of five movements:

> Prelude in E minor, Serenade in G, Humoresque in A minor, Minuet and Trio in G, and Dance in G.

The Musical Times, noting 'the busy pen of that very promising scholar', thoroughly approved:

> considering the lamentable dearth of good string quartet music by native composers, his *Fantasiestücke* should be in request; they certainly deserve to become well known, for they are thoroughly charming, remarkably free from reminiscences, and effective.

'Free from reminiscences' they may be, but at the concert the previous July at which his *Nonet* had been played, the programme had also included Schumann's *Fantasiestücke* for clarinet and piano. A case, one might think of emulating admired models — but only the title has been borrowed. Of the five movements, the Serenade (no. 2) and Dance (no. 5) are particularly striking. The energy of the latter is of the kind that would shortly earn the composer's work the description 'savage'. The simplicity of the former is of the kind that disarms criticism:

Ex. 16: Fantasiestücke No. 2, Serenade

In the previous year, (1894), Sir Alexander MacKenzie had introduced Tschaikowsky's *Sixth Symphony* (the 'Pathétique') to London; its second movement in five–four time suggested rhythmic possibilities to English composers, among whom Coleridge–Taylor was in the vanguard.

The *Fantasiestücke* helped to earn its composer what Parry described as 'quite a brilliant report' for the spring term. A more directly useful and tangible reward was the Lesley Alexander prize for composition which was worth £10. On the same programme of the concert on 13 March was Brahms's *Clarinet Quintet*. Stanford's association with Brahms went back to 1877, in which year, when the young organist of Trinity College, Cambridge, he had helped to persuade the University to offer Brahms an honorary degree. Brahms refused, but a link was forged and Stanford was henceforth responsible for a number of first performances of Brahms's music in Britain. The *Quintet* was a mere four years old in 1895; we can imagine Stanford urging his class to hear it, and their ensuing discussion. We know that he told them that it would be impossible, in the light of that work, for anyone to write a clarinet quintet without its influence showing. At that time, there were not many models, for apart from Mozart's *Quintet* and the Brahms work in question, few others were known. Coleridge–Taylor decided to accept his teacher's implicit challenge, and during the summer term he completed his *Clarinet Quintet in F sharp minor*. 'You've done it, me boy!' was Stanford's admiring response on studying the work.

The *Quintet* is a four–movement work, traditionally formed but with cyclic elements. It opens with a swinging sonata–form movement, reminiscent in its momentum of the first movement of Dvorak's *Seventh Symphony*. There follows a meditative Larghetto in which two ideas alternate with ever more elaborate decoration. The third movement is a three–four and nine–eight scherzo and trio; the work is concluded with a further sonata–form movement in which the coda brings back ideas from the earlier movements.

Had he in fact 'done it'? It was Hurlstone who, in discussions with his friend, carried the lance for Brahms. The Scherzo of Coleridge–Taylor's *Clarinet Quintet* certainly shows the influence of Brahms but, in the main, he continued to draw strength from his studies of Dvorak, whose most recent work he clearly knew: his *Seventh* and *Eighth Symphonies* were known here, as was the *F major Quartet*. Coleridge–Taylor was unlikely to have missed the first performance in England (by the Philharmonic Society, 21 June 1894) of the *'New World' Symphony*. Dvorak's music made a considerable impact here: Elgar, for example, playing in the *D major Symphony* at the 1884 Worcester Three Choirs Festival, spoke for many:

> It is simply ravishing, so tuneful and clever and the orchestration is wonderful; no matter how few instruments he uses it never sounds thin.

Not only were there tunes and fine instrumentation; there were also piquant harmonies, subtle rhythms, cyclic structures (in the *'New World' Symphony*) and the 'primitive savage' utterance.

From Dvorak's *Seventh Symphony* Coleridge–Taylor would have learned how to avoid monotony in six–four time with the use of a propulsive figure such as the one which opens the quintet:

Ex. 17a: *Clarinet Quintet, opening*

Ex. 17b: Clarinet Quintet, first movement

Melodically, he has assimilated Dvorak's fondness for the lowered
seventh (* in Example 17b above) which is apparent also in the second
idea of the first movement (Example 18a) — an idea interestingly echoed
in the second movement of Dvorak's *Cello Concerto*:

Ex. 18a: Clarinet Quintet, first movement

Ex. 18b: Dvorak, Cello Concerto, second movement

but the *Cello Concerto* was not heard in London until 19 March 1896,
in a Philharmonic concert conducted by Dvorak, long after Coleridge–
Taylor's *Quintet* had been written.

The soaring continuation of Coleridge–Taylor's melody shows
further Dvorak influence. One of the continuing delights of Dvorak is
the way in which a phrase will take flight in its after–song; as, for
example, in his *Seventh Symphony*, in the second subject of the first
movement. 'One of Dvorak's greatest musical paragraphs', said Donald
Tovey. Coleridge–Taylor learned from it. Dvorak's influence is appar–
ent right through to the final movement: here, Coleridge–Taylor takes the
melodic fifths of Example 17b and invests them with the energetic drive
characteristic of 'motoric' Dvorak:

Ex. 19: Clarinet Quintet, last movement

The structural approach is cyclic, but with the refinement that the ideas are subject to considerable rhythmic alteration — even complete transformation — on their re–appearance in another context. Thus, in the scherzo, Example 17a is reduced to its essentials to become first:

Ex. 20: Clarinet Quintet, scherzo

and, second, as the movement's trio:

Ex. 21: Clarinet Quintet, trio of scherzo

Similarly, at the conclusion of the final movement, Example 17b is heard in the following playful distortion:

Ex. 22: Clarinet Quintet, last movement

In this fine *Quintet*, not only is there a mastery of structure, but also a rich outpouring of lyrical melody, most marked in the serene Larghetto Affettuoso. One wonders what thoughts passed through Stanford's mind as he perused this offering; he would have recognised immediately its quality. Perhaps he might also have realised how few composers at work in the England of 1895 would have been capable of such an achievement — and how fewer still at the age of twenty.

On 10 July 1895, the *Quintet* received a first performance at the Royal College of Music. The review in *The Musical Times* for August 1895 is so remarkable, bearing in mind that Coleridge–Taylor was still a student, that it is quoted in full:

To do justice to this work we deliberately use a different standard from that by which pupils' compositions are generally judged. There is little or nothing in Mr Taylor's Quintet to betray the fact that he is still in *'pupillaris'*. His is, indeed, an achievement, not merely promise. Mr Taylor's themes are his own and very interest–ing the majority are, while the skill with which he handles the difficult form, the freedom and the artistic balance of his part–writing and even more, the variety and originality of his rhythms are quite remarkable in one so young. Nor are the higher qualities of imagination and emotion wanting, without which mere cleverness counts for but little. They are most conspicuous in the fine terse opening *Allegro Energico*, and in the Romance (*Largo Affettuoso*), which is as poetic and suggestive a movement as is to be found in English music. In the *Scherzo* a most complicated rhythm is handled with masterly ease, and in the Finale (*Allegro con fuoco*) the two–bar rhythm of a theme *à la* Dvorak kept up with strenuous persistence, produces a most spirited end. Towards the close, the expressive theme of the slow movement creeps in unexpectedly and helps to bring the work to a worthy close. Mr George Anderson (clarinet), Miss Ruth Howell, Messrs. Thomas Jeavans and Ernest Tomlinson, and Miss Ethel Uhlhorn Zillhart were the capable interpreters of Mr Taylor's fine but difficult composition.

Stanford showed the *Quintet* to his friend Joachim who rehearsed it in Berlin. The work is thought to have been offered to Breitkopf und Härtel, but it never appeared in their catalogue. Thus a work which could have had wide currency, and could have established its composer as a chamber music writer of stature, languished in obscurity until brought out by *Musica Rara* in 1974, sixty–two years after his death. It was then recorded and received some small measure of its due.

Coleridge–Taylor continued to teach at the Croydon Conservatoire, much preferring the more advanced pupils. About this time, he first took up the baton, and for ten years thereafter directed the string orchestra of the Conservatoire: a useful apprenticeship for one who would devote so much time to choirs and orchestras. Possibly it was also therapeutic, and evidence that his crippling shyness was at last being held at bay.

For their main tasks in the 1895–6 session at the College, Hurlstone was to work on a piano concerto, while Coleridge–Taylor devoted himself to a symphony. Time was also found for some trifles: the *Dance* and *Lament* for violin and piano, and a setting of a traditional tune, *The Three Ravens*. The works for violin and piano were played at a College concert and taken by Augener, who published them as *Two Romantic Pieces*, op. 9 (*Lament* and *Merrymaking*). *The Three Ravens* remains in manuscript but was written in two versions: one for voice and piano and another for voice and piano quintet. In the latter form, it found its way into the 1896 programme of the Bridlington Music Festival, a fact which speaks eloquently of the perception of him as a promising young composer. The four movements of the *Symphony* were completed, and Stanford tried it over with the College orchestra. He had invited Hans Richter to the College that day. Richter wrote in his diary:

> Heard a symphony by a nigger — Coleridge. Afterwards I con-ducted the *Tristan* excerpt.[27]

But the last movement did not satisfy Stanford, and its composer made no fewer than three further attempts to meet his teacher's criticisms by re-writing it, all of which proved unsatisfactory to him. The *Symphony* — in A minor and given the opus number 8 — remains in manuscript. The first three movements were performed by the College orchestra under Stanford at a concert on 6 March 1896 in St James's Hall, Piccadilly, at which Hurlstone also played his newly-completed *Piano Concerto in D major*. (Holst and Vaughan Williams were in the orchestra, playing trombone and triangle respectively.) Joachim, present to conduct his *Festal Overture*, heard both works. It is thought there may have been other performances in the north of England, but these have not been confirmed. In April 1900, Dan Godfrey and his Bourne-mouth Municipal Orchestra played it. In his memoirs, Godfrey claimed this as the first performance, which would seem to indicate that the work was now complete; Berwick Sayers does suggest that the work was com-pleted 'differently again' and this would accord with Avril Coleridge-Taylor's view that *five* drafts were made: the original, the three revisions mentioned by Sayers, plus the later final draft. Thus the Bournemouth performance could well have been the first complete one.

The fate of the various versions of the last movement is obscure. There are two versions in the Royal College of Music library, but it is not possible to say which in fact they are. Thanks to the efforts of Rutland Boughton and William J. Read, another version survived an attempt by the composer to destroy it; it turned up in recent years at a Sotheby's auction. The title page of this version states that 'it is the Finale of a Symphony by Coleridge-Taylor and is in his handwriting throughout'. When Coleridge-Taylor showed the manuscript to Stanford and he had expressed disapproval of the music, Taylor tore it across and threw it away; William Read, who was present, rescued it from the waste–paper basket and gave it to Boughton.

But, according to Coleridge–Taylor's widow Jessie, there was a further incident. The manuscript found its way from Read to a certain Mr Henderson of Hastings, where Read led a string quartet organised by him. Henderson placed the manuscript for sale with Maggs the book–sellers, whence it was purchased by Read, with Coleridge–Taylor advancing half the cost of three pounds and ten shillings. How it then found its way into Boughton's hands is not known. These circumstances are of interest but not important. The significant point is that Read, a life–long friend, read no pique into Coleridge–Taylor's attempted destruction of the manuscript; it was simply a matter of his implicit faith in Stanford.

The Piccadilly performance by the College orchestra seems to have been a good one, and *The Musical Times* was enthusiastic. For a student to be told that his work was 'probably the most remarkable piece of work yet produced by any pupil of the College' shows something of the distinction this mere student had attained. *The Musical Times* continued:

> For in Mr Taylor we have that genuine *rara avis*, a student who possesses distinct individuality. This was clearly shown in the *Larghetto Affettuoso* in Mr Taylor's work. He calls it a 'Lament' and well does the music answer that description. Chaste and yet deeply–felt expression are united to beautiful workmanship of which the subdued but fascinating colouring of the orchestration is not the least remarkable feature. The first movement, an elaborate *Allegro Appassionato*, is no less remarkable for the strength of the ideas than the play of its rhythms, the bright transparent scoring and the youthful vigour and buoyancy pervading every bar.

The *Symphony* is scored for normal full orchestra (double woodwind, four horns, two trumpets, three trombones, timpani and strings) with the addition of a tuba. The opening is arresting, with the timpani alone in fifths:

Ex. 23: Symphony, opening

The woodwind motif grows into an energetic first subject:

Ex. 24: Symphony, first subject of first movement

which generates the momentum for a large–scale movement. As always in Coleridge–Taylor's music, there is an abundance of ideas, none more striking than the expansive melody spread Tschaikowsky–fashion across the strings at the opening of the development:

Ex. 25: Symphony, first movement, development

The Lament which so impressed the critic commences with muted strings:

Ex. 26: Symphony, 'Lament'

and continues with an intense figure in the clarinet:

Ex. 27: Symphony, 'Lament'

which later flowers gloriously in the violins.

In the Scherzo, a tight little accompanimental figure sets off a
Ländler–like tune in the clarinet and bassoon:

Ex. 28: Symphony, Scherzo

With regard to the two versions of the Finale in the Royal College of
Music, one is filed separately; the other follows the first three move-'
ments in sequence, and could be either the original (first) or the final
draft. There are no signs of rejected ideas and little of revision in this
version. Whether or not it represents the composer's final thoughts, this
'in sequence' version would probably make a fine and fitting conclusion
to a performance of the *Symphony*. If this was one of the versions he
rejected, Stanford may have been tragically wrong. Marked 'Allegro
Maestoso ed Energico', it opens over a timpani roll and portentous brass
chords, leading to a long and passionate cello melody:

Ex. 29: Symphony, allegro maestoso ed energico

The intensity with which this grey mood is sustained has echoes of
Sibelius. It is relieved by the violas in warm D major:

Ex. 30: Symphony, allegro maestoso ed energico

But the movement, and the *Symphony*, concludes softly and tragically. Despite Stanford's opinion, the movement as it stands is not only a logical completion of the work but also the composer's most original concept thus far in his career. If it is the original movement, then first thoughts have a validity of their own, as the original versions of Bruckner's symphonies have shown us. Psychologically, the rejection of such a movement would have induced an inhibition of genius, when the genius is embodied in a person with a timid nature that is anxious to please; for Coleridge–Taylor at that time, the need to please was of prime importance. The rejection of so strikingly original a conception might make it all too likely that the young man would fall back on something more conventional.

In the context of the history of the symphony in this country, the yearned–for masterpiece — Elgar's *Symphony in A flat major* — was still a decade away. Coleridge–Taylor's *Symphony* is not in that league, but can at least hold its own in the company of those written by his teacher, and is superior to many others by English composers of the last quarter of the nineteenth century.

The rest of the session saw Coleridge–Taylor working on a chore and on a string quartet. The chore was the re–orchestration of a *Violin Concerto in F sharp minor* by Heinrich Ernst, for performance at the College on 21 July. The *String Quartet* was performed on 25 June. The score is lost, which is a misfortune, since it deprives us of the opportunity of appraising his most mature student chamber work.

Was it lost or destroyed? After a succession of glowing reviews, *The Musical Times* critic's response to the *String Quartet* was luke-warm: 'somewhat disappointing', decreed the journal, and 'less spontaneous in invention'. The review continued:

> here and there it seemed to us as if Mr Taylor were developing something like a mannerism where he sacrificed beauty to obtain his favourite 'barbaric' effects as they have been termed. These

remarks do not apply to the first movement, *Allegro agitato ed energico*, which is built on two fresh and engaging themes. The slow movement, a Romance and a Waltz, standing in place of the *Scherzo*, are as unlike the general run of romances and waltzes as can be, but they lack charm. The *Finale* is a set of ingenious and, in places, highly effective variations on a most melancholy but expressive theme. There is much capital, original music in these variations but it is sad that the aforesaid barbaric effects are laid on with somewhat too lavish a hand, so that they are liable to become monotonous. The performance ... was fair, but the tone was thin, the cello being sometimes all but inaudible.

The reference to 'barbaric effects' is significant, for these would be seen to be a feature of the *Ballade in A minor* which Coleridge–Taylor wrote a year later. Did he consciously feel that barbarism was expected of him, or were the critics reading into the music something *they* expected?

Clearly, the performance did not help, and Coleridge–Taylor was very sensitive to any adverse criticism. If Stanford had expressed reservations about the work, Coleridge–Taylor would without hesitation have destroyed his *Quartet*. Some support for the possibility of this might be found in what happened in 1916 when, some years after Coleridge–Taylor's death, his fellow student Thomas Dunhill wanted to include the *Quartet* in a series of concerts he was organising, to be played by the Philharmonic String Quartet. He wrote to Jessie to borrow the string parts, but she was unable to find any.

In the Autumn of 1896, he started his final year at the College. With his eye on possible markets for his work, he soon noticed that short salon works — pieces for piano or violin and piano — were saleable. The success of a piece like Elgar's *Salut D'Amour* would not have escaped him as he set about creating similar examples of his own.

He continued to read Longfellow, and his reading stimulated him not only to the *Hiawathan Sketches*, op. 16, for violin and piano, but also to the *Five Southern Love Songs*, op. 12, for voice and piano, the poems for two of which were by Longfellow. Brought out by Stainer and Bell, these were his earliest published songs. They are concise, economical of notes and attractively tuneful. They also have freshness and transparency, both of which qualities were occasionally to be lost in his later music when over–work took its toll. Of the five songs, 'If thou are sleeping, Maiden' and 'Minguillo' seem particularly worthwhile, but the set as a whole could well be revived.

Each of the *Hiawathan Sketches* is prefaced by a quotation from

Hiawatha's Wedding Feast:

> 1 *A Tale*: O good Iagoo, Tell us now a tale of wonder, Tell us
> of some strange adventure ...
> 2 *A Song*: Sing to us, o Chibiabos! Songs of love and songs
> of longing That the feast may be more joyous ...
> 3 *A Dance*: O Pau–Puk–Keewis, Dance for us your merry
> dances, Dance the Beggar's Dance to please us ...

These, too, are effective pieces, directly inspired by the lines at the head of each. But, a year later, when he came to set the whole poem, he used none of the ideas from the *Hiawatha Sketches*.

Other salon music from this time include the *Valse Caprice*, op. 23, the *Two Moorish Tone–Pictures* and the *Three Humoresques*, op. 31. The *Valse Caprice* is an unsatisfactory work: erratic, awkwardly written and hardly blessed with melody. Its publication is evidence either of pressing need for money, or of deficient self–criticism, or both. There is little Moorish colour in the *Two Moorish Tone–Pictures* which appeared in 1897 and were his first published works for piano solo. So little, in fact, as to call into question the title of these unpretentious but thoughtful pieces. It is a curious feature of much of his work of this period that, despite a title suggesting Spain, Morocco or elsewhere, the music remains resolutely mid–European and favours in particular the influence of his beloved Dvorak. *Zarifa*, the second of the *Tone–Pictures*, is perhaps more effective in the simplified arrangement made by Alex Roloff and published posthumously.

The *Three Humoresques*, op. 31, appeared during the following year; the style of these miniatures amply justifies their title. With their delicate wit, they mark a considerable advance on the *Moorish Tone Pictures*. There is much greater enterprise in the piano writing and a determined attempt has been made to eradicate the influence of Dvorak, although echoes of Schumann and (in no. 3 in A) Schubert, take over. Their rhythms show a refreshing originality, especially those of no.1 in D:

Ex. 31: Humoresque No. 1 in D

Contemporary reviewers of the songs and instrumental music of this period often commented on the originality of his work. From the perspective of nearly a century later, this originality may seem mild, especially if considered against the musical fireworks shortly to be sparked off on the continent by Richard Strauss (eleven years older), Arnold Schoenberg (one year older) and Igor Stravinsky (seven years younger). But originality is there, nevertheless, in the rhythmic exuberance, in the avoidance of two- and four-bar phrases and in the melody, which is free and natural, but which in its relationship to its harmony does not always follow the traditional usage, or obey the 'rules'. This was never going to be the all-rejecting revolution of some of the great Europeans, but it was a small rebellion: Coleridge-Taylor, having established complete technical mastery of the traditional style, now struggled not to overthrow it but to assert his individual voice.

For the College, his time was principally spent writing his *Légende* for violin and orchestra (op. 14, published by Augener). The piece is dedicated to a fellow scholar, Marie Motto, who gave the first performance at the College, 15 February 1897, when the orchestra was again conducted by Stanford.

The *Légende* is scored for full orchestra, but one with certain differences which reflect the nature of the music: there are no trombones but there is an important part for the harp. It is a poetic piece with an elegantly ornate solo violin weaving high over the delicate writing for the orchestra. In some ways, the opening anticipates the mature Delius:

Ex. 32: Légende, opening

The work is in ternary form, with a contrasting central section in G major:

Ex. 33: Légende, central section

But not too contrasting; both ideas seem to dwell on the sub–mediant of
the scale (the note A in one, and E in the other), and it is this emphasis
which contributes to the 'soft' effect. Did he take the 'savage' criticism
to heart? The gentle lyricism of the *Légende* makes it a miniature tone–
poem of great appeal — Vaughan Williams's *The Lark Ascending* and
Julius Harrison's *Bredon Hill* are its successors. But this softening had
its dangers. Criticism from Stanford was one thing, when it resulted in
a sharper, cleaner technique; but the voice of the critics was another. In
listening to them, and perhaps in attempting to please them, Coleridge–
Taylor may have departed, over a period of time, from his natural
expression. The lyricism so attractive in the *Légende* could all too easily
congeal into a cloying sweetness; the savage barbarity (if such it was)
was to be replaced by a blandness all too prevalent in some of the works
to come in the new century.

    A few weeks after the performance of the *Légende*, Coleridge–
Taylor's time at the Royal College of Music came to an end. He was in
his twenty–second year and his apprenticeship there (very nearly the
traditional seven years) had been one of rare distinction. His distinguished fellow students, Gustav Holst, Ralph Vaughan Williams, John
Ireland, Clara Butt, Agnes Nicholls, Leopold Stokowski, and Muriel
Foster — all names taken at random — would probably all have agreed
with John Ireland that 'The most admired pupils were William Hurlstone

and Samuel Coleridge–Taylor ...'

Had he but known it, some of Coleridge–Taylor's best music had already been written. If we take the year of one of the finest pieces — 1895, the time of the *Clarinet Quintet* — we find that Delius (aged thirty–three) had by then written only *The Magic Fountain* and *Paa Vidderne* and a few other minor pieces, many of which he subsequently cannibalised. Elgar, at thiry–eight, was making a provincial reputation, but had only *The Black Knight, Froissart,* the *Serenade for Strings* and a few salon pieces in his catalogue. Vaughan Williams and Holst, at twenty–three and twenty–one respectively, had written virtually nothing. Coleridge–Taylor, aged twenty in that year, had already published, and was the composer of at least one work, the *Clarinet Quintet,* which had achieved rather than merely promised.

Little has been said of colour in this chapter. There are two questions to consider, the first of which is: to what extent did Coleridge–Taylor suffer at the College because of his colour? The answer must be that, apart from a few slighting references, very little. From the frequent performances at the College of his music through to the staggering number of performances given and the appointments he held in his later life, there is no evidence that he suffered professionally on account of colour. He may indeed have derived some benefit from it. Although proud of his colour, he does not seem to have thought of himself as anything other than a young Englishman. At the age of twenty–two, it seems unlikely that he had even considered the possibility of promoting his father's race and culture. But others would soon make him aware of what was expected of him.

5 ELGAR, GLOUCESTER AND THE *BALLADE*

For some while before leaving the Royal College, both Hurlstone and Coleridge–Taylor had been working independently of it to lay found–ations for their careers. Hurlstone had taken on an orchestra in Addiscombe, while Coleridge–Taylor (as we have seen) taught violin in the evenings at the Croydon Conservatoire of Music, in addition to conducting the Conservatoire String Orchestra. As time went by, he added other groups, among which were a ladies' choir — the Brahms Choir — and (in 1898) the Croydon Orchestral Society. In the spring of that year, the Conservatoire Orchestra took the Small Public Hall in Croydon for a concert. The reviewer (*The Musical Times*, Jan/June 1898, p. 192) noted 'the results of careful training' in performances of Grieg's *Holberg Suite* and *Elegiac Melodies*. A few months later, in contrast, (December 1898) the critic of the local paper found the Brahms Choir had 'need for further patient work'. In Croydon, the town which would be his base for the rest of his life, he was nevertheless consoli–dating a reputation for solid professionalism. In this town, just as in Elgar's Worcester, there were certain prominent musical families who ran musical life; women were prominent in them, and Coleridge–Taylor was fortunate at such an early age to have the patronage of such families as the Downs, the Carrs, and the Pethericks. Indeed, at the concert in December 1898 mentioned above, the majority of the small string orchestra consisted of members of the Down and Petherick families.

His creative work had to be carried out against a background of teaching in one form or another. So had that of Holst, but where he found it stimulating, for Coleridge–Taylor it was draining and exhausting: 'Everything you give your pupil is something taken from yourself,' he said. And he well knew that some pupils came to him only because they were aware of his financial need.

One of the works of this period was the 'cantata operetta', *The Gitanos*. The very description shows the composer looking towards the theatre which was to call him throughout his career; it was published by Augener as one of a series of works that could be either performed in a concert hall or be staged. It is a short *scena* featuring linking recitatives, written for three–part female chorus and soloist, and accompanied by piano. There is some superficial Spanish colour, with Spanish dances and percussion (castanets and tambourines). *The Gitanos* does not seem to have been prompted by a specific commission, and was probably tailor–made for the Augener series.

Just as in his formative years Stanford and Colonel Walters had been the major influences, so now three new figures assumed importance. Of these, the most enduring was a young fellow–student, Jessie Fleetwood Walmisley. She, too, came from Croydon, and from a musical family. She was the niece of Thomas Attwood Walmisley (1814–1856), a musician of great brilliance. Walmisley, a friend of Mendelssohn and a pioneer of the Bach revival movement, had at the early age of twenty–two been appointed Professor of Music at Cambridge University. He is remembered today for some fine anthems and two much–loved evening services.

Jessie was an attractive girl with a beautiful singing voice. Her parents held musical soirées and it was at one of these that Coleridge–Taylor met her; he played his *Légende* for violin and she accompanied him. She then pursued their acquaintance: needing more accompaniment practice, she wrote to the College to ask for his address. From then onwards their relationship blossomed. It marked one of the final stages in Coleridge–Taylor's halting progress to social confidence, for until now he had never been entirely at ease in the company of women. As a child, he had been embarrassed when he went for tuition to Arthur Hatchard, who had five young sisters. Hatchard related that, in an effort to escape the young girls' attentions, Coleridge–Taylor would in desperation barricade the music–room door by pushing a sofa against it.[28]

But it was one thing to have a charming young coloured man as a soloist at your soirée; it was quite another to have him as a prospective son–in–law. Her relatives disapproved. However brilliant a composer, he could have no prospects, and his colour would mean ostracism for Jessie and social ruin for the pair of them. Jessie herself faltered a little in the face of her parents' opposition, but only to the extent that, as a good High–Church woman she asked her priest for advice about marrying a man of another race. Jessie's great–niece, Linette Martin, later wrote:[29]

> My family's attitude to race was typical for their class and generation. Grandpa [Jessie's brother] once turned down the chance of having a cook–cleaning woman in their Purley house because she was black. He declared he couldn't possibly have a black woman working in his home. That was, I think, some time after the Second World War. Had he forgotten about his

brother–in–law? May be it was the combination of race *plus* class that made her unacceptable.

There is a parallel in Edward Elgar's treatment at the hands of the family of his future wife. Here, though, the reason for ostracism by Alice's family was purely class snobbery, because Elgar was the son of a tradesman. This, we now know, spurred Alice to turn her musician jack–of–all–trades into the leader of his profession. Here the parallel must end, for Coleridge–Taylor needed no spur to work. But he sold his work cheaply, and his Jessie had not Alice's modest income. Nor did the couple's suburban friends match the means of the Elgars' circle of landed gentry who could afford to invite 'the genius' and his wife to holiday in luxury and to allow him congenial conditions for creative work.

Coleridge–Taylor always saw himself as an English composer, and certainly the music written up to the time of leaving the Royal College would support his contention. Paradoxically, in common with that of his teacher and most of his contemporaries, this meant that his music looked to continental Europe. But in the U.S.A. the first stirrings among the coloured community were manifesting an awakening to its potential. Then the black poet and novelist Paul Laurence Dunbar (1872–1906) visited Britain and Coleridge–Taylor met him.

Dunbar, of Coleridge–Taylor's generation, was the son of a former Kentucky slave. His hatred of racial injustice was fuelled by his association with the black rights campaigner Frederick Douglass, by whom he was employed. In 1896, Dunbar published his *Lyrics of Lowly Life*. This is a substantial volume of poems, most of which are written in an elegant English style, although some are in a Southern Black dialect. Their subjects are plantation life and aspects of love and philo-sophy by turns. It was the success of this publication which led to invitations to lecture and thus to travel, bringing him in due course to London. Dunbar exercised a considerable influence over Coleridge–Taylor, who in 1897 set a number of his lyrics, including the *Seven African Romances* and *A Corn Song*. Despite the occasional lapse of technique, these Dunbar settings are finely fashioned. The accom-panimental figures usually work independently of the melodies, which themselves seem to manage an unexpected turn of phrase (or even a single note) which lifts them out of the ordinary. In the following example from the first song, the accompaniment establishes its own rhythm, while the voice moves serenely in longer notes; the melody contrives to avoid an obvious starting note:

Ex. 34: Seven African Romances, no. 1

The poet and composer joined forces in January 1897 for a recital in Croydon, given under the auspices of the U.S. Ambassador. They collaborated again on 5 June 1897 for a recital at the Salle Erard in London at which *A Corn Song* and two of the *African Romances* ('How Shall I Woo Thee' and 'Over The Hills') were performed. *The Musical Times* for July 1897 expressed 'astonishment at a composer barely out of his teens who produces work after work showing remarkable originality in almost every bar'. Nevertheless, the critic noted a reservation (using a euphemism, perhaps, for persistent 'barbarity'): 'that element of beauty, as we understand it, seems as yet somewhat dormant in his music'.

Another work dating from this time was the *African Suite*, a four movement work for piano. In fact, the last movement, a Danse Nègre, was originally written for strings and in this form the manuscript bore a quotation from Dunbar. Nowhere in the score is there any suggestion that actual African songs are used, but it is probable that Dunbar made him aware of some. Moreover, the work of the Fisk University Jubilee Singers, from Tennessee, was increasingly well-known in England from the 1870s onwards; indeed in the 1890s their manager, Frederick Loudin, established a similar choir here. Coleridge–Taylor would have been aware of the work of these groups, and would have benefitted from the spread of the vocal heritage that they engendered; but the *African Suite* may well have been conceived before this awareness.

The second movement, A Negro Love Song, might possibly derive from an actual song, and the third, Valse, has a feeling of authenticity about it. At first glance, it sits oddly in the *Suite*, but its jaunty dotted rhythms have some parallels in the music of the urbanised negro, echoes of which were picked up years later by John Dankworth in his *African Waltz*. The concluding Danse Nègre has had a life independent of the rest of the suite; it, too, offers some intriguing parallels. In his *Florida Suite*, Delius included a 'Danse Nègre' (described thus on the MS.) as part of the 'Sunset' movement. This work was written in 1887; it was revised in 1889 when it received a rehearsal–performance in Germany. But it was not heard again until Beecham revived it in the 1950s, by which time Gershwin had already used a tune reminiscent of it for 'I got plenty of nuttin' in *Porgy and Bess*. The Delius/Gershwin relationship is perhaps more obvious than the Delius/Coleridge–Taylor one, but there is enough similarity between the latter to point to their common origin in 'Plantation Song':

Ex. 35a: Danse Nègre, allegro assai

Ex. 35b: Delius: *Danse Nègre ('Sunset', from Florida Suite)*

There are other stylistic similarities between the early, black–influenced music of Delius and that of Coleridge–Taylor in the first flush of his enthusiasm for his racial roots. Time and again, for example, in the work of both men a phrase will be stated in the tonic major, to be repeated in the mediant major (e.g., C major to E major). However, Delius, in his quest for what Eric Fenby aptly calls 'The Idea', moved on, but Coleridge–Taylor never strayed far from his early style: he never followed Delius in exploring the deepest springs of human emotion.

Possibly the *Danse Nègre* was the first work to be conducted by its composer, for he included it in that Conservatoire string orchestra programme given at Croydon in the spring of 1898. Hurlstone performed it shortly afterwards with his Addiscombe orchestra; in various arrangements, it went on to become one of Coleridge–Taylor's most popular pieces.

His first venture into purely dramatic music for the stage was to set words by Dunbar; the work, named *Dream Lovers*, was given at the Croydon recital (16 December 1898) of the Brahms Choir to which reference has already been made. The 'dream lovers' are a quadroon lady, Katherine, and a mulatto prince, Torado, 'who dream of each other, come together, recognise each other and wed in double–quick time'. 'It passed off very agreeably,' said the *Croydon Advertiser*.[30]

Avril Coleridge–Taylor believed that it was Dunbar who made him conscious of his father's racial origins and deepened his pride in them. Certainly the years 1897 to 1898 show a marked change of direction in his work, away from the abstract music that had occupied his student days and towards work which as often as not bore exotic titles which were derived from overseas scenes and stories. This change of direction may be pin–pointed exactly by a letter to the *Croydon Advertiser*, 12 August 1897, where he joins in a controversy over the respective merits of abstract and operatic music. At this point he is firmly in the abstract camp:

> By all means let us honour operatic composers and their works, but not by taking the music from its proper sphere and thus robbing it of much of its effect.

His own art was subsequently diverted from 'its proper sphere' (i.e., as represented by continental abstract music). Quite possibly it was Dunbar who convinced him of the necessity of using his art and talent in service of the black cause. Three months later (4 November 1897), Coleridge–Taylor wrote a letter to Miss Carr. The letter itself is of no significance: what is significant is that it was written on the headed paper of the African Society of Literati, Musicians and Artists.

But there are degrees of espousing a cause. That Coleridge–Taylor was proud of his paternal descent is undoubted. That he considered himself the equal of any man, we have on the authority of his own word. That he considered himself an Englishman, we have on the same authority. Throughout the remainder of his life he sporadically attempted to turn his mastery of the European idiom to the service of his father's race with the composition of *Negro Melodies, African Dances, African Suite, Variations on an African Air,* and *African Romances*. It seems possible that the impact of Dunbar in bringing home to him the plight of the black races may have brought about a crisis of identity which may never have been finally resolved, for the pull of his English environment and his European creative tradition was too strong ever to be completely vanquished by his coloured paternity.

The third prominent figure in Coleridge–Taylor's life at this time was August Jaeger, immortalised for music–lovers as 'Nimrod' among the 'friends pictured within' Elgar's *'Enigma' Variations*. A publisher's editor, Jaeger had by 1897 been assigned by Littleton, the proprietor of Novello's, to deal with Elgar's work. Just as he had perceived Elgar's genius, Jaeger recognised Coleridge–Taylor's real worth at an early stage. A three–cornered relationship began, in which for a while Coleridge–Taylor was helped and promoted by both Elgar and Jaeger.

Although he was born in Germany, Jaeger had lived in England for a number of years, and had acquired a love and enthusiasm for English music. He had married Isabel Dunkersley, a pupil of Henry Holmes at the Royal College of Music, and he was in the habit of attending the College students' concerts whenever he could. At one of them he heard a work by Coleridge–Taylor and told his wife: 'I have long been looking for a English composer of real genius and believe I have found him'.

The work which prompted this enthusiasm was the *Ballade in D minor* for violin and orchestra, brought out by Novello in 1895. Jaeger's association with Coleridge–Taylor's music thus commenced as early as that with the music of Elgar: this had begun seriously with the publi–cation of *Lux Christi* and *King Olaf* in 1896.

Jaeger's critical faculty was never thrown off balance either by Elgar or by Coleridge–Taylor. Along with Stanford, he thought that Coleridge–Taylor lacked self–criticism. He also thought he was a poor accompanist. Of this he had plenty of opportunity to judge, for Coleridge–Taylor and Jessie became frequent visitors to his house in Kensington, where Jessie would sing newly–composed songs to the composer's accompaniment.

Elgar was first made aware of Coleridge–Taylor in a letter from Jaeger (dated 15 September 1897) where he speaks of him as 'the coming man',

> the young nigger (he is only 21!). That boy (a very nice, dear boy!) will do great things. His originality is astounding. When he grows older and develops beauty a little more (in his music, I mean!) he will be a 'power'. Novello's published five anthems of his while he was 16 or 17. Now he develops his originality and strength they will take nothing of his! I have before me a Morning and Evening Church Service which I consider splendidly fresh, ORIGINAL and yet simple and effective and devotional which we won't do because the editor thinks it is not the English Church style (precious English Church Style!!) He says that of *your* work! You see: to succeed always write as others did before you!!

Poor Taylor is disheartened because we refuse all his things lately and yet he writes better and better every month! He is a genius I feel sure, if ever an English composer was (his mother is English, his father a full–blooded nigger!). Have you seen his *Seven African Romances*? (Augener). They are strange and yet beautiful when one gets used to his peculiarities or *originality*. Do get them! He is a fellow sufferer! A word of appreciation from you (if you DO see anything in them as I do in my amateurish way!) would give him courage! And such poor devils *want* cheering up! I am awfully sorry for him. If I had any means I would back up my enthusiasm to the extent of publishing his Service at my own expense.

Elgar was impressed and did better than sending him merely a word of appreciation. He had recently been appointed as conductor of the newly–formed Worcester Orchestral Society and was looking for works to perform so he asked Jaeger, 18 October 1897: 'has Coleridge–Taylor anything?'

He now showed that impulsive streak of generosity so characteristic of him. He had been asked by the Three Choirs Festival for a new work for the 1898 meeting, due to be held at Gloucester. He demurred, as he was under pressure to complete *Caractacus* and, in a postcard to the Gloucester conductor Herbert Brewer, he set about securing a commission instead for Coleridge–Taylor, 'far and away the cleverest fellow going among the young men'. He reported this to Jaeger (17 April 1898):

I have strongly urged them to make the offer (alas! an honorary one) to Coleridge–Taylor. I don't in the least know if they will do so, but if it should come and he should consult you, you had better advise him to accept — nicht wahr?

There is a sting in the tail of this letter:

It is not a bad introduction and I should dearly like to see a clever man get on and upset the little coterie of 3 Choirs hacks.

But Brewer was not immediately convinced. So Jaeger wrote in support, 12 May 1898, to tell Brewer that Coleridge–Taylor

is most wonderfully gifted and might write your committee a fine work in a short time. He has a quite Schubertian quality of invention and his stuff is always original and fresh. He is the coming man, I'm quite sure. He is only 22 or 23 but there is nothing immature or inartistic about his music. It is worth a great deal to me — I mean I value it very highly, because it is so original and often *beautiful*. Here is a real melodist at last.

Why not try him and make the '98 Festival memorable ... by the introduction of the young C–T? He scores very well, in fact he conceives everything orchestrally and never touches the P.F. when composing! I suppose you know his father is a negro. Hence his wonderful *freshness*.

Why not give him a commission? He would rise to the occasion and do something good.

His symphony in A major [*sic*] is a most original work. We are doing a short cantata of his, *Hiawatha's Wedding Feast*; delightful stuff! Won't that do for your Festival? You want a secular work, don't you? I'll send you the M.S. score (P.F.) if you like (though at present in the printer's hands).

At any rate, keep your eye on the lad, and believe me, he is *the* man of the future in musical England.

Brewer still hesitated; indeed he suggested Edward German as a possibility for the vacant commission. But on 28 May, he finally recommended Coleridge–Taylor to his committee, leaving the composer only three months to write the work. Jaeger gave Elgar the good news, and Elgar now manifested the first signs of trepidation at what he may have unleashed (Elgar to Jaeger, 2 June 1898):

I hope he won't write anything *too* startling — that is, founded on too remote a subject — of course he will want to show the critics what's in him but the easy–going agriculturalists who support these things also want a tiny bit of consideration and, if he can please them, *without the slightest sacrifice of his own bent of course* it would be well in view of future commissions.

You had better not tell him this from me, a stranger, or he will kick me if we ever meet, and — well I'm thin and bony and it might Hurt.*

* I don't know — I've never been kicked.

1898 was proving to be a busy year for Coleridge–Taylor. He also had a work in hand for Henry Wood's fourth season of Queen's Hall Promenade Concerts. Jaeger sent Elgar a copy of the work — the *Four Characteristic Waltzes*. Elgar responded (5 June 1898): 'I like what I see'. The *Waltzes* were duly heard at the Proms — a first London performance and the first Coleridge–Taylor work to be heard at these concerts. He included a version of them for strings and piano in his December 1898 concert at the Croydon Public Hall, but probably derived more satisfaction from the fact that the Queen heard one of the *Waltzes* performed at Osborne by her private band. Elgar must have been in charitable mood, for the *Waltzes* are unenterprising. There is little of the originality over which Jaeger enthused in other work, and they must have been a disappointment to Wood. It is not known if Coleridge–Taylor was familiar with the work of Johann Strauss, but he certainly knew the waltzes of Brahms and Tschaikowsky. Nowhere does he emulate their skill in disguising the basic rhythm of the dance. *The Musical Times* review of the published score makes perplexing reading today:

> The adjective 'characteristic' is not seldom applied to pieces which virtually possess no character save that of conventionality but in Mr Coleridge–Taylor's waltzes its use is thoroughly justified ...

for 'no character save that of conventionality' is exactly what the waltzes offer.

One of Coleridge–Taylor's practices appears for the first time in these waltzes. Always under extreme pressure of work, he would never waste material from a composition he considered to have no future life. He would quarry such a work for ideas, as he did here for the third piece, 'Valse de la Reine'. In it, the fugue subject from the *Piano Quintet in G minor*, op. 1 (see Example 6, p. 28) is turned into waltz time to provide a contrasting idea for the middle section.

The Three Choirs Festival work was for orchestra only, and Coleridge–Taylor could think of no title for it. According to Jessie, it was she who suggested the simple name *Ballade in A minor*. The September issue of *The Musical Times* ran a preview of the new music to be heard at the forthcoming Festival. There were pictures of both Coleridge–Taylor and Herbert Brewer, whose first festival as conductor this would be, and who had composed for it a setting of Psalm 98. *The Musical Times*'s comments on the *Ballade*, based on a perusal of the piano score, seem lukewarm:

> Melodic ideas are not abundant, but the few are so elaborated and emphasised by repetition that they serve the purpose of the piece sufficiently well. The modern spirit is easily recognised, while it seems no less evident that a great deal depends upon the nature of the orchestration, which, judging by such indications as a pianoforte version can give, should be brilliant and effective.

Elgar (in a letter, 27 August 1898) commented to Jaeger: 'Brewer is very lucky — or rich — to get it into *The Musical Times* before he's done ANYTHING — Samuel Coleridge–T deserves it and I rejoice thereat'. The performance was drawing near and, as was the custom, the preliminary rehearsals were held in London. The composer was to conduct his own work, and the importance of the occasion imposed some strain on him. At one of these rehearsals, held at The Queen's Hall, Coleridge–Taylor and Elgar met for the first time:

> It was a real refreshment to me to see Coleridge–Taylor and to know him. I don't think the *opening* of the *Ballade* too fast when the 'chaps' are familiar with it — but, as I told him, the cantabile sections would gain infinitely by being taken slower (and rubato?) — the fiddles could then draw '3 souls out of one weaver' in many expressive places — I *liked* it all and loved some and adored a bit.

It must have encouraged Coleridge–Taylor when, at one of these rehearsals, the 'chaps' accorded him a standing ovation.

The programme given at the Shire Hall, Gloucester, on 12 September 1898 was formidable, as was the custom of the time. Apart from the *Ballade*, it included the overture to *Die Meistersinger*, Sullivan's *Golden Legend*, and a choral ballad *Henry of Navarre* by Rosalind Ellicott, daughter of the Bishop of Gloucester. Bishop Ellicott was not fond of music (he tended to take his holidays away from Gloucester during Festival time), but his daughter Rosalind (1857–1924) had studied at the Royal Academy of Music, and from 1882 onwards there had for a few years usually been a work by her included in the Gloucester meetings. *The Musical Times*'s 'Special Correspondent' (1 October 1898) dismissed poor Miss Ellicott and Sir Arthur Sullivan with little ceremony, but welcomed Coleridge–Taylor's *Ballade*, which

> met with extraordinary success, and assuredly it is stimulating, highly coloured and sonorous even for the present generation of hearers. It has barbaric moments, moreover, and is by no means unworthy of a youth who follows Tschaikowsky. Mr Taylor will tone down in course of time. He is at the stage of crude feeling now; presently will come the tempering influence of judgement. The composer conducted his own work and received a perfect 'ovation'.

A decade later, he had not thrown off the then still–clinging epithet 'barbaric' but, perhaps sadly, the 'tempering influence of judgement' did indeed come in due course.

One local Festival critic scored an 'own goal' when he suggested that Coleridge–Taylor could profitably study the orchestration of Brewer's *Te Deum*. He was evidently unaware that, because of pressure of events leading up to the Festival, Brewer had asked Coleridge–Taylor to orchestrate his work for him. (Three years later, Elgar orchestrated Brewer's cantata *Emmaus* for the 1901 Gloucester Festival.) *The Musical Times* had perceptively seen Tschaikowsky as the principal stylistic influence; if there is a specific model in Tschaikowsky, it could well be *Francesca da Rimini*. But this work has a centre of repose around which the storms swirl; the *Ballade* has no comparable point of contrast. Its chief virtue is probably the orchestration. It does seem lacking in ideas, with much repetition and little growth. In a frankly popular style, with few of the interesting textures which so distinguished the student works, it was perhaps the victim of too much haste. As for the 'barbaric' moments noted by the critic, only the opening of the work seems at all savage:

Ex. 36a: Ballade in A minor, opening

The trouble is that this figure nowhere becomes more than it already is. The idea that Elgar wanted slower and rubato in performance (though in fact it is marked 'a tempo') again shows Russian influence:

Ex. 37: Ballade in A minor, 'a tempo'

The work has faults but is nevertheless attractive. Elgar had performed a service, and the performance of it was a turning–point for the composer, who became something of a celebrity when he returned to Norwood.

*

Ex. 36b: Ballade in A minor, opening brass chords in its composer's writing (from 'The Musical Times', 1 September 1898)

6 HIAWATHA'S WEDDING FEAST

Henry Wadsworth Longfellow died on 24 March 1882. Although he is nowadays somewhat patronised and remembered mainly in the parodies of his work which are all too easily made,[31] he was among the most widely–read and influential poets during the last quarter of the nineteenth century. That his work then found its way into innumerable households is testified by the number of copies now to be found mouldering in charity shops and flea–markets. His poetry was seized upon eagerly by composers seeking suitable texts: his translations provided Elgar with the libretti for *King Olaf* and *The Black Knight*, and his original work, *The Golden Legend*, was set by Sullivan. *The Song of Hiawatha* (1855), which sold in huge numbers, gave to the world its imaginary portrait of the 'Red Indian' (as the native American was then called) as a prophet and teacher and as the Noble Savage in tune with the Rhythms of Nature.

This picture was an idealised one, for Longfellow eliminated from his portrait of Hiawatha anything discreditable and romanticised his squaw Minnehaha into the comely maiden of the poem. In this country, the spread of Longfellow's *Hiawatha* coincided with the news reaching here from about 1865 onwards of the plight of the native American 'Indians'. With the ending of the Civil War, the opening up of the Great West gathered pace. In the ensuing stampede for land, agriculture, gold and land for settlement, native Americans were perceived as a nuisance. They were massacred along with their buffalo; they were starved and decimated by disease. Innumerable treaties and promises were broken — usually by the rampant whites and their government. And, on 15 December 1890, in an attempt to arrest him, the authorities killed Sitting Bull, the old chief of the Sioux tribe. The American Indian Nation died in what came to be called the 'Massacre of Wounded Knee'.

All this was reported in Great Britain. The prevailing ·white American view could be summed up in the words of its government agent, General George A. Custer: 'The Indian is capable of recognising no controlling influence but that of stern, arbitrary power'. The British view was sympathetic to the native 'Indian'; hence the circumstances were propitious for settings of Longfellow's work.

Over the winter of 1897 to 1898, having already tested the water with the *Hiawathan Sketches*, Coleridge–Taylor immersed himself in his setting of *Hiawatha's Wedding Feast*. He was not the first to attempt it: as early as 1860, the American composer Charles Converse had set lines from *The Death of Minnehaha*. Even while Coleridge–Taylor was writing his work, Frederick Cowen was here bringing out his setting of *Onaway, Awake, Beloved*. Jaeger showed Coleridge–Taylor the early proofs of it; Coleridge–Taylor replied:

> Very many thanks for Mr Cowen's *Onaway*. Some of it I like very much; but why has he missed one beautiful section out altogether, and repeated another? Evidently Onaway's lover in Mr Cowen's conception is a very different — and less sentimental, less languid — person from mine.

Dvorak might have set it, just as he came close to setting Newman's *Dream of Gerontius*. During his stay in Spillville, U.S.A., during the nineties, he had interested himself in native Indian music, and there was no want of urging from Mrs Thurber, his patron, to get to work on a *Hiawatha* opera. In 1888, Delius did complete a 'Hiawatha' work: a tone poem. It was never performed and, according to Eric Fenby, some of it was incorporated into the Nocturne, *Paris*.

The Evans family had by now moved again, this time to 30 Dagnall Park, Selhurst, Croydon, and it was here that Coleridge–Taylor worked on his setting. (A blue plaque on the house now commemorates him.) When the tenor solo 'Onaway, Awake, Beloved' was completed, he proudly took it to Jaeger, saying, 'This is the most beautiful melody I have ever written'. He sang it, but his voice, by now thin and reedy, revealed nothing of the music's beauty. Jaeger was mystified.

The work proceeded rapidly, and was in the hands of Novello by the spring of 1898. Jaeger showed Elgar an early copy, as the postscript of Elgar's letter of 30 June 1898 to Jaeger shows:

> P.S. I have Taylor's theme jigging in the vacuities of my head — have sent the book to Forli, but the tune remains.

Littleton, the proprietor of Novello, had not wanted to publish it, and had only agreed to do so under the personal urgings of Jaeger. He expected to make nothing from it, for the negotiations took place well before the enthusiastic reception at Gloucester of the *Ballade*. For his part,

Coleridge–Taylor was typically shrinking:

> Of course, I shall be perfectly willing to leave *all* arrangements
> regarding *Hiawatha* with Mr Littleton. Will you tell him this on
> my behalf, or would it be advisable to write to him personally?

Littleton offered a fee of fifteen guineas, and a note on the
correspondence in Jaeger's handwriting confirms that Coleridge–Taylor
'accepts £15.15.0'. This was for the outright purchase of the copyright
of *Hiawatha's Wedding Feast*, and the composer considered himself
fortunate to get it. Littleton was a business man; not insensitive, but
simply unable to perceive much profit in an unknown young coloured
man whose chamber music was admired by *cognoscenti* but whose
previous work published by Novello had yet to make a respectable
return. Coleridge–Taylor was ever in immediate need of money, and was
flattered that a major publishing firm would take on a substantial choral
work. With all the timidity of his person and the insecurity of his up–
bringing and of his racial and class background, he could not find it
within him to press for better terms.

How Elgar's life would have been transformed if he had not
similarly sold outright his interest in *Salut D'Amour*! So too would that
of Coleridge–Taylor if he had retained a percentage interest in his
masterpiece. But, in due course, the repercussions of his loss went
beyond both publisher and composer, for the whole profession of
composers was building up pressure for a better deal from their
publishers. Stanford was a leader in this, and he tried to enlist Elgar's
help in persuading the Society of Authors to do something for
composers. Although he did eventually help, Elgar was at first hesitant.
Stanford wrote to him:

> I am of course glad that your experience leads you to think that the
> big publishers are often everything that is considerate. I can tell
> you of many cases where they are not. Some horrible cases. One
> e.g. of a man out of whom a big firm made a £1,000 (out of one
> of the 'small works to take care of themselves') and gave nothing
> and who is now precious near starvation. But if you and other
> prominent men won't move, it makes an amelioration all the more
> difficult. I shall do my best but it will be an uphill job, I think. If
> by accident you saw the accounts of Messrs Novello concerning
> Hiawatha, it might open your eyes a little as regards the
> 'considerate treatment of your composers'.

None of this would benefit Coleridge–Taylor, for he died before the eventual outcome: the establishment of the Performing Right Society. For Novello, it must be said that they took the work without it having even the prestige of a festival commission.

Hiawatha's Wedding Feast was to be heard first at the Royal College of Music. Excitement among the R.C.M. students grew as they learned the work, but they were asked not to reveal too much about it. Sullivan, by then very ill, met the composer by chance in Novello's showroom, and told him that he would be coming 'even if I have to be carried into the room'. On the day of the concert, Elgar wrote to Jaeger (11 November 1898):

> ... today I think is the Hiawatha at the College: good luck to it and the young man. I saw in a local paper that the committee of the North Staffs propose asking him to do something for them.

That evening, Sullivan as usual made up his diary:

> Dined at home and went to Roy. Coll. Music Concert to hear Coleridge–Taylor's *Hiawatha*. Much impressed by the lad's genius. He is a composer ... not a music maker. The music is fresh and original ... he has melody and harmony in abundance, and his scoring is brilliant and full of colour ... at times luscious, rich and sensual. The work was very well done.

Stanford conducted a programme that also included Beethoven's *Fifth Symphony* and Rossini's overture to *The Barber of Seville*. The orchestra was led by William Read, who was to become one of Coleridge–Taylor's closest friends. The chorus lacked balance, and all the performers, probably only too conscious of a sense of the occasion, were nervous. So was the composer, who still found the gaze of an audience unbearable. Shrinking from any contact, he listened to his work from behind a screen. Afterwards, terrified by the enthusiasm his creation had unleashed, he dodged into a doorway out of sight of the audience. The correspondent of *The Times* brought the evening vividly to life (12 November 1898):

> The circumstances under which *Hiawatha's Wedding Feast* — a new cantata by Mr S. Coleridge–Taylor — was produced at the Royal College of Music last night were for many of the hearers well nigh as uncomfortable as they could have been. The heat in the concert–room was stifling and apparently far more tickets had been issued than were justified by the number of seats, in consequence of which many people were compelled to stand

throughout the concert or leave the room without hearing a note. So rapid and sure has been Mr Coleridge–Taylor's rise into a position of distinction among contemporary native composers that every work he produces is looked forward to with pleasurable anticipation. His latest work, the cantata aforesaid, is as clever, musicianly and masterly in its way as anything its author has yet done. Moreover, it is full of a picturesqueness and freshness that are rare even among much older composers. The part–writing is clear and eminently singable without ever being obvious, and the orchestration is vigorous and sometimes brilliant, though never too obtrusive. But it is even more in the invention of his themes than in his treatment of them, whether for voices or instruments, or both, that Mr Coleridge–Taylor shines. Often and often again he happens upon a haunting theme or phrase, which clings to the ear because it is fresh and hitherto unheard. The first part of the tenor solo — the tenor being the only soloist employed — for example, is of exquisite beauty. Little wonder, all things considered, that Mr Coleridge–Taylor's quondam fellow students played and sang *con amore*. Their task was a pleasant one and a grateful one, and, on the whole, they acquitted themselves well of it under Professor Stanford's direction. Mr Gwilym Evans was a little over–weighted by the solo, but sang bravely.

After reading the above, the composer must have been perplexed by the *Manchester Guardian*, who thought his vocal part–writing 'though effective ... the least individual part of the work' and said of the tenor solo 'though extremely peaceful, [it] might have been written by almost any modern composer'. And how was the *Guardian*'s 'extremely peaceful' tenor solo to be reconciled with that of *The Referee*, which claimed that *'Onaway* is a gem of impassioned melody which all tenors who are in the throes of courtship should learn ... at once'? We might have imagined that 'Onaway' — 'the most beautiful melody I have ever written' — would be the composer's own favourite passage; but that was in fact the bitter–sweet alto setting of 'So he told the strange adventures of Osseo the magician'.

The piece is symphonic in construction, and so has scarcely any precedent in English choral music. Its unity springs from the fact that only three basic ideas supply its working material; its diversity is derived from the Wagnerian plasticity of their transformation. Of his contemp–oraries, Delius hardly ever seems to have used the technique to the same extent; and Elgar, although he used a 'leitmotif' technique to a limited extent in his choral works, mainly reserved thematic transformation for his symphonic orchestral music.

Hiawatha's Wedding Feast is, with the exception of the set piece 'Onaway', through–composed. But its form bears some resemblance to a rondo, the principal subject of which 'jigged in the vacuities' of Elgar's head:

Ex. 38: Hiawatha's Wedding Feast, principal subject

The episodes of the rondo use the second and third ideas, or combinations of them, and these, too, are heard in the opening pages:

Ex. 39: Hiawatha's Wedding Feast, second and third ideas

Below are some of the transformations of these ideas which are heard in the episodes. Longfellow's detailed description of Pau–Puk–Keewis's apparel is introduced in the woodwind by a six–eight version of Example 39c:

Ex. 40: Hiawatha's Wedding Feast, woodwind

The description itself is split between the women and the men, each group singing in four–part harmony. Their tune is made from a simple graft of the end of Example 38a onto the beginning of Example 39b:

(transposed)

He was dressed in shirt of doe-skin.

Ex. 41: Hiawatha's Wedding Feast, graft of themes

For Pau–Puk–Keewis's mystic dances, idea Example 39b is used, turning the music to a dark F sharp minor and incorporating the falling third and lengthening its descending scale:

First he danced a so - lemn mea - sure.

Ex. 42: Hiawatha's Wedding Feast, mystic dance

The wedding guests turn next to Chichiabos for entertainment. Their appeal to him for a song, and their thankful aftersong, change Example 39c into some of the most moving unaccompanied choral passages in the work:

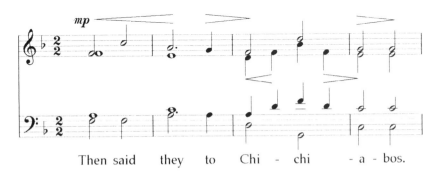

Then said they to Chi - chi - a - bos.

Ex. 43: Hiawatha's Wedding Feast, choral appeal

(The aftersong is in G flat: 'Thus the gentle Chichiabos'.)

Hiawatha himself is not heard in the *Wedding Feast*. His love–song is sung for him. Chichiabos, we are told, is 'the sweetest of all singers', the 'best of all musicians', and he sings 'in tones of deep emotion'. After such an introduction, the love–song 'Onaway, Awake, Beloved' is in a crucial position, akin in the cantata to that of the Prize Song in *Die Meistersinger* or the Dance of the Seven Veils in Strauss's *Salome*; in each case, the composer is 'out on a limb' and risks an anti–climax. And we are indeed conscious of the composer turning on all his power in this song, which remains one of the most eloquent of its kind. Perhaps this eloquence derived from the fact that Grove's belief that an artist needed to have experienced love had now, for Coleridge–Taylor, been vindicated. He was now in love, and 'Onaway' surely expresses not only Hiawatha's love for Minnehaha but also the young composer's love for Jessie. Example 38 supplies the foundation of the 'most beautiful melody'; only a slight adjustment of intervals is needed:

On-a - way,   A-wake,___ be - lo - ved___
Thou,   the   wild   flower   of   the

Ex. 44: Hiawatha's Wedding Feast, love song

Iagoo the storyteller is jealous of the reception accorded the singing of Chichiabos; but he is known as a boaster, and the guests deride him:

Moderato energico

Ne - ver___ heard he   an   ad - ven - ture but him -
self   had   met   a   grea - ter.

Ex. 45a: Hiawatha's Wedding Feast, the guests' derision

The music is loosely related to Example 39b:

Ex. 45b: Hiawatha's Wedding Feast, relationship of Ex. 39b and 45a

But the guests recover their good humour and request a story, using the same phrase as they had used to seek a song from Chichiabos. Iagoo responds with the tale of Osseo the Magician (Coleridge–Taylor's favourite passage):

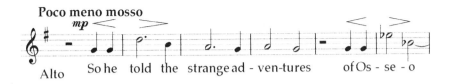

Ex. 46: Hiawatha's Wedding Feast, tale of Osseo

In the *Wedding Feast*, Iagoo and his boasting are treated with amusement and disbelief, and in part two of the *Scenes from Hiawatha* (*The Death of Minnehaha*) an even more unlikely story from him will receive unexpected support from no less than Hiawatha himself. We are not ourselves told the story of Osseo, for at this point the cantata draws to its close:

> Leaving Hiawatha happy with the night and Minnehaha.

Dvorak did not write a 'Hiawatha' opera, but he may well have written a 'Hiawatha' symphony. At the time of its composition, it was widely believed that the scherzo of the *'New World'* *Symphony* had been inspired by the dancing of the Iroquois Indians that Dvorak witnessed at Spillville, Iowa, U.S.A., and that the slow movement reflected a visit by the composer to the Minnehaha Falls. The trouble with these theories is that he had probably completed much of the *Symphony* before taking up residence in Spillville. Nevertheless, Dvorak himself said that the second and third movements were linked to specific incidents in Longfellow's poem: the Scherzo with the Wedding Feast and the Largo with the Funeral of Minnehaha. More recent researches[32] have made a convincing case for considering the whole work to be a 'Hiawatha' *Symphony*.

Dr John Clapham has already shown that Dvorak was familiar with

a number of Iroquois tunes before writing his symphony.[33] Some of
these tunes are shown below:

Ex. 47: Iroquois songs

There is no evidence that Coleridge–Taylor knew any Iroquois music at
the time of writing *Hiawatha's Wedding Feast*, but he was familiar with
the *'New World' Symphony*. It is possible that Dvorak unconsciously
refined some of the above ideas; one possibility might be:

Ex. 48a: Dvorak: *'New World' Symphony*

— the skeleton of this being:

Ex. 48b: Dvorak: *'New World' Symphony*

It is possible that Coleridge–Taylor, equally unconsciously, transmuted this into the 'jigging tune' (Example 38a). Fourths, fifths and octaves appear to be the common language units of Dvorak, the Iroquois and Coleridge–Taylor, in this instance.

Why did Coleridge–Taylor's work blow like a fresh breeze through dusty concert halls the world over? It is a truly original work, carried through with complete assurance. It is tuneful and its harmonies are poignant, particularly those in some of the unaccompanied choral passages that often seem to echo those found in Delius heard from his African workers as he sat on the verandah of his hut in Florida.

Even a cursory reading of Longfellow's poem will reveal the size of the problem faced by any composer in setting it. In particular, its metre is unbending and each line ends regularly with the same accentuation. Yet the challenge has the reward of Longfellow's verbal energy which, properly harnessed, can release similarly energetic music. Coleridge–Taylor said[34] that the 'essential beauty of the poem is its naive simplicity, its unaffected expression, its unforced idealism'. His resource in dealing with this material is almost infinite. Moreover, in his setting every word can be heard, for his accompanimental figures, and his orchestration of them, offset rather than duplicate each vocal phrase. He may have constructed the music this way because he knew that his work was initially to be given by music students rather than by a massive amateur choir, and he could therefore expect confident singing without the need to double up orchestrally every vocal part, as was the custom: this materially helped to create the feelings of transparency and lightness which are such striking characteristics of the work.

It is easy to take the originality of the choral writing for granted. Elgar used to say that he included fugues in his earlier cantatas and oratorios because he supposed they were expected of him. In *Hiawatha's Wedding Feast*, there is much counterpoint, but there are no fugues. Women's voices are often set against the men's, and their voices may be divided into as many as four parts each. Or, in contrast, only a single line of altos or basses is used if the colour is appropriate.

The work has its mannerisms. The listener can tire of the 'jiggy' tune, and the orchestra does tend to repeat each choral phrase, but even this is useful punctuation which allows the singers to breathe. The work has faults but, as Dan Godfrey pointed out, 'it was a complete novelty'.[35]

Now began its triumphal progress around the world. Even before the performance conducted by Stanford, *The Musical Times* was drawing attention to other presentations scheduled for Plymouth, Torquay, Glasgow, Bridlington, Middlesbrough and at the People's Palace in the East End of London. This trickle became a flood as performances took place in the United States, in Canada, South Africa and even as far away as New Zealand. For a period of perhaps ten years, no other choral work except *Messiah* approached it in popularity.

But the composer seems to have considered a performance which he conducted in Sunderland, six days after that directed by Stanford, to be the first public one. He clearly made a distinction between the student event given before invited friends and parents, and a commercial one before a paying audience. The Sunderland performance, given on 16 November 1898, is interesting because the choir there was under the direction of one of Elgar's closest friends, the Sunderland iron merchant and musician Nicholas Kilburn. Kilburn and Elgar were much in contact over the late summer and autumn of 1898, and it is likely that Kilburn's interest in Coleridge–Taylor was fostered by Elgar.

Choirs and festivals liked to have the composer to conduct and, for a working composer, an inordinate amount of time was spent on trains. We can picture Coleridge–Taylor rushing up north in time for the rehearsal, and then catching the overnight express after the performance, for he could spare only one day between commitments in London. Kilburn's young son Paul aspired to composition,[36] and Coleridge–Taylor treated his efforts very seriously:

> I hope you will not forget to post me a copy of Master Paul's 'symphony' as you promised — I shall prize it *very* much indeed.[37]

and, after the manuscript had been sent to him:

> The 'symphony' I intend putting in my album and some day when Master Paul has made his name, I shall feel particularly honoured by possessing his first opus number.[38]

The overwhelming success of these early performances of the *Feast*, coupled with those of the *Ballade*, radically altered the direction of Coleridge–Taylor's creative and personal life. They led directly to his visits to the United States of America; they led also to professional jealousies on the part of some colleagues. He was famous and had somehow to meet the expectations engendered by fame. He was expected to judge, to give interviews, to offer opinions, and to conduct. The great provincial festivals demanded new choral works from him: not the least of their demands being for more 'Hiawatha' settings to complete a trilogy which he had not at first even contemplated.

His successes as a student had been in chamber and symphonic work — in abstract work — and he had hoped that this would lead to a future for him on the continent. Germany was seen as the musical Mecca where, in the first years of the dawning new century, Delius and Elgar would both achieve distinction. But, after the *Feast*, Coleridge–Taylor was not perceived as a profound or philosophical composer; he was sentenced to the English cantata market, from which later forays to the United States provided but little relief. What this meant for him was almost constant overwork for small reward.

While chamber music was uneconomic, its down–market relative, salon music, would sell. Symphonic orchestral music was not wanted either, as even Elgar eventually found. Festival commissions for choral work meant at least a performance and a commissioning fee, while the theatres fuelled a fairly constant demand for incidental music. The overwhelming impact of *Hiawatha's Wedding Feast* inevitably over–shadowed some of the instrumental music written in or around 1898. Two works for violin and piano, the *Gypsy Suite* (op. 20) and the *Sonata in D minor* (op. 28), were not published until some years later: the *Suite* in 1904 and the *Sonata* posthumously in 1917.

In the four–movement *Gypsy Suite*, some desultory nods are made in the direction of the title, but not too many. Coleridge–Taylor contents himself with some 'snap' phrase endings he had learned from the con–sciously–Slavonic music of Dvorak and Liszt. The *Suite* is music purely for entertainment and is appropriately light in style, with a succession of attractive melodies and almost no development. As he had shown in the *Wedding Feast*, he was a master of thematic transformation and variation techniques, but in the *Suite* and a number of other light works, he clearly thought that the use of anything of this kind would not be called for. As usual, the violin writing is superbly idiomatic, whereas that for the piano could have been pruned. The American violinist Maud Powell took up the *Suite*; it was her first acquaintance with his music. A few years later he was to write a violin concerto for her.

There was a market, too, for songs. They could be written quickly and he wrote them regularly throughout his life, but at no time was he more prolific than during the last two years of the century. In these two years alone, he published the *Six Little Songs for Little Folks*, op. 6, the three rhapsodies *In Memoriam*, op. 24, the *Three Songs*, op. 29, and the *Six Songs*, op. 37.

With the success of *Hiawatha's Wedding Feast* and a ready sale for his other music, he had hoped at least to be able to give up teaching. But sheer financial necessity forced him to continue with it, with the result that, towards the end of 1898, pressure of work caused him to fall ill.   Among the engagements he cancelled was one to conduct the *Ballade* in Gloucester, the city in which he had first found fame. Berwick Sayers pointed out that for most of his life he harboured a dread of chest weakness, for coloured folk in Britain were thought to be more than usually susceptible to chest infection.

Financially, the *Wedding Feast* had done little for him.   At the height of its popularity, Littleton sent him a further £25, and from time to time he would send other gifts.   But, like Mozart's snuff–boxes, these were little help in providing for a family, and Coleridge–Taylor's aspirations for family life were no less than those of any other man.

7 THE DEATH OF MINNEHAHA

As the new century approached, many British composers had reason to bless the 'Proms', the Crystal Palace and the Bournemouth Orchestra, together with their percipient directors of music: Henry Wood, August Manns and Dan Godfrey respectively. From their creation in 1895, the Queen's Hall Promenade Concerts provided a shop window for orchestral novelties, and while there was inevitably a high percentage which did not survive, many present–day orchestral standard works were first heard there. In south–east London, Sir August Manns presided from 1855 to 1901 at the Crystal Palace. On the south coast, Dan Godfrey (like Manns, at first a military band–master) directed the Bournemouth Municipal Orchestra from 1893 to 1934. Whatever was new would almost certainly be heard at one of these centres, and more often than not at all three.

On 4 November 1898, August Manns invited Coleridge–Taylor to conduct the *Ballade in A minor* at the Crystal Palace. During the following month, Dan Godfrey included the *Four Characteristic Waltzes* at Bournemouth. Writing of *Hiawatha* in his autobiography some years later,[39] he expressed the widely–held view that 'the manner was in every respect thoroughly British'.

Concert–givers liked to have composers conduct their own works; composers were not averse to this, since (having as a rule sold their work outright) the occasional conducting fee was welcome. It is difficult to reconcile a twenty–three year old Coleridge–Taylor who was supposed to be still trying to avoid the public gaze with the indisputable fact of his growing number of appearances as a conductor both of his own music and of others. Few composers in recent years have managed to avoid conducting altogether, and Coleridge–Taylor became proficient at it. To what extent he was more than that is a matter of conflicting opinion. According to Herbert Antcliffe he 'never became more than a second–rate conductor even of his own works'.[40] Against this, the singer Julien Henry thought he did his own works better than anyone else. But for such a naturally reticent man, the struggle involved in forcing himself to overcome his chronic shyness can well be imagined.

The extent to which in later years he did overcome it is evident from press reviews. Coleridge–Taylor, said one, 'conducted with his usual fiery energy ... always forceful and energetic'.[41] He conducted 'with splendid verve', said another.[42] One of the groups to benefit from his rehearsing and training was a recently–formed local orchestra.

The Croydon Orchestral Society was formed as an amateur orchestra in 1897; Coleridge–Taylor conducted it from the 1898–99 season onwards, and stayed with it for six years. Its membership varied from year to year, but averaged some seventy players — most of the string players being women and all of the woodwind and brass being men. The Pethericks played in the orchestra; one of them, Ada, was also an able pianist who played Beethoven's *'Emperor' Piano Concerto* in the second concert of Coleridge–Taylor's first season. Their conductor did not spare himself; that, and the atmosphere in the room, meant he had to change his collar halfway through the rehearsal. A confirmed tea–drinker, he liked a large mug of it to be brought to him in the interval. The players gave him their loyalty and he, although firm, would always be pleasant and easy in his relationship with them; his loyalty to them would be tested later when it came to choosing between friendships and musical standards. He would sing difficult passages to them, always intoning almost *sotto voce*; gradually, too, he developed a rhythmic language, similar (one imagines) to that used in later years by Sir Malcolm Sargent. But Ada remembered one peculiarity; an inability to pronounce the letter 'h'.

It is clear from his correspondence that he was not good at delegation. Letters reveal a concern for details more properly the responsibility of an orchestral secretary: the engagement of extra players, seating arrangements, music hire and similar matters.

The Society's concerts were held in the Pembroke Hall, Wellesley Road, Croydon, and for them he would write the programme notes. His programmes were prudent rather than adventurous. Only the first move–ment, for example, of Beethoven's *'Eroica' Symphony* was attempted at the second concert of the 1899–1900 season, probably because the orchestra's horns would have been mercilessly exposed in the scherzo. But he must have felt some confidence in the violins, for he included overtures by Weber: *Preciosa* in January 1899 and, more daringly, *Euryanthe* in February 1900. Schubert's *'Unfinished' Symphony* found a place (his programme note claimed it to be 'the most glorious of all symphonies'), as did Grieg's *Piano Concerto*. But of his own music, there was surprisingly little: *Danse Nègre* was played in the concert on 6 April 1899, and cries of 'encore' were heard, but the composer did not respond. This was less attributable to over–modesty than to his

experience of over–long provincial festival programmes. He timed his
own concerts precisely to a two–hour limit.

Marjorie Evans noted that many of his friendships were derived
from the orchestra. She thought, however, that 'he didn't make really
close friends with many people at all'.[43] Ada Petherick was perhaps an
exception; to the end of his life he visited the Petherick house regularly,
playing and singing whatever had just been written. For Ada's album he
wrote the following few bars, based on her name:

Ex. 49: 'A–D–A'

By the end of 1898, Coleridge–Taylor could look back with satisfaction
on a year of achievement remarkable in one who had left college only
eighteen months before. There had been successes at Bournemouth and
the Three Choirs Festival; *Hiawatha's Wedding Feast* had begun its
triumphal progress with a maximum of publicity, and in his home town
his position was assured with the conductorship of the Orchestral
Society. And there were commissions: the North Staffordshire Festival,
the Three Choirs Festival and the Norwich Festival had all asked for new
works for 1899.

It may be that, far from regarding all this with quiet pride, he was
unsettled by it since so much of his activity was suburban. He had
glimpsed a wider horizon but was tied to teaching and conducting within
the constricting boundary of Croydon. The New Year was a time for

resolutions and re–appraisals. On 2 January 1899 he wrote to the
Croydon Conservatoire:

> As I have so many commissions to complete within the next three
> years, my friends have strongly advised me to give up my teaching
> after this term, more especially as I am expecting to go to
> Düsseldorf at Easter for a time.
>
> So will you kindly arrange so that I may have no fresh pupils
> during this term? ... but these arrangements rest with Mr Jaeger,
> who is now in Düsseldorf, and I cannot say for certain until I see
> him again.

He had never forgotten Joachim's group playing his *Clarinet Quintet*,
and he was sufficiently attracted to the German people and their literature
to learn the language. August Jaeger had been born in Düsseldorf; he
realised the importance for English musicians of the vast continental
market, and promoted Novello's composers in his native country. It was
the performance of *The Dream of Gerontius* at the Lower Rhine Festival
that finally brought international recognition to Elgar. Ethel Smyth and
Stanford had successes in Germany, and Delius was to be known there
well before any notice was taken of him in England. At Düsseldorf in
particular, Julius Buths had shown himself eager to try out new English
music. From time to time throughout his life, Coleridge–Taylor tried to
arrange a visit but never managed to get there. Nor did his music,
despite a performance in Berlin of *Hiawatha*, ever achieve acceptance
there. It would not have been in tune with the philosophical *gravitas* of
the Teutonic approach to Art at that time. Perhaps Coleridge–Taylor
attempted to accommodate his style to this, for some of the works
written in the new year of 1899 approached the seriousness of purpose
of his student chamber works.

One of these was the sequel to *Hiawatha's Wedding Feast*, commissioned by the North Staffordshire Festival; this, *The Death of
Minnehaha*, occupied him for most of the early months of 1899. There
is no evidence that at this stage he was contemplating the ultimate part
of the trilogy, although the decision to write a third cantata was
prompted shortly afterwards by an invitation from the Royal Choral
Society to write something. But the growing number of *Wedding Feast*
performances must have convinced him of the richness of this seam,
even had there been no commissions for sequels.

Godfrey was continuing his support at Bournemouth with performances of *Danse Nègre* on 27 February 1899 and the *Ballade in A minor*,
following this up in April with a *Ballade for Violin and Orchestra*.

(This particular *Ballade* is not clearly identified but is probably the one in D minor published by Novello as op. 4.) Support continued from Nicholas Kilburn, too; the correspondence between the two charts a growing friendship as well as providing evidence of the composer's rapidly filling diary. Kilburn was organising performances of the *Wedding Feast* at Bishop Auckland and Middlesbrough, and he was expressing interest in the *Ballade in A minor*. Coleridge–Taylor's response shows something of the problems of a composer (and indeed of a publisher) trying to cope with a burgeoning demand:

> I greatly regret I have no score of the Ballade myself and Novellos only have two so I wondered if anything can be done with the piano arrangement?
>
> It is awkward — Novellos ought to publish the score as they *are* doing in the case of the 'Wedding Feast'.[44]

The same letter reveals the name originally intended for the second part of the trilogy and the nature of the work in progress for Norwich:

> I have completed the new section of *Hiawatha* — Novellos are going to call it *The Death of Minnehaha* and not *The Famine*. I'm also engaged on an overture to the whole for the Norwich Festival ...
>
> Please excuse this abrupt note, and with kind regards to Mrs Kilburn and the 'Coming Man' [Paul Kilburn who, it will be remembered, was trying his hand at composition] ...

Creative work was continually interrupted by concerts: at Bournemouth for the *Ballade*, a Croydon Orchestral Society concert (6 April 1899) and performances of the *Wedding Feast* at Coventry and by Kilburn at Middlesbrough (12 April 1899).

In the following month, he and Jessie were in London to give a recital at the Salle Erard. He played a *Romance for Violin and Piano* and she sang the three rhapsodies collectively entitled *In Memoriam*. She was, by her own admission, 'nervous'. The *Romance* was probably that in G published by Novello the following year as op. 39. This is for violin and orchestra but it was, as usual, issued in violin and piano form. Precisely when it was written cannot be stated with any accuracy; it may well have been composed expressly for the London concert — an important one, for in it Coleridge–Taylor and his future wife would appear together in public. Musically, the *Romance* is soft–centred and weakened by over–indulgent harmony. But it is superbly written for the violin; as he apparently played it, the work testifies to his own

instrumental prowess. As will be discussed in chapter 21, the principal
idea of the *Romance* is identical (though in halved note–values) to that
of the central movement of the *Violin Sonata*. Its treatment in the
Romance is superior to that in the *Sonata* movement, especially in its
accompaniment, which has greater subtlety.

The three *In Memoriam* songs sung by Jessie are settings of the
poems: 'Earth Fades, Heaven Breaks on Me' by Robert Browning;
'Substitution' by Elizabeth Barrett Browning, and 'Weep Not, Beloved
Friends' by Chiabrera. The pervading solemnity of *The Death of
Minnehaha* spills over into these songs. There is some insensitive word–
setting, and the thick piano writing needs pruning for the composer
thinks more as an orchestral writer than as a pianist. (Indeed it is
possible to imagine effective orchestral versions of these accompaniments.) But, as a group, the songs are striking — especially the
sombre austerity of the Robert Browning setting:

Ex. 50: In Memoriam

With his student days now well behind him, Stanford was no longer at
hand to advise and criticise Coleridge–Taylor; but he needed some such
figure, and Nicholas Kilburn now joined Jaeger as one of those to whom
he could send his work for perusal. *The Death of Minnehaha* was set
down for performance at Hanley (in the North Staffordshire Festival) in
the autumn; before embarking on the orchestration, Coleridge–Taylor
sought Kilburn's approval of the vocal score:

as you know, I think a great deal of your opinion.[45]

There was even more pressing work to occupy the summer of 1899, for he had to complete the promised new works for the Three Choirs and Norwich Festivals. That for the Three Choirs, the *Solemn Prelude*,[46] was for full orchestra and explored yet further the elegiac mood of *Minnehaha* and *In Memoriam*. With it, Coleridge–Taylor's affection for Kilburn could take more tangible form:[47]

> May I have the honour of dedicating my *Solemn Prelude* (Worcester Festival) to you?

Kilburn was a fortunate man; a few years later, Elgar would dedicate *The Music Makers* to him.

The *Solemn Prelude* was the only novelty of the 1899 meeting. It was first performed at Worcester on 13 September, sharing the morning programme with Elgar's *Light of Life* and the *'Enigma' Variations* — the latter performed with the new ending which had been prompted by Jaeger. Elgar wrote to Jaeger giving his impressions of Coleridge–Taylor's work:

> Taylor's prelude went *well* except a trifle of unsteadiness in the scale passages and one other place — at least that's all I (a barrel man) could discover; I revelled in the opening and the close but I could not 'sequentiate' the middle. He is a dear chap and it's all so human and yearning ...[48]

A week later, Elgar wrote again to Jaeger, finding common cause with Coleridge–Taylor over criticisms of the *Solemn Prelude*:

> I wish the critics had a little more imagination when British music is concerned: if it's cut and dried they sneer at us and if we do show a bit of real feeling and emotion they laugh at it — I'm sick — and so are you of me ...[49]

Set in the episodic form of a rondo, the *Solemn Prelude* has a spacious–ness and breadth which make it an impressive piece of work. It is constructed from hardly more than three ideas, of which the middle 'sequencing' is, as Elgar suggested, not wholly convincing. But the second idea in particular has a fine sweep to it — 'such as Elgar might have writ', and as Hans Richter might have said:

Ex. 51: Solemn Prelude

The influence of Tschaikowsky, already noted in the *Ballade in A minor*, is again apparent. By 1899, knowledge of Tschaikowsky's work was spreading rapidly in England. Henry Wood was an advocate of it; as was Stanford, who was largely responsible for the Russian composer's visit in 1893 to receive an honorary Cambridge doctorate. Coleridge–Taylor thought him a great master, although he recognised the inconsistent quality of his work.

The overture mentioned in Coleridge–Taylor's letter to Kilburn had by the summer acquired a name and function. It was to be called *Overture to the Song of Hiawatha* and was intended to act as a prelude to the trilogy. Having said that, its musical connections with the *Wedding Feast* are minimal and those with *Minnehaha* are non–existent. This is not a criticism — the composer himself considered the overture to be an independent work; its inspiration seems to have been un–connected with either Longfellow or his *Hiawatha*, but with the visit of the Jubilee Singers already mentioned in chapter 5. Coleridge–Taylor was impressed by the spirituals in their repertoire; one of them, *Nobody Knows the Trouble I See*, was to be turned by him into a one–in–a–bar Allegro in three–eight time to form the principal subject of his overture:

Allegro ma non troppo

Ex. 52: Overture to the Song of Hiawatha, first theme

Clearly identifiable as it is, the tune also bears a family resemblance to one in Dvorak's *Amid Nature* overture; indeed anyone hearing the *Hiawatha* overture for the first time might be forgiven for thinking he was hearing an unknown Dvorak work. Why would Coleridge–Taylor use a specifically black American theme for a work concerning a great Indian leader and teacher? Why, too, use a Christian spiritual for a pagan subject? Possibly in his on–going process of identifying with the cause of his paternal race, he saw little distinction between the real plight of the one and the legendary or imaginary plight of the other, and this over–rode the inconvenience of his theme's religious associations.

Structurally the overture is simple. After an introduction, there is an Allegro with but two basic ideas: that in Example 52 above and the following lyrical melody:

Ex. 53: Overture to the Song of Hiawatha, second theme

There is some sequential development of the spiritual idea (Example 52) and (for Coleridge–Taylor) a somewhat unusual episode of alternate five–eight and three–eight bars. Belatedly, in the closing pages, the composer remembers his subject; he creates a coda from his spiritual — now a two–four Allegro Vivace — welded to the 'jigging' *Hiawatha* theme (Example 38). Inconsistently, in view of its possible function, the work is cast to finish in B major. The *Wedding Feast* to follow starts in G.

The overture is a well–made piece; it is tuneful, immaculately orchestrated and sure in its management of key and musical logic. It is, in short, something that a graduate of a composition course might produce at will. But nowhere is there that spark of pure imagination that so frequently lights the pages of the unschooled Elgar or the little–schooled Delius. Berwick Sayers claimed that it quotes a Weber phrase at one point, but I have been unable to identify this. His assertion that in his turn Edward German used a phrase from the overture in his *Welsh Rhapsody* is also problematical; the opening of the *Rhapsody* certainly uses a phrase of Example 52, but this is really the first phrase of the featured Welsh song 'Loudly Proclaim o'er Land and Sea'. Coleridge–

Taylor conducted the first performance of his new overture at the 1899
Norwich Festival (7 October 1899) and in the following year Wood gave
it at the 'Proms'. Elgar was present at Norwich to conduct his *Sea
Pictures*. His letter to Jaeger, some months later (10 January 1900)
marked a turning point in Elgar's erstwhile championship of Coleridge–
Taylor:

> I was cruelly disillusioned by the Overture to Hiawatha, which I
> think really only 'rot' and the Worcester prelude did not show any
> signs of cumulative invention or effect; the scoring is altogether
> uninteresting and harsh of both these works: wherever I've been
> people are sympathetic and kind on account of the colour question
> and he is well advertised and backed but his later work is insincere
> and cannot do any real good: this is what I feel: I have never
> worked so hard for any man before — on *your* recommendation —
> and I took a real pleasure in him.

Here for the first time is a suggestion that, far from encountering
opposition on account of his colour, this factor may even have helped
him, albeit in the patronising way of double standards.

With the orchestration of *The Death Of Minnehaha* complete,
Coleridge–Taylor wrote again to Kilburn:

> The orchestration of *The Death of Minnehaha* is, as far as
> instruments are concerned, exactly like the *Wedding Feast*. I have
> purposely avoided any unusual instruments because I know what
> obstacles they are to present performances of any [mark?]. The
> first performance takes place at Hanley on October 26th together
> with the overture and *Wedding Feast* after which I can tell you if
> it is worth doing or not![50]

The *Wedding Feast* was by now scheduled for performance at the
People's Palace, and by the Bermondsey Settlement Choir, the Highbury
Philharmonic Society and two Birmingham choirs. Performances were
starting to pile up, and several societies were prepared to take the as yet
unpublished and unperformed *Minnehaha* on trust, as Joseph Bennett
(music critic of the *Daily Telegraph*) revealed in his article on 'the
musical man of the hour'. He was able to tell his readers that the
composer was at work on a third cantata, *Hiawatha's Departure*, and that
the whole trilogy was to be sung for the first time by the Royal Choral
Society, who had commissioned the third part. His article posed the
question that must have occurred to many:

Is not such a blazing success enough to turn the young musician's head? The answer depends, of course, upon the strength of the head and we can only hope for the best.[51]

Coleridge–Taylor had not yet reached his twenty–fifth birthday; his problem was now the expectation encouraged by the brilliance of the *Wedding Feast*.

To coincide with the North Staffordshire Festival, *The Musical Times* lavished columns measured in feet rather than in inches on a full–scale analysis of *The Death of Minnehaha*, replete with many musical illustrations and spread over the November and December 1899 issues. The concert took place in the morning of 26 October; it was of heroic duration, including as it did Schumann's *Paradise and the Peri*, the *'Eroica' Symphony* and Tschaikowsky's *'Pathetique' Symphony*, with the Coleridge–Taylor works (the *Hiawatha* overture, the *Wedding Feast* and *Minnehaha*) as dessert.

A coloured man was still very much a rarity outside London, let alone a coloured composer, and the natural curiosity of the potters probably helped to account for the packed house. But if they came to stare, they unleased a tumultuous ovation at the concluding chord:

> The little work worked a great wonder: we saw gray–bearded critics moved to tears and there were many in the audience who made no attempt to hide their emotion.[52]

The general dampness of eye is confirmed by Jaeger:[53]

> It was a sight for the *Gods* to see *Bennett* and *Stratton* and *Shedlock* and other old stagers 'wipe their eye'. As for my little wife, she cried half the time. I was too much concerned about the bad orchestral performance to cry (I have done that at home over the vocal score and at the piano!) ...

The performance of the orchestra certainly was bad. It would be hard to think of a more effective prescription for orchestral disaster than a programme that was, by today's standards, at least an hour–and–a–half too long, and was played by an orchestra plagued by deputies. *The Musical Times* sternly condemned the band:[54]

> We must raise a protest against the treatment which the work received at rehearsal. It can hardly be believed that the composer had no rehearsal with the orchestra alone for a first performance of a cantata which was absolutely new to the orchestra. It is not our concern to apportion the blame for such an inartistic, aye,

dangerous piece of false economy. We merely place the fact on
record, and express our opinion that Mr Taylor would have gained
the approval and deserved the thanks of all creative musicians if he
had left Hanley in disgust and made the performance of his new
work impossible. The result of this lack of rehearsal was seen in
performance. The accompaniments were inefficiently played, many
of Mr Taylor's best effects 'missed fire' completely, and occasion–
ally certain instruments took long rests that were not in the score.

But he at least had the consolation of a fine choir who had learned the
work thoroughly because they loved it. Within a year, with an equally
important first performance, he would be denied even this luxury.

There is but one thematic connection between *Minnehaha* and the
Wedding Feast, and the reason for that is readily apparent. The *Wedding
Feast* is all about joy; the Great Day of Hiawatha and his young bride,
surrounded in their happiness by their friends and relatives, is therefore
expressed in bright sounds and dancing rhythms. In *Minnehaha*, the joy
has evaporated in the attrition of famine. The work depicts Minnehaha
succumbing to it, and her funeral and Hiawatha's lament at her loss.
Hiawatha is now a mature figure. He was never heard in the *Wedding
Feast*, but he is heard here, singing as a baritone. An orchestral prelude
sets the sombre mood with an idea which the chorus will later use to
depict Longfellow's powerful imagery of Winter and Famine:

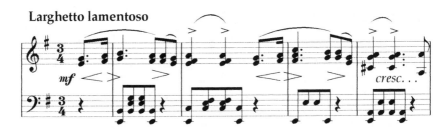

Ex. 54: The Death of Minnehaha, prelude

Not the least remarkable characteristic of Coleridge–Taylor's work is his
ability to sustain such a mood. Here it is sustained throughout the
cantata.

There follows a scene set in Hiawatha's wigwam, where the dying
Minnehaha is visited by the awesome figures of Famine and Fever.
Deep in the forest, her husband is hunting desperately for food:

Ex. 55: The Death of Minnehaha, the hunt for food

He prays to his god, Gitche Manito, for help for his tribe and for his wife. In the distant wigwam, Minnehaha is comforted by Nokomis (Hiawatha's grandmother), but at the moment of her death, she cries out to her husband. Far away in the forest he hears her. The approach of this climactic moment is heralded in the orchestra by that one thematic connection with the *Wedding Feast* as the Hiawatha theme (Example 38) peals out. Too late he returns, and with the chorus sings a lament — dangerously sentimental in its chromaticism, but placed unerringly for maximum effect:

Ex. 56: The Death of Minnehaha, lament

The music for Minnehaha's funeral is arguably the finest in the score. Against Example 55, used as an orchestral ostinato, the voices of the chorus move in unison and octaves to form a stark two–part texture, enhanced by the effective use of deep brass:

Ex. 57: The Death of Minnehaha, funeral

Within a few years, both Delius and Elgar would also meditate on Death and loss, in *Sea Drift* and in *The Dream of Gerontius* respectively: 'O past, O Happy Life', sings the he–bird in *Sea Drift*; and, with 'Softly and Gently', the Angel bids farewell to the Soul in *The Dream of Gerontius*. Sadly, Coleridge–Taylor lacks the imaginative resource to rise to the challenge of the corresponding moment in *Minnehaha*. Hiawatha and his tribe sing her to the Islands of the Blessed with nothing more than a variant of the opening famine idea:

Ex. 58: The Death of Minnehaha, farewell

The comparison is a cruel one; Coleridge–Taylor's genius matches neither the agonised yearning of Delius nor the nobility of Elgar. His style here is unashamedly popular, and is perhaps also further evidence of his leaning towards the theatre: a point somewhere between opera and operetta. He had on occasion expressed admiration for the operas of Puccini, but there was little chance in England of emulating him. If he had not the resources, circumstances and sheer determination to follow Delius or Ethel Smyth to the continent in the faint hope of production, an English composer had better at that time resort to the unsatisfactory form of dramatic cantata.

8 *HIAWATHA'S DEPARTURE*

At Novello's, the management was now alive to the potential of their young composer. As things turned out, they were lucky to be able to buy outright *The Death of Minnehaha* and *Hiawatha's Departure* for £250. In addition, Coleridge–Taylor was given a five–year contract which guaranteed him a retainer of £100 per annum in return for the publisher having first refusal of anything he might write. The terms, set out in Novello's letter of 17 January 1899, are (for their time) liberal, and it is clear that the publisher hoped to relieve the composer of his need to teach for a living. The agreement was to run from 1 January 1899. His prospects were further enhanced when in November 1899 the Birmingham Festival asked for a new work.

Now possessed of something like financial security, he felt able to marry Jessie, but it was difficult for a busy musician to find even a small gap in his diary in which to fix a wedding date:

> Thank you for sending the circular for the Sunderland Philharmonic Society's concert.
>
> I was hoping to be present (accidently!) as I expected to conduct the 'Wedding Feast' at Newcastle a day or two before.
>
> Unfortunately (for them) I am to be married on Jan. 1st and so many of my engagements will have to be broken, I'm afraid ...[55]

He was mistaken here; the wedding took place on 30 December 1899 at Holy Trinity Church, South Norwood. The best man was the organist, Dr J. W. G. Hathaway — a circumstance that prompts the question of why there was no closer friend to shoulder this pleasant duty. In a letter to his friend Mrs Petherick of the Croydon orchestra, he wrote that he and Jessie hoped it would be secret, but the news leaked out and the church was full. Having told Kilburn, he can hardly have been surprised that some of the Northern choral societies sent their good wishes.

On the morning of the wedding, he sent his bride a telegram, quoting loosely from *The Song of Hiawatha*:

> You shall enter in my wigwam
> For the heart's right hand I gave you.[56]

Coleridge–Taylor was too much of a celebrity to escape the attentions of the press, and the Boer War was only six weeks old:

> It is an odd coincidence that while we are struggling in Africa the
> first coloured subject of the Queen who has acquired eminence as
> a composer is the young Anglo–African, Mr S. Coleridge–Taylor
> who was married on Saturday last at Selhurst to Miss Jessie
> Walmisley. If the Boers would study music instead of the art of
> entrenchment how different things might be!

Clearly the paper had but the vaguest idea what a Boer might be, and
cheerfully lumped together everyone coming from the African continent.
The couple went on honeymoon to Shanklin, on the Isle of Wight, where
Jessie came up against the special problems of marriage to a musician
right from the outset.   Her new husband had brought *Hiawatha's
Departure* with him to work on and, in any case, had to interrupt the
holiday to travel to Manchester to conduct a performance of the *Ballade
in A minor*.

On their return to Croydon, the couple lodged at St James's Road;
but, after a while, Alice and George Evans moved out of 30 Dagnall
Park and the Coleridge–Taylors moved in.   For a few years they moved
house frequently, never staying in one place for more than a year or two:
Fernham Road, Dagmar Road and Upper Grove, Norwood followed in
succession, and none was more than a mile or so from another.   It was,
incidentally, about this time that the hyphen came into his name through
a mistake made in a printed score by his publisher.   From then on, the
composer retained it.

> Never was a marriage, so disapproved of by well–meaning friends,
> more triumphantly justified in its results.   For Coleridge–Taylor it
> was the happiest and most successful period of his life.[57]

And this, generally, was to be so.   Alice Evans approved of Jessie but,
years later, her daughter Marjorie (Samuel's half–sister) commented:

> Jessie had a short temper, you know, and that made Coleridge more
> inclined to come and see mother whenever possible.   I think he was
> sure of a cup of tea and a biscuit at our home ...[58]

Like many another lower–middle–class family, the couple managed to
employ a maid, but the turnover was fairly constant:

> Jessie was not very kind to them and they would leave.   It wasn't
> a question of working for a black man, but Jessie.   Coleridge never
> mentioned it to mother, but she knew from what the girls told her

— not knowing she was Coleridge's mother.[59]

Against this may be set the perception of Jessie by her great niece Linette Martin:

> There was a great gentleness — a disciplined gentleness — about her.[60]

But, from Jessie's point of view, there must have been times when the ceaseless drudgery and travel which the life of a composer and conductor inevitably involved made life well–nigh intolerable; one made bearable only by her belief in her husband's genius and her deep love for him. Linette Martin remembers in her

> that special combination of sweetness, precision and no–nonsense toughness that I have come to associate with Edwardian ladies and retired headmistresses. When she spoke of him, the love in her face was something quite unforgettable. As a more cynical adult I have sometimes wondered if she may not have idealised and idolised him but it must have taken a great deal of hard–headed practical love to survive a mixed marriage at the beginning of this century.[61]

In her memoirs, no hint of dissatisfaction with her lot appears.[62] When her chores were done, there was little else for her but to settle down and read aloud to her husband as he toiled at his scoring. She survived him by many years, living on into the 1960s, mellowing greatly in old age into:

> The sort of grown–up who looks directly at a child with interest and respect for that child's personality.[63]

*

It had not been plain sailing to get *The Departure* to the point where it could be scored. He submitted the cantata to Novellos for printing — the Royal Choral Society performance in March 1900 was approaching fast, and the singers had to learn the work — but the composer can hardly have been prepared for the reaction when the score reached August Jaeger. Fearless and uncompromising, Jaeger's insistence that the notoriously touchy Elgar must recast the passage in *The Dream of Gerontius* where the Soul is taken for a moment before his God is well known. He savaged *The Departure*, declaring that the choruses were commonplace and some were no better than mediocre hymn–tunes:

This will never do, the public expects you to progress, to do better work than before; this is your worst.[64]

Just as he had done for Stanford with the last movement of the *Symphony in A minor*, Coleridge–Taylor set about re–writing the whole cantata. Inevitably there was a casualty. There would now be no time to write a new work for Birmingham, whose festival would have to be content with a performance of the *Hiawatha* trilogy.

Writing to Kilburn on 14 March, eight days before the first complete performance, he gave vent to his feelings about the Royal Choral Society with rare and bitter eloquence:

> I'm pleased with the [finale?], particularly the baritone scena, which I suppose you'll like as well as anything in the whole work.
>
> But the Albert Hall Chorus!!
>
> Heavens! how I long for Sunderland and Middlesbrough!
>
> There is neither [voice?] nor pathos nor humour nor anything — and they are so *heavy* to move along — remind me of very muddy roads and huge waggons — each waggon having only one horse, and that one stolid to an incredible degree.
>
> ... they sing with pained and strained faces...
>
> ... I write:

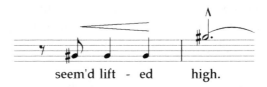

seem'd lift - ed   high.

> ... they sing:

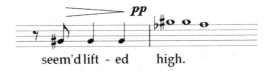

seem'd lift - ed   high.

> Woe is me! for my spirit is troubled within me, and so would yours be if you could hear 'England's Premier Choral Society'.
>
> I'm glad you live in Bishop Auckland or you might feel inclined to sever friendship with the man who wrote those sounds! ...[65]

And so he was led to the slaughter, for the performance was very much as he expected. *The Times* review is masterly in the way it deals with a choir whose musical qualities were at that time not as elevated as its aristocratic membership and connections, and one which it would have been dangerous to offend by overt criticism:

> The choir sang with excellent tone throughout though their entry was not very certain after the soprano solo of the last part, and in a few other places they seemed not quite familiar with the music. Their phrasing was, however, so good that this cannot have been the case ...[66]

This inauspicious performance was in fact to prove the start of a long and fruitful association with the work by the Royal Choral Society. One member of the audience that night was the future black leader, W. E. B. Du Bois, whose influence on Coleridge–Taylor will be discussed in chapter 12. For Du Bois, the shortcomings of the choir's presentation of the work would have paled into insignificance in view of the fact of its performance at all by so august a body; it was the work of a black man. As for Jaeger, he was shortly to receive the first few pages of something much more to his taste: *The Dream of Gerontius*.

*

Hiawatha's Departure, part III of *The Song of Hiawatha*, is almost as long as parts I and II put together. It makes musical references to the earlier parts, and thus the whole trilogy has parallels with the cyclic symphonic forms to be found in the late nineteenth century. Coleridge–Taylor was to describe his work as a kind of choral symphony in which *The Death of Minnehaha* formed the slow movement (a funeral march; he was, of course, familiar with that in the *'Eroica' Symphony*) and the first half of *Hiawatha's Departure* was the scherzo; in this analysis, the second half of the *Departure* was a peroration.

It is questionable whether or not this third cantata is justified dramatically. Marriage ceremony, famine, death and funeral: these, the subjects of parts I and II, follow one another with a natural rhythm. In part III, life has returned with the coming of Spring, but Hiawatha, now a much older man, finds neither happiness nor fulfilment without Minnehaha. Iagoo returns from journeys afar, but his traveller's tales are met with derision by the tribe, just as they had been years before. Hiawatha silences the mocking braves, for he has seen in a vision all that Iagoo describes. What Iagoo has met on his travels is the advance of the White Man, and what Hiawatha has seen in his vision is the dis–integration of the Indian nation. It is at this point that the story loses credibility: as Hiawatha awaits the coming of the White Man who, with his companions, arrives in the person of the Black Robed Chief. He brings with him the message of Christianity, which the sages of Hiawatha's tribe solemnly agree to consider. Hiawatha entrusts his guests to Nokomis and his tribe's well–being to the young braves, bidding them listen to the words of the white men who he believes have been sent by The Master of Life. His life's work done, Hiawatha departs for the Land of the Hereafter.

A scenario that tests credulity — certainly in the light of history — and dramatically difficult to justify. But the musical justification is powerful indeed, for a ternary form (which this work is, considered as a whole) is a fundamental musical one in which the basic musical device of recapitulation can be deployed. Thus, for the return of Iagoo, the orchestra pointedly reminds us of the tribe's derision at his earlier stories:

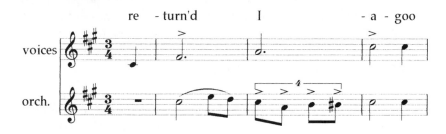

Ex. 59: Departure of Hiawatha, return of Iagoo

And, to the same music that the tribe had bade Chichiabos sing to entertain them at the wedding feast (Example 43), the scene is set for Hiawatha to sing his farewell. But with this memory of earlier, happier times it has now a doubled emotional force. The *Hiawatha* theme itself (Example 38) is used throughout, never paraded but worked subtly into the orchestral texture.

As with the *Symphony*, it would be interesting to see just what was re–written and what, if anything, was retained from the original version. Was it all as bad as Jaeger thought? Or was it that Jaeger (and perhaps other critics of the time) judged the work for what it was never intended to be? In his visits to the Royal College of Music concerts years before, Jaeger had perceived the young Coleridge–Taylor to be a composer of chamber music firmly in the European mainstream tradition — a possible successor to Brahms or Schumann. But Coleridge–Taylor had left serious abstract music behind and had gone on to produce not a major philosophical statement but a work of picturesque detail and colour. From his perspective, Jaeger had identified the weakest part of the

Departure: the appearance of the Black Robed Chief does seem, even in the revised version we have, to sink to the low level of late Victorian religiosity.   But to judge by the worst is to overlook the wonderful opening pages, alive with youthful energy — for which the composer could elicit no corresponding response from the Royal Choral Society:

Ex. 60: Departure of Hiawatha, opening

It overlooks, too, the inspired music of Hiawatha's vision, where in a baritone solo of effortless flow and flexibility, the composer suggests a wisdom and humanity not unworthy of Hans Sachs himself.

Finally, there is the orchestration.   There are passages of such sumptuous sound (the passage, for example, where Hiawatha tells his people of his impending departure) that Elgar might have been pleased to have written them.   The touches of sharp colour as Iagoo describes the white man's 'canoe' on the water; the derisive woodwind as the tribe mock him, and the fine trombone passage as Hiawatha greets his white guests — all these and many more show the hand of a master. Sir Malcolm Sargent described the trilogy as the best–orchestrated choral work he knew. The claim merits attention because Sargent's experience of orchestrally–accompanied choral music was vast, and because he probably conducted more performances of the trilogy than anyone else, excepting perhaps the composer. Essentially it is a question of texture. More than most composers of his time, Coleridge–Taylor lets in the daylight. The choir is not continually supported, and the orchestral patterns are set *against* those of the singers, in strongly–contrasting colours. Coleridge–Taylor is one of those composers (Berlioz is another) whose orchestral work rarely impresses in piano score, but which comes alive only in orchestral performance.

The *Departure* may be uneven in quality but there is enough fine music in it to ensure that a performance of the whole trilogy will always be more affecting than the separate parts. But it does have mannerisms which can be irritating, chief of which is the constant repetition by the orchestra of the ends of vocal phrases. There is also some faulty word–setting; it is simply not true to say, as *The Musical Times* analyst claimed, that there are no false accents to be found in it. Coleridge–Taylor would never sacrifice a good tune for the sake of a misplaced verbal accent. Sargent is again interesting on this point:

> The whole of Longfellow's poem is set in lines that don't rhyme: each consists of four trochees ... It would seem impossible to set a work lasting in all its three parts nearly two hours always in this scansion ... but it is so cleverly done and so amazingly varied in its musical rhythm that one forgets the monotony of the poem.[67]

The received view is that, with the completion of the trilogy, Coleridge–Taylor had reached the apex of his achievement:

> it seemed to be Coleridge–Taylor's particular mission on earth to give us that wonderful choral picture.[68]

and then burned out:

> The fate of half–dozen other works in cantata or oratorio form which he wrote between 1900 and his early death suggest that after the *Hiawatha* series he had little left to say.[69]

However, Sargent shall have the last word:

> I have been told by the highbrows that Coleridge–Taylor does not rank absolutely on the top shelf. This is not my opinion. I have

done his works so often that all the 'weaknesses' should have hit me.... He's a first–class composer, completely equipped technically, with a remarkable and individual charm of melodic invention.[70]

The Birmingham Festival of 1900 is remembered for one of the most famous fiascos in the history of English music: the first performance, on 3 October, of Elgar's *Dream of Gerontius*. Coleridge–Taylor's trilogy followed the Elgar work that evening. *Hiawatha* was cheered whereas Elgar's masterpiece fell flat — literally at times. But even for *Hiawatha* things had not looked promising at the rehearsal on 29 September, the only one with the full company:

> Soon after 7.30 Mr Coleridge–Taylor's *Hiawatha* trilogy was taken in hand, and it lasted until after ten, in spite of the fact that the composer, whether from satisfaction with the results or because he was too diffident to put forward his views, did not take the initiative in suggesting any improvements.[71]

From the review in *The Musical Standard*,[72] it is clear that Coleridge–Taylor's work fared better in performance than Elgar's only in respect of note accuracy:

> The Birmingham choir was particularly unintelligent throughout the festival ... very seldom did it give us the right tone colour. This was particularly noticeable in Coleridge–Taylor's *Hiawatha*. The performance was bright and vigorous to a degree — accurate, too. But point after point of fun and pathos was missed — especially the pathos. Although I say the chorus sang unintelligently, I do not mean to infer that the enthusiastic ladies and gentlemen composing it had no sense of the fine shades of musical meaning ... is it not possible that the rough–shod energy with which the chorus trampled out the fun and pathos of *The Song of Hiawatha* was a good deal due to Richter's want of sympathy with the score? Of course I do not know that he was really less sympathetic, but his straight–forward conducting certainly looked as if he were.

Hans Richter's diary (for 3 October 1900) confirms the surmise of *The Musical Standard*'s reviewer:

> In the evening conducted that rubbish *Hiawatha*. It was well received. Oh!

The generally accepted reason for the Elgar debacle was the death of the choirmaster Swinnerton Heap in the middle of the rehearsals and the subsequent poor preparation of the choir by his aged replacement, Dr W. C. Stockley. But Coleridge–Taylor himself was not impressed with Richter as a choral conductor; as for sympathy, it is possible that Newman and his theology appealled more to Richter's rigorous mind than Longfellow and his Indians. Thus ended Coleridge–Taylor's association with the great conductor. He would later recount with much amusement that, at a party after the concert, Richter played the overture to *Tannhauser* on a pianola.

One immediate postscript to the symbiotic relationship of *Gerontius* and *Hiawatha* can find a place here. G. H. Johnstone (Chairman of the Birmingham Festival) had negotiated with Alfred Littleton (of Novello's) a fee of £200 for Elgar for the publication of the *Dream of Gerontius* and, of course, the firm had already agreed to pay £250 for parts II and III of the Coleridge–Taylor trilogy. But it was also Johnstone's recollection that a royalty per copy had been agreed for *Gerontius*. Littleton tenaciously disputed this, giving way on the point only when it was pointed out to him that *Gerontius* was considered by the publisher to be a commercial failure and that the payment of the royalty was scheduled to come into effect only when Novello's had recovered their costs. Which, everyone felt, would never come about.

But, as Johnstone wrote in his letter to Littleton dated 22 November 1900, 'the success of *Hiawatha* is very marked'. No question, therefore, of a royalty per copy for Coleridge–Taylor, and he was far too timid to push for one on his own account.

9 ORCHESTRAL MUSIC: A FIRST FALTERING?

The newly–sprawling housing estates of south–east London hardly seemed an ideal environment in which a young composer might work. Delius, in the heady atmosphere of *fin–de–siècle* Paris and idyllic Grez–sur–Loing, John Ireland in his windmill or even Vaughan Williams by the Thames at Cheyne Walk — all these seem better placed than Coleridge–Taylor in south–suburban Croydon. But it suited him; it was convenient and he was to live in the district for the rest of his life. Our pictures of him come from Jessie, from his daughter Avril, from his half–sister Marjorie and from his friend and biographer Berwick Sayers. Sayers makes a thought–provoking observation:

> I never heard him utter a sentence which could ruffle the serenity of the most sensitive mind.[73]

The point is confirmed by Marjorie:

> I never remember Coleridge complaining about anything.[74]

This self–effacement has parallels in a certain impersonal quality that occasionally creeps into his music. But where the *performance* of music was concerned, he could be fierce and uncompromising. He demanded absolute silence before commencing a performance; at one Croydon concert his impatience showed:

> Will those people who want to talk please go outside?[75]

There seemed to be sharp contrasts within his personality. While the newly–weds welcomed into their home all and sundry, on his frequent travels around the country Coleridge–Taylor sought the anonymity of a hotel room. In congenial company he would relax, usually standing with a cigarette in his hand, listening intently and occasionally interjecting an 'is that so?' into the conversation.[76] Marjorie's picture of him at home is drawn with clarity and affection:

> He had a high speaking voice, sort of quacky. It was slightly high for a man, but not a silly voice. His sense of humour was gentle, and if he was telling a story he would impersonate their voices and he often acted out the part, portraying the people he was describing.

He was quite fussy over his clothes as was mother. He smoked
cigarettes, and sometimes had one with a cup of tea. He got his
clothes in Croydon, not in some expensive fashionable tailor in
London. He had no sense of being grand.[77]

Avril, too, notes the addiction to tea: innumerable cups of it, even in the
middle of rehearsals. He was clearly a creature of routine, with a
passion for order, neatness and tidiness amounting to obsession. Jessie
tells of the unvarying timetable when he was at home:

8.30 am Breakfast.
9–12 noon Composition.
12 noon–1 pm Long walk — usually with a book of poems.
1–2 pm Dinner.
2–4 pm Rehearsals or private lessons.
4 pm Tea.
Then more composition, proof or editorial work until 10 pm.[78]

Retiring to bed would be accompanied by an apple and a glass of water.
And then, more often than not, some study of German: a pointer to
where he thought his future lay. Eventually he learned to speak German
reasonably well.

With Mozart, we are told, the creative process took place at the
billiard table. With Coleridge–Taylor, it probably took place on those
walks. He used the piano only to try the occasional chord, or for playing
over a completed stretch of work. As with so many composers, he
showed a jealous secrecy while his work was in progress and he hated
to be either overheard or overlooked as he worked. During his walk, he
would quietly hum to himself and on his return would often say: 'don't
talk to me for a moment' as he jotted down his thoughts. All composers
will recognise this characteristic elusiveness of fleeting musical ideas.

But what inspiration could Croydon and Norwood provide?
Marjorie reminds us:

Croydon was the country then, and you could get out into the fields
around Beddington in a short time[79]

She had no doubt that poetry was another source of inspiration:
Longfellow's obviously, and Browning's too, but lesser lights also found
favour — poets such as Lady Florence Dixie, Katherine Easmon or
Marjorie Radclyffe Hall. Shakespeare he liked read aloud to him.
Paradoxically, Marjorie did not remember seeing many books in the
household, and presumed he must have frequented the public library.

Work was the hall–mark of Coleridge–Taylor's existence in the twelve years of life and marriage left to him. He was always in need of money, perhaps through his own faults of kindness and generosity; hardly faults. This generosity, shown in particular to coloured folk, had to wait until his death to be recorded:

> The number of his benefactions to needy coloured people visiting England will, perhaps, never be known.[80]

He was always in need of 'cash crops', such as could be provided by songs. They were quickly written and could be sold outright for an immediate sum.

Concerts, rehearsals, lessons and travel meant a framework of engagements which in turn generated the labour of a considerable correspondence. The constant travelling meant that he would have to send deputies to regular standing engagements such as the Croydon Conservatoire orchestra. More often it meant rushing from a rehearsal to catch a train to distant parts. The completion of the *Hiawatha* trilogy in 1900 had, for example, to be carried out against a counterpoint of competing pressures, including concerts at Bournemouth, Worcester and The Queen's Hall, London, to name just a few.

At the end of April 1900 he went to Bournemouth to conduct the *Symphony in A minor*. Described in the *Bournemouth Visitors' Directory* as the work of 'the young West African composer', the *Symphony* was reviewed (2 May 1900) as 'striking and characteristic' and was said to be well played and enthusiastically received. The next day, he conducted the Municipal Orchestra and Festival Choir in the *Wedding Feast*, prefacing this with the *Hiawatha Overture*. There was, said a local critic, 'a very favourable reception'. This review, pasted into Dan Godfrey's scrapbook, is not identifed; the reviewer found the tenor solo 'Onaway' to be 'not very interesting'.

Coleridge–Taylor much admired Dan Godfrey and his work at Bournemouth; for his part, Godfrey pointed out that Coleridge–Taylor was 'the first coloured man to achieve musical distinction possibly since Beethoven's Bridgetower'.[81]

Two days after the Bournemouth concert (3 May 1900) he was in Worcester to conduct the Worcester Choral Society in *The Wedding Feast* and *Minnehaha*. Later that month (20 May 1900) he was present at The Queen's Hall in London to hear a complete performance of the trilogy conducted by Allan Gill for the National Sunday League. He was back there again on 24 May to conduct the Philharmonic Society.[82] This was a signal honour given to a twenty–five year old composer by the august Society. The work he presented for the occasion was the *Miniatures of an Everyday Comedy* for full orchestra. This, at any rate, was the title he proposed to his publisher Novello, but when it was printed, the work was named *Scenes from an Everyday Romance: A Suite for Orchestra in Four Movements*. The movements are:

1 *Allegro* in E Minor
2 *Andante* in G
3 *Tempo di Valse*
4 *Presto* in E Minor

By chance, Richard Strauss was to produce his *Sinfonia Domestica* three years later, and only the previous year Elgar had written his *Variations* about his 'friends pictured within': three instances of a cosy romanticism.

Elgar at least gives a clue, in the initials which head each of his movements, to guide the listener to the subjects of his variations, but Coleridge–Taylor offers nothing, and in consequence we are left to respond to his *Scenes* as best we can. The critic of *The Times* (25 May 1900) responded ecstatically:

> The music is of an order that is, alas, not met with everyday. Not in the Golden Age of English music, not even at the best part of its classical period in Germany, can such music as this have ever been common. Fresh, full of imagination and of originality. Masterly in design and execution, these four movements would always have commanded the admiration due to a creation of the highest class.

The Musical Times reviewer was more perplexed by the new work:[83]

> Opinions will doubtless be strangely at variance as to the merits of this, his latest achievement — in fact even in the concert–room after the performance, it was quite possible to learn that one critical hearer bestowed upon it the laudation 'perfectly lovely' while another, equally competent to judge, dismissed it as 'awful stuff'. Time, the great tester, will judge as to these differences of opinion.

Time has judged, quickly. The work soon sank without trace, which seems a cruel fate for a *Suite* which is substantial in length (150 pages of full score: about 23 minutes in performance) and of considerable interest. Not the least striking feature is the orchestration which encompasses all the effectiveness of that of his earlier work but now adds a new virtuosity in handling the medium. The first movement uses the violas, against a throbbing accompaniment of low harp and 'cellos to express something of a romantic ardour:

Ex. 61: Scenes from an Everyday Romance, first movement

This same idea also forms the basis of the last movement, where it is compressed into a two–four *Presto*. The second movement moves dangerously towards sentimentality, but in its langour could still have the attraction of forbidden confection to a dieter. The waltz which forms the third movement soon shows its indebtedness in its harmony, key structure, counterpoint figures and above all melody to that of Dvorak in his G Major *Symphony*:

Ex. 62: Scenes from an Everyday Romance, waltz

That is to be expected, but perhaps more interesting are its hints of a song Coleridge–Taylor wrote just a year earlier. *Eleanore*, to words by Eric Mackay, was published by Novello as one of *Six Songs*, op. 37, and it soon achieved enormous success as a vehicle for tenors (amateur and professional) resounding in its full–throated romanticism throughout both drawing–room and concert–hall.

The *Suite* hardly seems to be inferior to the *Petite Suite de Concert*, written eleven years later, which is still seen as one of the masterpieces of light music. The *Scenes from an Everyday Romance* is light music too, and pointed the way in which Coleridge–Taylor should go. But commissions from festivals and from Beerbohm Tree, not to speak of the continual longing to write an opera, distracted him, and it would be some years before he again found this path. By then, little time was left to him, and others, most notably Eric Coates, inherited his mantle.

It might be thought that the writing of the *Scenes from an Everyday Romance* so soon after Elgar's *'Enigma' Variations* was a mere coincidence, were it not for the fact that there are other instances where Coleridge–Taylor seems to shadow Elgar.   He had been present the previous year at Norwich to conduct his *Hiawatha* overture, and there he had heard Elgar's *Sea Pictures* for contralto and orchestra. When he was commissioned to write a work for the 1900 Three Choirs Festival, it seems probable that he remembered the success of the Elgar work, and this may have prompted him to write settings of four sonnets by Elizabeth Barrett Browning for the same forces, under the title *The Soul's Expression*, op. 42. The Festival was held that year at Hereford, and the composer conducted the first performance there on 13 September, with Marie Brema as his soloist.

The critic of *The Times* liked the work, noting the harmonic transitions as an 'exquisitely faithful reflection' of Elizabeth Barrett Browning's words.   'All four songs most cleverly and effectively orchestrated', he enthused.[84] Jaeger had, as usual, been preparing the score. He mentioned it in passing in a letter to Elgar:

> ... Taylor's songs (Sonnets) for Hereford (The Soul's Expression) really good and big ...[85]

This was one of the last occasions on which Jaeger found anything complimentary to say about Coleridge–Taylor's work, and few would disagree with his judgement here. Whilst, like the *Sea Pictures*, they would make their best effect with orchestral accompaniment, the composer's own piano accompaniment is well laid out and grateful to play. The *Sea Pictures* may have prompted the concept, but are in few respects the model; the songs are carefully wrought in the Brahms manner with an accompaniment that complements, but is in no way subservient to, the voice. They represent his very best work; a labour of love, perhaps, for him and Jessie to perform themselves when the occasion for their creation, the Festival, was past. Now that their kinship with music of the nineteenth rather than the twentieth century no longer makes them seem insufficiently up–to–date, as it did at the time, these songs could well be rehabilitated.

The Musical Times announced that 'the fortunate young composer has been commissioned to supply the incidental music to Mr Stephen Phillips' drama *Herod*, which is announced for production at Her Majesty's Theatre'.[86] This was commissioned by Beerbohm Tree, who produced the play. Jessie commented that 'she didn't think Tree knew anything about music'.

For his part, Jaeger doubted whether Coleridge–Taylor knew anything about the theatre; his comment to Elgar was derisory:

> I *do* wonder what *he* will do with the music to a play. I don't think he has ever been to a theatre in his life, at least I've never heard him say so. Really nothing succeeds like success. Produce one work that will become *really* POPULAR and you get com-missions chucked at you! It's extraordinary.[87]

Tree lived in a flat high over his theatre; his rooms were hung with Shakespearian tapestries made for his past productions. Here he enjoyed an everyday role as almost a caricature of the 'actor–manager' stereo-type, whether he was on stage or not. He may not have known much about the technique of music but

> his instinct for it in relation to the needs of whatever play he was producing was marvellous. Many a fiery conductor has flung down his baton in a rage because Herbert has stopped him in the middle of a phrase saying 'stop there — exactly there ... you must cut out all that tra–la–la–la–ing' he would say, imitating the sounds. The conductor would break his heart — the first violin his bow; but Herbert had to be right ...[88]

Because theatrical incidental music is more often than not a background to conversation, it has often been delegated to hack musicians. But a number of composers of distinction have produced incidental music which has passed into the popular repertoire: Schubert's *Rosamunde*, Grieg's *Peer Gynt*, Fauré's *Pelléas et Mélisande* and Delius's *Hassan* come to mind. Coleridge–Taylor's problem was the expectation aroused by the promise of his early work. Each new piece was measured against *Hiawatha*. Berwick Sayers thought that adverse criticism may actually have inhibited his work:

> I know that he would have done better work had a wider under-standing and a saner sympathy been extended to him. In his thirties he gained the detachment and independence which made him entirely indifferent to [critics], and the sense of values which enabled him to gauge the character of his critics and to appraise their work.[89]

Critics have been generally unfavourable to the work produced by Coleridge–Taylor over the next few years. In appraising this music at a distance of just under a century, one hopes to find that their judgement was unjust; one looks at each work impartially in the hope of finding that the early promise really was maintained.   Unfortunately, it is difficult to make a case for some of the music written in the first few years of the new century; the question is not so much whether or not it is inferior, as why it is so.   With regard to the *Herod* music, it might have been expected that since *The Musical Times* was the house magazine of Coleridge–Taylor's principal publisher Novello, it would have found something enthusiastic to say, even though the music was published by a competitor, Augener.   At best, its review was tepid:

> the impression gathered in the theatre is that it shows less of that originality and maturity which have made most of Mr Taylor's compositions so remarkable.[90]

Already, it seems that expectations were not being fulfilled.   The perception that he was some kind of musical savage which had surfaced a few years before was still evident, but it seems that now he could be criticised for work that was too civilised.   His previous work:

> on first principles, would have seemed to make him the man most fitted to illustrate a semi–barbaric subject.   But Mr Taylor's barbarism is Western — *Herod* is Eastern.   Perhaps it was consciousness of this that has made Mr Taylor write what is perhaps the most civilised music that has come from his pen.[91]

Melodically undistinguished and harmonically bland, this music does show an alarming drop in quality.   This might have resulted from his new experience of domesticity or been a by–product of that professional training which would have shown him how to continue producing even when inspiration was lacking.   (Working to order will always carry the risk that inspiration will fail; it is hard to imagine a Delius doing much work to order.)

Or was it that, for this work and few works afterwards, there was no Jaeger to say 'this will never do'?   Nor indeed anyone else, now that Stanford was part of his past; Jessie was unlikely to question her husband's work in the same way as Caroline Alice Elgar would occasionally gently question her husband's work.   Coleridge–Taylor would in later years be re–united with his muse; but by then little time would be left to him.

*

On the 13th of October, Jessie gave birth to a son. The day after, Coleridge–Taylor wrote to tell Kilburn — an indication, perhaps, of how much this man's friendship meant to him:

> I write to tell you that my wife presented me with a very fine baby boy yesterday, whose name shall be Hiawatha.
> P.S. Mother and child are exceedingly well.[92]

The child was registered as Hiawatha Bryan Coleridge, and his father was described as 'Professor of Music'. Berwick Sayers noted that the name was subject to confirmation upon the child's coming of age. He was christened at St Michael's Church, West Croydon. With much younger brothers and sisters, Coleridge–Taylor had some experience of children, and loved especially Marjorie:

> When I was a small child Coleridge would lift me up on to the mantelpiece and sit me on one of the tea canisters, and when I began to cry he would lift me down and cuddle me .... He would put his hat on crooked when he left — just to make me laugh ...[93]

He identified with children and they were drawn naturally to him; in some ways a certain child–like innocence was never entirely to leave him. But Marjorie was a good girl; Hiawatha turned out to be such a naughty boy:

> He got hold of his father's violin, the one he had been given years before by Mr Holmans. Mother had kept it and gave it to Coleridge when he said that he thought that Watha should begin music lessons. She was dubious, but she handed it over, and the very next time she visited Coleridge's home it was broken; in pieces under the piano. Watha was a perfect little terror at times. His father had that shed to work in, the 'music shed', because Watha would make such a noise. He would say to us 'Father's trying to work — let's make a noise' and he would run up and down the hallway.[94]

A far cry from the repressed Carice Elgar, packed off down the road to boarding school, or from her mother, standing guard in the woods on the approach to Birchwood, lest anyone disturb Edward at work on *Gerontius*. Watha was certainly a trial to his father; but he grew up to be a musician, who on occasion even conducted the masterpiece after which he had been named.

10 TOILING FOR THE FESTIVALS

A fourth reason for any discerned falling–off in the quality of Coleridge–Taylor's work became all too apparent as 1901 dawned: overwork.

At the beginning of the century, and indeed for many years after, a career in composition was hazardous for those without private means. In the eighteenth century, a composer might serve a great aristocratic house; probably as overworked as ever, but at least with some security and a settled routine. These days, he might be a university academic who, one hopes, would not be too outraged at the suggestion that over–work is not a problem. But in 1901, if he had not the contractual cunning of a Beethoven or the awesome financial 'borrowing' capacity of a Wagner, a composer without an independent income had perforce to accept any and every part–time job. Coleridge–Taylor must have discovered that the music–loving fraternity loved singers, players and conductors more than they did (and would) composers. Through sheer need, he took all the work he could get. And when he had money, he was generous in giving it away.

> Mr Coleridge–Taylor has been appointed conductor of the next Westmorland Music Festival, to be held in 1901, when his *Death of Minnehaha* is to be performed.[95]

The Westmorland Festival, held biennially at Kendal, had been founded by Mary Wakefield, a contralto singer in her younger years, and one of the pioneers of the festival movement. Coleridge–Taylor described his first festival there for the benefit of his American friends:

> a huge gathering, held in the beautiful Lake District ... . The first one you will be pleased to know was a great success, and the singing (the choir was 600 strong) was magnificent.
>
> Moreover, the famous Hallé band from Manchester was engaged for my benefit, and we had a really wonderful performance each evening.[96]

The press agreed:

> The choir and orchestra, inspired by the composer's presence and

119

remarkable skill in conducting, did extremely well, and the whole performance was a brilliant success.

The Festival was a curious hybrid, with a competitive element (judged by Dr William McNaught) as well as the choral and orchestral per–formances. Coleridge–Taylor did not conduct the purely orchestral work, but did stray from the choral works to direct the Hallé Orchestra in the accompaniment of Wagner's 'Prize Song' (from *Die Meistersinger*) for the tenor soloist Whitworth Mitton.

Croydon continued to appreciate his conducting too, as he worked week by week with the orchestral society. Over in Worcester, some of his friends had organised an amateur choir and orchestra for Elgar to conduct, and a comparison between the fortunes of the two organisations is illuminating. At Worcester, Elgar's programmes were adventurous, as he explored music that made an appeal to him as a composer. But he was not good with amateurs, employing a vague beat, losing patience quickly and lacking analytical explanatory skills. After a few years, he walked out of a practice and abandoned the bemused Worcester Philharmonic to Granville Bantock.

At Croydon, Coleridge–Taylor's programmes seemed by compari–son distinctly unenterprising, and showed little evidence of a quest and thirst for new musical experience. Where Elgar occasionally put in some of his own work, Coleridge–Taylor rarely included any of his. But while Elgar fulminated and finally exploded in frustration (unable either to live with or to alter his members) Coleridge–Taylor worked on patiently, biding his time. Overtures by Weber and Mozart, and symphonies by Beethoven, Schubert and Dvorak were standard fare, leavened occasionally by the work of Grieg or Smetana. *The Bartered Bride* overture is, as the music critic of the *Croydon Advertiser* well knew,

> very far from child's play. However, the members of the orchestra mastered the difficulties with comparative ease, and with the confidence born of the experience they had gained in the last five years ... . Mr Coleridge–Taylor, to whom naturally the atmosphere of the piece peculiarly appealed, was able to impart to the rendering the fire and fervour which it demands.

But now he had taken his amateurs as far as they and he could go together. There was a running disagreement with the committee over wind players, the lamentable quality of whom was such that listeners had difficulty in identifying which instrument was being played. This, and difficulties with an over–bearing soloist, led to Coleridge–Taylor's resignation in the 1902–3 season after six years of service. The Croydon Orchestral Society disintegrated. But now, in August 1903, he acted with a ruthless energy surprising in one apparently so timid. The following circular letter tells what happened next:

COLERIDGE–TAYLOR ORCHESTRAL CONCERTS
(season 1903–1904)
Conductor — S. Coleridge–Taylor

Dear

The Croydon Orchestral Society having been dissolved, a new series of first–class Orchestral Concerts is now being organised, of which I shall have entire control.

... The Concerts will be given in the Large Public Hall, Croydon, and the assistance of professional wind–instrument players and an eminent vocalist will be secured on each occasion.

A limited number of Amateur String Players will be admitted to the Orchestra; all such players must submit themselves to an examination.

... Each member must attend at least five–sixths of the weekly rehearsals ...

Yours faithfully

'I shall have entire control'; clearly he was exasperated by committee management. 'A limited number of amateur string players'; these would be the more able players from the rump of the deceased orchestral society. Those not invited but who applied would be auditioned. But the string players were more proficient than the word 'amateur' would normally suggest; they were 'R.A.M. and R.C.M. girls who live round about and they do play magnificently'.[97]

He solved his problems with the wind players equally efficiently, and the engagement of 'eminent' soloists suggests that he had had his fill of 'local talents' being foisted on him. No detail escaped him: he even undertook the drudgery of writing to or visiting his acquaintances to elicit subscriptions. The Coleridge–Taylor Orchestral Concerts, with a band of sixty players, ran for three seasons and, as they briefly illuminated the Croydon musical scene, were accounted an artistic success. But the Public Hall, although always well filled, was too small, and the churches would permit only sacred performances. Running the concerts on a shoestring, the Coleridge–Taylors did all the administration themselves. Even step–sister Marjorie was pressed into service to sell programmes. With no subsidies and no other organisation to back them, the concerts had by 1905 lost a total of around £80, and they had to come to an end.

Thus both Elgar and Coleridge–Taylor ultimately failed in their work with amateurs; but the manner of their failures seems to reflect, or symbolise, their respective characters: Elgar, neurotic, depressive and ultimately eruptive; Coleridge–Taylor, patient, professional and ultimately unable to compromise where musical standards were in question.

Over the same period (1900 to 1906) he accepted other regular posts. In 1902 he took over the Rochester Choral Society, and with them his programmes included *The Golden Legend* (Sullivan), *The Spectre's Bride* (Dvorak) and *The Banner of St George* (Elgar). His particular and frequently expressed admiration for the Sullivan work is disquieting: it is not an obvious model for a young composer at the start of a questing new century. He had also joined (in 1903) the staff of Trinity College of Music as a professor of composition, and a year later became conductor of the Handel Society (a post he held until his death). He was not an admirer of Handel, whose music he found 'crude and bare', and he worked into the programmes as much music by other composers as he reasonably could. The Handelians also found them–selves singing *The Spectre's Bride*.

It is against this background that his compositions of the first years of the twentieth century must be considered, for clearly there was little time for meditation, or for the prolonged gestation of a new composition such as Delius had indulged in by communing with Nietsche's philo–sophy or Elgar with Newman's theology.

The major undertakings which occupied Coleridge–Taylor in 1901 were various: a cantata commissioned by the Leeds Festival, an overture, a further commission from Beerbohm Tree for incidental music, and a commission for the 1901 Three Choirs Festival.

Faced with such a programme of work to complete, it is not surprising that the composer looked for corners to cut. Herbert Brewer at Gloucester had asked for an orchestral work; as the *Symphony in A minor* had not been heard there and was still in manuscript, he was not to know that Coleridge–Taylor's response to the commission, an *Idyll*, was a re–working of the *Symphony*'s slow movement, the 'Lament'.

The *Idyll* is considerably larger than the movement from which it is derived, which was also completely re–orchestrated with the addition of trombones, tuba and harp. Its performance took place on 11 September 1901. *The Times* critic was enthusiastic:

> A single, very beautiful movement ... giving ample room for the composer's love of original rhythm and rich and individual orchestral colouring ... the little work is sure of popularity and is a worthy example of the clever young author's work.[98]

The Times critic of this occasion was not given to over–praising; in the same review he speaks of the work of the choir in Cherubini's *D minor Mass* as 'little short of disgraceful'.

The Musical Times, hardly to be blamed for not realising the *Idyll*'s relationship to the work it had reviewed a few years before, noted again the composer's melodic gift:

> The principal theme is of quite reposeful character; it is, however, a real theme, not a short phrase or mere figure to be afterwards twisted and tortured by cunning devices[99]

The Leeds cantata was the *Blind Girl of Castel–Cuillé*, once more to a poem by Longfellow or, rather, a translation by him of a Gascon troubador's poem *Jasmin*. With Madam Albani and Andrew Black as soloists, the composer conducted the first performance at Leeds on 9 October, 1901. The audience and chorus seemed to like it; the composer, who conducted, was cheered by both. But most of the critics were tepid, seeing no progress from *Hiawatha*. Worst of all for Coleridge–Taylor, it found little favour with Stanford, the Leeds Festival conductor, who had been instrumental in securing the commission for him. The comments of *The Musical Times* were hard:

> Why Mr Taylor should have selected a poem as Adelphi–melodramatically tinctured as *The Blind Girl* we are at a loss to understand. The music of the new cantata, although strongly resembling *Hiawatha*, cannot be said to equal the older work. There are some characteristic touches here and there, especially the pathetic solo of Margaret in Part II; but Mr Taylor must free himself from the snare of over–elaboration and ultra–colorations of orchestral effect, if he is to maintain his high position as one who has something spontaneous to say.[100]

The critic of *The Times* was even more severe:

> The great bulk of it is as conventional as the works of those English composers who in former years were wont to bring out pieces as insincere as they were monotonous at the successive provincial festivals, and whose names were scarcely heard of between one festival and another.

... in spite of the many skilful passages throughout the work, it is impossible to call it a great success. Much of the choral writing is sadly wanting in the very quality of inspiration which brought Mr Coleridge–Taylor so suddenly to the front.[101]

He considered the possibility that the failure was largely due to an impossible libretto which needed far more adaptation than had been made; but in the end he concluded that the problem was

the over–production which is the usual consequence of success.

The Yorkshire Post was generally kinder; indeed, of all his critics, Coleridge–Taylor retained throughout his life a belief that Herbert Thompson of *The Post* was the fairest. Thompson was not to be prejudiced by an early warning from Jaeger who had, of course, seen the score in advance at Novello's:

I fear you won't like Taylor's Leeds cantata much. I leave him severely alone now, for he is too big a celebrity now ever to come near me. He sent me the other day another new choral work to this address without even a letter of explanation and I haven't even looked at it yet. I'll teach that youngster manners yet, *though* his Hiawatha sells like hot cakes. It is I should think the biggest success Novellos have had since *Elijah*.[102]

Within one short month his fortunes had changed; his golden image had tarnished. From this point onwards, for at least a few years, there would more often than not be a question–mark hanging over each new work.

He was hurt by the reception of *The Blind Girl*, and this must have been a factor in a letter he wrote (dated 17 October 1901) to Littleton at Novello's:

I ... want to know if it will be possible for you to release me from the agreement I made with Novellos three years ago. I want to have quite a long rest from all kinds of composition, and may not write anything for a number of months.

Two days later the firm wrote a soothing letter which effectively retained him on a long, but secure, lead:

It seems to us that the object you have in view, viz. a somewhat prolonged rest from all kinds of composition, can be equally well obtained if we mutually agree to eliminate the year 1902 bodily from the agreement, which we would take up again on Jan. 1st, 1903.[103]

Coleridge–Taylor wrote to thank Kilburn, in a letter which also showed his awareness of the dramatic absurdities forced on a composer by Festival economics and the conventions of the 'dramatic' cantata which all too often required one singer to represent two or more characters:[104]

> I had your letter and thank you for it most heartily — you were the *one* friend in need! — and at any rate my Leeds experience has opened my eye in *that* particular way ... Thank you, yes, I saw the Daily Telegraph notice. Bennett is the only one who seems to understand that I deliberately set the dramatic element on one side, and even had I not, it's no better than *Hiawatha* in that respect.
>
> For instance, Nokomis in *The Death of Minnehaha* speaks through the chorus — Minnehaha herself is 'Famine' and after she is dead she sings 'Spring has come'!
>
> There is strong dramatic consistency for you! In an opera, of course, I should be the first to take care of these things.

Henry Wood continued his support by including the *Ballade in A minor* and *Hiawatha's Vision* (sung by Harry Dearth) in his 'Prom' on 22 October 1901. It was probably overshadowed there, for it was preceded by Elgar's first *Pomp and Circumstance* March which was encored upon receiving its first hearings. Four days later, Coleridge–Taylor was back at The Queen's Hall for the first performance of his overture *Toussaint L'Ouverture*.

A brief reminder of the historical place of Pierre Dominique Toussaint L'Ouverture will serve to explain Coleridge–Taylor's interest in him as he sought ways to use his art in the service of his brothers. Toussaint (1743–1803) was a Haiti slave, the grandson of an African chieftain, who took advantage of the outlawing of slavery in France in 1789 to lead the liberation of Haiti at the end of the eighteenth century. He appointed himself Governor–General of Haiti for life, but Napoleon sent a force there and brought him back to France where he died in prison.

The Musical Times commented:

> In its entirety the overture shows advance on Mr Coleridge–Taylor's previous writings for orchestra.[105]

But *The Times* was scathing in its condemnation:

> It is a piece of nondescript form, a good deal too long for an ordinary overture, too monotonous in style and treatment for a symphonic poem and too organically conceived for a mere fantasia.

It presents the warlike and tenderer sides of the negro patriot in a style of contrast of which Mackenzie's *Coriolanus* overture affords one of the best recent examples; the usual negro characteristics are duly presented, according to Dvorak's recipe, in the first subject, and the second is appropriately suave, not to say sentimental. The whole, it must be confessed, is rather disappointing, for the music has far less than the composer's usual individuality and although it is skilfully scored, it is far too long.[106]

The overture was repeated at the beginning of December, after which the composer attempted to remedy some of the structural weaknesses, re–writing also the coda in the process. In this revised form it was heard in January 1902 at Bournemouth, together with the *Herod* music.

Jaeger's jibe about Coleridge–Taylor never having been in a theatre may have been valid at the time it was made but, once he tried it, he soon acquired a taste for it. He was never happier than when in a theatre, and Tree had so liked his *Herod* music that he looked no further when he needed music for Stephen Phillips's *Ulysses*, produced at His Majesty's Theatre that January. Coleridge–Taylor greatly admired Phillips's blank verse; it is a worrying thought, nevertheless, that he apparently placed it on a higher level than that of Shakespeare. All that appears to have been published are two songs: 'O Set the Sails, for Troy is Fallen' and a drinking song, 'Great is he who fused the might of Earth and Sun'; but in addition to these he also wrote an overture, a part–song ('From the Green Heart of the Waters'), a Nymph's song, interludes, entractes and music for a storm scene. From *Herod*, and much sub–sequent theatre music, he was able to put together suites but, according to Berwick Sayers, the theatre retained the unpublished music of *Ulysses*, which in any case may not have been adaptable. He comments that the part–song was 'one of his best' and that the storm scene was 'remarkably dramatic and effective'.

It may be that the remaining music is still in existence, rotting deep in some theatre store. In the meantime, we have the songs, which are of considerable interest. 'O Set the Sails' would not be out of place as an extra *Sea Picture* (as if by Elgar): it is one of very few Coleridge–Taylor works to show any Elgar influence. The drinking song marks a welcome return to the rhythmic energy of the *Wedding Feast*, and is particularly striking in the independence of its accompaniment:

Ex. 63: Ulysses, drinking song

Music, perhaps more than words, can suggest other times and places. But nothing in these two songs transports the theatre–goer very far in either place or time from the Haymarket in 1902 — a fact that the composer ruefully recognised:

> I hope you and Mrs Carr will go and see *Ulysses* — nothing has ever been seen on the stage to equal it — and I think you'll like my music though it is not Grecian and therefore not ugly enough for certain critics![107]

He should have conducted at the opening night, but 'King Influenza reigned supreme'[108] and he had to hand over to the music director of the theatre, Adolph Schmid, missing also a trip to Glasgow to conduct the Scottish Orchestra. Schmid admired Coleridge–Taylor's theatre music, and became a lifelong friend.

None of this was allowed to hold up the production line of choral work for the insatiable music festivals. Work on his choral seascape *Meg Blane* for the 1902 Sheffield Festival had started as early as the Autumn of 1901 while he was holidaying at Hastings. He had known Robert Buchanan's poem for some time, but the conception of the cantata seems to have been sparked on a particularly rough day, as he stood at his Hastings window watching the seas break over the esplanade. A year later he was putting the finishing touches to it while again staying in the district, this time at Bexhill. (It says much for the evocative power of these south–eastern resorts: a mere three years later, along the coast at Eastbourne, Debussy was finishing *La Mer*.)

The 1902 Sheffield Triennial Festival was directed by Sir Henry Wood. Coleridge–Taylor conducted the first performance of his new seascape there on the morning of 3 October, when his work shared the programme with Dvorak's *Stabat Mater*, Bach's *Jesu Priceless Treasure* and one of Sir Henry's war–horses, the *Symphony No. 6* in B minor by Tschaikowsky. Also in the Sheffield Festival that year was *The Dream of Gerontius*; the performance of which, after the Birmingham debacle, marked the true beginning of that work's establishment in this country. Both *Meg* and *The Dream* benefitted from the rigorous choir training of a choirmaster of genius: Henry Coward (1849–1944), a master cutler by trade, who had educated himself musically as best he could and became the director of a number of choirs with whom he accomplished something of a revolution in choral standards.

Described as a 'Rhapsody of the Sea' and dedicated to Mary Wakefield (the composer's deference leads to her being simply 'Miss Wakefield' on the score), *Meg Blane* is scored for mezzo–soprano, chorus and orchestra. The soloist at Sheffield was Louise Kirkby–Lunn (1873–1930) whom Coleridge–Taylor had known as a fellow student at the Royal College of Music. The work was well received as 'one of the most pleasing and effective compositions submitted at the 1902 Festival'.[109]

A prayerful prologue sung by the soloist, and an epilogue in which she sings the same words but is joined by an eight–part chorus, sandwich a simple story. At the height of a storm, fishermen line the shore, powerless as they watch a ship foundering on a reef. A woman, Meg Blane, rallies some of the men to brave the breakers and row out to rescue. All in vain; the wreck slips under the waves even as the rescue craft draws near. The work, which lasts about half–an–hour, is immaculately written for both soloist and chorus, with an unfailing care for both phrasing and word–setting. It is structurally simple; as the local critic pointed out:

> The entire work is, in fact, built up on three motifs, easily written on a quarter–sheet of note–paper.[110]

The climaxes are well–placed and the choral textures expertly varied. Yet the cantata is ultimately disappointing; for this the text, despite the fact that the composer thought it greatly superior to that of *The Blind Girl*, must take much of the blame. The plethora of hand–on–heart exclamations encourage Coleridge–Taylor less to drama than to melo-drama; all too often these emotions are clothed in threadbare diminished sevenths or augmented triads which have today lost much of their potency. But this was his style and at the time it was still a valid one. Perhaps unjustly the work is a victim of changing taste and fashion.

Sea subjects were popular. A perusal of any of the back pages of the original buff–coloured Novello vocal scores would yield Gray's *Legend of the Rock Buoy Bell*, C. A. E. Harris's *The Sands of Dee* and J. F. Bridge's *The Inchcape Rock*. All the ingredients for popularity were there and *Meg Blane* had a number of other performances, including one by the Central Croydon Choral Society in the early spring of 1903, conducted by the composer. But, along with the *Blind Girl*, within a few years it was virtually forgotten.

While these and other cantatas never established themselves in the repertoire, there was never any problem in securing either a publisher or a hearing for each new Coleridge–Taylor work. There was always the hope that it might prove to be another *Hiawatha*, and performances of *Hiawatha* had grown to flood proportions.

He was well able to work on a number of different projects at the same time, and three orchestral works were also written in 1902. By the September of that year, Novello's had published the full score of *Novelletten*, op. 52, a suite for strings, tambourine and triangle. Sheer volume of work put him under pressure and, because of this, corners were again cut; the cannibalising of the *Symphony* which had begun with the *Idyll* for the Three Choirs Festival continued in this work; its third movement was taken from the *Symphony*'s Scherzo (see Example 28). This was probably done simply to save time, for the other movements, which were original, show no faltering of the spring of melody. The fourth movement, a gentle waltz, is typical of the work's attractive style:

Ex. 64: Novelletten, fourth movement

The second of these three works, this time for full orchestra, is the unusually–named *Hemo Dance*, op. 47, no. 2. No explanation is given on the score, but he would have had in mind the rhythmic idea of *hemiola*; not the Handelian use of the term, but rather the super–imposition of two notes in the time of three and vice versa. Within a basic one beat in a bar, the bassoons and timpani establish a duple pattern, against which the violins play in a triple pattern, both of these being contained within three–eight time. He probably had the work in mind some years later when, again under pressure, he was at work on a dance for his *Othello* incidental music:

Ex. 65a: Hemo Dance

Ex. 65b: Othello, dance

A few days after the first performance of *Meg Blane*, he travelled to Bristol to conduct the *Hiawatha* Trilogy, as part of the Tenth Bristol Music Festival. The Festival had not been held in 1899 because of the destruction by fire of the Colston Hall; but a new and superior hall had been built, and a Festival Chorus of five hundred voices assembled for Grieg, Elgar and Coleridge–Taylor to conduct their own works. Elgar conducted the second performance of his *Coronation Ode*, written for the coronation of King Edward VII which had been postponed because of the King's illness. Coleridge–Taylor preceded the Trilogy at Bristol with his new Commemoration March, *Ethiopia Saluting the Colours*. (The Bristol programme wrongly described it as a 'Coronation March'.) The march, which is dedicated 'To the Treble Clef Club, Washington, U.S.A.', is headed by some lines from Walt Whitman:

> Who are you, dusky woman, so ancient hardly human,
> With your woolly white and turban'd head, and bare bony feet?
> Why rising by the roadside here, do you the colours greet?

The Treble Clef Club was a society of black women which we will encounter again in the next chapter, when negotiations for his first American visit are discussed. A work for them was opportune; that it was a march may have been prompted by Elgar's enormous success the year before with the first two *Pomp and Circumstance* marches. If, as is likely, Coleridge–Taylor attended that 'Prom' on 22 October 1901 to hear Harry Dearth sing a *Hiawatha* excerpt, he would have heard Elgar's work encored. He certainly heard the marches a few days later, on 26 October 1901, when they were included that night at The Queen's Hall 'Prom' at which his overture *Toussaint L'Ouverture* was performed. Where composition is a profession, composers tend to watch one another very closely for successes and failures.

Ethiopia was issued in its orchestral form but also as a piano duet. In neither version did it match the success of the Elgar marches. Competent though it is, the tunes simply do not have Elgar's panache and exuberance.

Ex. 66: Ethiopia Saluting the Colours

For Elgar, these qualities were the natural reverse of his predominantly dark melancholy. Further, the essential vulgarity of his marches belie the aristocratic overtones of their title. Coleridge–Taylor had little or no pessimistic side; no dark side, in fact. Moreover, his attempts at a popular style belie his essentially refined nature and are to that extent artificial. His bid to match Elgar's common touch results only in the commonplace.

11 A LOW EBB: THE RECEPTION OF *THE ATONEMENT*

All three works — the march, the *Hemo Dance* and the *Novelletten* — were given by the ever–supportive Dan Godfrey at Bournemouth in February, 1903. A few days later, on 8 March, Jessie gave birth to the couple's second child: a girl christened Gwendolen. In later years, Gwendolen decided to use the name Avril, and as Avril Coleridge–Taylor she pursued a distinguished career as a composer and conductor in her own right, at all times championing her father's music.

It was in this year that the family moved to South Norwood, to 10 Upper Grove. Most of the year was taken up with work on a major composition for the Three Choirs Festival which was to be held in Hereford, in the smallest of the three cathedrals. The organist and conductor there was George R. Sinclair (1862–1917), who was immort–alised with his inseparable companion, a bulldog called Dan, in Elgar's *'Enigma' Variations*. The 1903 Festival saw the first performances of *The Wilderness* by Bantock, *Indian Rhapsody* by Cowen, and *Voces Clamantium* by Parry. It was distinguished by a performance of *The Dream of Gerontius* with the original text; a performance which seemed finally to overcome the scruples of Church of England clerics towards the expounding of Roman Catholic theology in an Anglican Cathedral. It also afforded a platform for the major Coleridge–Taylor work: *The Atonement*, described as a cantata, but in fact a cantata of exceptional length. Its performance on 9 September shared a programme with a Bach cantata and Mozart's *Symphony No. 40* in G minor.

At Novello's, the staff were under pressure, for not only did they have to produce the material for *The Atonement* but also that for Elgar's second oratorio *The Apostles*, due for performance later in the year. Jaeger gives a picture of the publisher at work, as he wrestled with all the proofs:

> Brause is using every available man .... He is driven right and left over these Apostles and Taylor's new long thing for Hereford ...[111]

Following in the wake of the *Ballade* (Gloucester, 1898), the *Solemn Prelude* (Worcester, 1899), *The Soul's Expression* (Hereford, 1900) and the *Idyll* (Gloucester, 1901), the new work was to be his first choral music for the Three Choirs Festival. It was to be not only the composer's bid to be a 'Three Choirs composer' to be reckoned with, but also a statement such as all composers with pretensions to importance were expected to make: a statement such as *Gerontius* or the *Mass of Life*. At twenty–eight, Coleridge–Taylor was perhaps young to be staking his claim to the moral high ground; at that age, Delius had not yet even found his authentic voice, let alone his ecstatic message, while Elgar had hardly graduated from quadrilles and lancers, and had certainly not found his song of 'heroic melancholy'.[112]

But the English School, in the shadow of Beethoven, Brahms and Wagner, hankered after an ill–defined concept of 'greatness': Sullivan, for example, was forced by his gambling debts into his true milieu of light opera and away from his preferred path of oratorio and grand opera. Elgar as a boy, down by the river, also dreamed of 'something great'. And to be great, it had to be continental or, more specifically, Austro–German. The English way was the way of the amateur; the Germans were the ones who really knew. Thus, artistic affairs tended to be controlled by them — Hallé, Richter, Manns or Jaeger. Many of the friends of Elgar and Delius were German. Notwithstanding the fact that the Hallé Orchestra was founded by a German, Delius on one occasion lambasted its English inefficiency in turning up without certain instruments necessary for his *Appalachia*:

> Call yourselves an orchestra? You're no better than a bloody village band. My God, if this country ever goes to war with Germany what a hiding you will get![113]

'Aspiration' was the admired quality: the hallmark of European Romantic Art. Along with the others, Coleridge–Taylor was determined to break out of insular England onto the great European musical uplands. The accepted vehicles were the symphony and the opera; but, despite his early success in the sonata forms, his work was now favouring dramatic development. In his own country there was little practical opportunity for opera and it could be argued that both Delius and Elgar wasted time in their early years working on opera and cantata respectively, but both lived on into old age and could make up this early waste. Coleridge–Taylor, who similarly wasted much time — in his case on unworthy words, bad models and genres alien to his light–dramatic genius — was not to be afforded a full life–span. It would take composers such as Vaughan Williams, Edward German and Eric Coates (to name a random few) to bring some realism to English music: Vaughan Williams to forge a national style in which to express profound thought and German and Coates to bring respectability to music without a message; music for purely immediate enjoyment.

The performance of *The Atonement* had the benefit of a team of distinguished soloists (Albani, Emily Squire, Kirkby–Lunn,[114] Andrew Black and William Green), and the chorus liked the work. But critical reception was again mixed. A few praised it, but others found it 'uninspired' and 'lacking in reverence' or even actually irreverent. The orchestration was 'not rich enough' and there was 'tiresome repetition of the words'. Normally, Coleridge–Taylor shrugged off criticism; in his view, critics were always at least trying to be constructive and kind. He himself pointed out one of their problems:

> The fact is there has never been a religious work written by a coloured man before, so they had only English and German works to guide them, and my efforts [are] fearfully misunderstood.[115]

But the reception this time caused him grief and depression. Never again, he told Leila Petherick, would he undertake a festival commission. The day after the performance, he reacted just as he had after the criticisms at Leeds of *The Blind Girl*. He sought once more to break his publishing agreement with Novello's:

> I really think I shall do better work if I feel quite free — perhaps I am superstitious! I didn't think the people disliked *The Atonement* so much as the critics, and I am afraid they have judged my work from an entirely wrong point of view.[116]

It seems unlikely that in this he was intending to sever his connection with the firm; rather it is almost as if he felt that, in the failure of his cantata, he was in some way letting Novello's down. On receiving this second entreaty, the publishers felt bound to release him, although they were in due course to bring out several more of his larger works. The misunderstanding (as he saw it) depressed him. His gloom would have deepened if he had been aware of the shaking heads of those whose opinions he most valued. A few days after the first performance Jaeger wrote to Elgar:

> Poor Taylor! And yet Maitland and Thompson praise it muchly! Where *are* critics with taste?[117]

and Elgar replied:

> Taylor's work was a disgrace to any civilised country! The utter want of *education* is the curse of this chap. The clergy condemn it as blasphemous.[118]

Elgar's insecurity was showing, as Michael Kennedy noted:

> Elgar's attitude to Coleridge–Taylor is incidentally symptomatic of his own vulnerability. In 1899 he could describe the younger man's music as 'all so *human* and yearning' ... but by 1900, when Coleridge–Taylor had had outstanding success with *Hiawatha*, his work becomes for Elgar only 'rot' and 'insincere and cannot do any real good'.... The conclusion is inescapable that once a younger composer became a potential rival, he became a target for the dismissive remarks which so often betray Elgar's insecurity ...[119]

Jaeger, in a letter to Thompson (4 March 1901) had attempted to prejudice him by comparing Coleridge–Taylor unfavourably with the composer W. H. Bell, who:

> though he may lack Taylor's easy invention of tune, has certainly vastly more meaning than the young Blackie, and more depth and poetic imagination. Why I should bother about these youngsters at all I don't know ...

A few months after the Hereford performance, the work received its first hearing in New York.[120] That is not so surprising as the fact that shortly afterwards it was heard in Calgary, Alberta. Back in England, on 17 February 1904, the Royal Choral Society performed the work at the Royal Albert Hall. With memories of the last time the Society performed his music still searingly painful, he must have looked forward to this with dread. But as it happened, he was gratified by both performance and reception, as his letter to Hilyer a few days after makes clear:

> *The Atonement* has been much abused by a portion of the English press, but not by the leading papers such as *The Times* which puts it above Gounod's *Redemption*! The strange thing about it is this, that it was received more enthusiastically at the Royal Albert Hall than ever *Hiawatha* was. I was recalled twice in the middle, and three times at the end, and the audience nearly smashed a magnificent performance by applauding in the course of a trio towards the end — almost an unheard–of thing. The choir, numbering a thousand voices, sang it as they have never done anything before, at least that was the opinion of most people, so *The Atonement* can afford to wait for a little.[121]

It waited and waited. There was talk of it replacing Gounod's *Redemption* as the annual Lenten performance of the Royal Choral Society, but it came to nothing. Instead the Society continued to offer

Hiawatha — a much more certain money–spinner.

Some of the specific criticisms made after the Three Choirs per–formance are valid. The setting does use much repetition of words, and the text itself, the work of Alice Parsons, does need revision. If Richard Strauss had been faced with unsatisfactory passages of libretto he would probably have referred them back to his Hofmannsthal. And if, for example, a sequential passage was thought musically necessary, the writer would have been asked to provide suitably varied words for the phrase–repetitions. Taking the score as published, it would today be a comparatively straightforward task to re–write the words of the few unworthy passages if an enterprising society wished to sing the work.

The orchestration was criticised, but the playing at Hereford was probably inadequate; it is worth pointing out that 1903 was the last year in which an 'ad hoc' orchestra was employed at the Three Choirs Festival. Admittedly, this orchestra employed many London musicians, some from Wood's Queen's Hall orchestra, but it would have had no corporate identity. From 1904, the newly–formed London Symphony Orchestra was used.

The cantata is cast in five scenes with an orchestral prelude and a concluding chorus. Within this framework, the work tells the story of Christ's seizure by the mob, his desertion by his disciples, his treatment at the hands of Pilate and his crucifixion. It covers, therefore, the same ground as a Passion setting, but with important differences: there are no chorales to involve a congregation or audience and there is no Evangelist to narrate. Since it is not a strict setting of the Gospels, certain liberties have been taken: the words of Christ are liberally extended, as is the part of Pilate. A role is even found for Pilate's wife, whose pleadings for Christ to be left alone are rejected roughly by her husband. The intention was probably to inject a greater sense of drama; indeed, the dramatic moments are more striking than the spiritual ones: Christ at the mercy of the baying mob, for example, or the contemptuous Pilate handing Christ over for crucifixion. At moments such as these it seems as if Mendelssohn's Elijah confronting the priests of Baal may have been in the composer's mind. (Confirmation of the influence of Mendelssohn is there in the eight–part 'Prayer of the Holy Women and Apostles' which is clearly suggested by 'Lord, Bow Thine Ear' from *Elijah*.) After the savagery of these confrontations, the sweetness of the final chorus of apotheosis is distinctly anaemic. It may be that the very direct and dramatic language of parts of *The Atonement* appealed to the Americans whereas it embarrassed the English.

A feature of the cantata, and one which acts structurally as a unifying factor, is the march form. This is used at various times: (i) the growing menace of the approaching Roman soldiers at the conclusion of the Gethsemane scene:

Ex. 67: The Atonement, Gethsemane scene

(ii) the orchestral prelude to the Pontius Pilate scene, clearly visualised operatically by Coleridge–Taylor as a scene in which Pilate and his dignitaries assemble ceremonially for Christ to be brought before them:

Ex. 68: The Atonement, prelude to 'Pilate scene'

and (iii) the savagely ironic march as the mob leads Christ away, crowned with thorns:

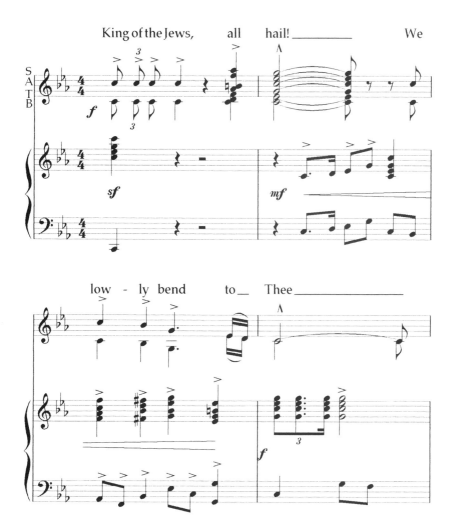

Ex. 69: The Atonement, Christ being led away

All of these 'marches', together with the dragging procession to Calvary, were as realistic as the composer could make them. Despite this, the Three Choirs listeners, at that time more used to the religiosity which had been their standard fare, may well have found that much of the work seemed to be as irreverent and blasphemous as some critics alleged.

Coleridge–Taylor composed nothing else for them; they took *Hiawatha* in later years, but not *The Atonement*. The irony is that, later on, instead of Coleridge–Taylor, who professed a real but simple faith, the Three Choirs Festival asked Delius, an assertive atheist (had they but known), to conduct his *Dance Rhapsody* in 1908. Vaughan Williams, who they took to their hearts, was an agnostic and even the faith of Elgar, the quintessential 'Three Choirs composer', was and is in doubt.

What Coleridge–Taylor had written was an embryonic opera, albeit dressed in cantata or oratorio apparel. For this, his stylistic models were Mendelssohn and Dvorak (as might be expected) and (less to be expected) Tschaikowsky. This was not only a matter of half–remembered Tschaikowskian phrases:

Andante con moto

Ex. 70a: The Atonement, 'It is finished'

but also (particularly in the Prelude) of Tschaikowsky's moods:

Molto moderato

Ex. 70b: The Atonement, Prelude

The English loved both Dvorak and Tschaikowsky, but found it difficult not to recoil from Slavonic excess when they were offered it in sacred music by Coleridge–Taylor.

With regard to the remaining criticism of 'lack of inspiration' it is difficult to judge since no opportunities to hear the work now occur, and with this composer any lack of effect one registers on reading the score, or even playing it on the piano, may well be confounded by its actual sound in performance. Even making this reservation, it must be acknowledged that, while he achieves a remarkably consistent standard, Coleridge–Taylor does not seem to be able to transcend his text to produce the searing, blinding moments which, for example, inspire Delius at crucial points in the *Mass of Life*. Thus the concluding chorus 'It is finished, He hath triumphed' is a sad disappointment, for which Coleridge–Taylor can find only Example 70a above.

Even so, *The Atonement* is a notable achievement which represented an enormous expenditure of time and energy by its twenty–eight year old composer. It should not be dismissed unheard. The composer himself fought for his work as best he could. His anxiety lest adverse criticism of it affect the opinion of his American friends has been noted; he was anxious, too, that such valued colleagues as Kilburn should not have their judgement prejudiced. Writing to Kilburn the day after the Royal Choral Society performance, he told his friend:

> I was recalled twice after the first part and three times after the end. I mention this not for the sake of it, but because I always had great faith in the work in spite of the dishonest newspaper criticisms, many of which I found were written in the neighbourhood of Berners St a *fortnight before* the Hereford performance.
>
> So you can tell how pleased I was last night to *feel* that the people who were performing it were making it live, and that the usually dull West End audience remained to the very end and to hear music which has none of the tuneful attractions of Hiawatha.
>
> I do hope you will do it at Sunderland or Middlesbro' — it isn't terribly difficult and has no *extra instruments*.[122]

Perhaps some enterprising choir and orchestra will give it an airing so that we can judge whether or not it comes alive in performance as successfully as other, at first apparently unpromising, music by him. *Hiawatha* was adapted for stage performance — so might *The Atonement* be; it might well present fewer problems.

In the last analysis, Coleridge–Taylor's problem was that his 'times were out of joint'. On the one hand, his models — Mendelssohn,

Dvorak and Tschaikowsky — tended to make his compositions appear to 'date' in a way that those of Elgar and Delius (Brahms and Wagner) did not; on the other, his concept of a sacred work was premature, at any rate for the church. It would not be too many years before such 'irreverent' works as Walton's *Belshazzar's Feast* and Britten's *Noyes Fludde* found ecclesiastical acceptance — or at least tolerance.

12 AN AWARENESS OF COLOUR

Was Coleridge–Taylor an African living in a foreign country or a coloured Englishman? A difficult question even to approach, since it is in the field of perception: how he perceived himself and how others perceived him. And the 'others' themselves would have a varying perception according to whether they were in the United States or the United Kingdom. In any case, many people have no settled 'persona'. It may vary with circumstances or with whom the subject may be interacting. Avril has no doubt that he thought of himself as an Englishman — coloured, certainly, but not a 'colonial'. Marjorie described his 'medium light coloured skin which looked light compared to those Africans who were quite black'.[123] She added that it was in no way odd to have a coloured brother, and that 'he was proud to be a coloured man'.[124]

The perception of coloured people in this country changed as the nineteenth century progressed. In the first half of the century, attitudes were influenced by the anti–slavery movement which reached its climax in the eighteen–thirties. Throughout the controversy coloured speakers toured the country; few experienced serious abuse. A few years later, in 1852, Harriet Beecher Stowe's *Uncle Tom's Cabin* had an enormous influence, her fictional characters forming opinion even more than the real ones had done.

One man's experience can hardly hold true for an entire community, but may be worth observing here. The coloured violinist and composer Joseph Emidy worked as a teacher and performer in Cornwall until his death in 1835.[125] He seems to have suffered little from prejudice on account of his race or his hue. But, in the second half of the century, 'blacks' (as they were then called) tended more and more to be identified with the lower orders of society. At the same time arose the claims of Dr James Hunt (1833–1869) and the Anthropological Society of London (founded in 1863) who asserted a 'scientific' basis for making distinctions between White Europeans and Black Africans which included totally unjustified suggestions about the inferiority of the latter. By the time of Queen Victoria's Jubilee, matters had deteriorated even further: 'boys threw stones and rotten eggs at visiting black troops'.[126]

Specifically in music, the original high moral purpose of the Fisk

Jubilee Singers in bringing their spirituals on tour with them in 1874, 1876 and 1884 gradually broke down as commercial interests corrupted their work into 'nigger minstrel' shows and other coarse caricatures.

By 1900, with more achievements to be proud of than most, and in a town of white people, Coleridge–Taylor was naturally becoming a magnet for others like him — as Marjorie relates:

> Of course there were very few coloured people in London, although when Coleridge became famous they came to visit him and to meet mother, and I remember visitors from Africa calling in the 1900s.[127]

Some came begging:

> I remember one coloured fellow turning up, dressed like a tramp, and asking for Coleridge's help. For some reason coloured people didn't have portmanteaus in those days; this fellow had a bundle on his back.[128]

And some needed counsel:

> Being a coloured man, other coloured people looked up to him, and sought his help and advice.[129]

There were many coloured visitors to his home, among them Kathleen Easmon, the artist and poet from Sierra Leone, and John Alcindor, a Trinidad–born doctor whose home in Bayswater (London) often served as a base for visiting coloured American musicians.

In 1900, the first Pan–African Conference was held at Westminster Town Hall. The conference was organised by the Trinidad lawyer Henry Sylvester Williams and The African Association (an association of Africans resident in England which later became the Pan–African Association), and it took place from 23 to 27 July 1900. Its participants included Frederick Loudin (manager of the Fisk Jubilee Singers), Professor W. E. B. Du Bois and representatives from Africa, U.S.A., Canada, the West Indies and Great Britain, a number of whom were lawyers and clergymen. The conference passed various resolutions which seem innocuous enough today, submitted a petition to Queen Victoria specifying grievances in South Africa, and made an appeal 'To the Nations of the World':

> The problem of the twentieth century is the problem of the colour line, the question as to how far differences of race, which show themselves chiefly in the colours of the skin and the texture of the hair, are going to be made, hereafter, the basis of denying to over

half the world the right of sharing to their utmost ability the opportunities and privileges of modern mankind.

As conferences go, this one might seem insignificant since only thirty–two persons took part. Coleridge–Taylor was one of these. Beyond the probability that he organised some musical entertainment for the delegates, nothing is known of his part in the conference activities or how far he was politically involved. But that at the age of twenty–five he was a delegate and that subsequently he was elected to the executive committee of the Pan–African Association speaks much for the esteem in which he was already held by his fellows.

Within the white English musical community, too, he received the respect which was his due, but he seems to have assumed that he would suffer rude behaviour in the streets. Both his daughter Avril and his wife Jessie testify to the petty insults and audibly offensive remarks which were directed at him. Jessie, for instance, recalled a performance in which he accompanied Ada Crossley in the *Six Sorrow Songs* at which she overheard one member of the audience remark to her neighbour:

What a killing little nigger![130]

In his own country, he would endure this kind of thing patiently when it happened, taking comfort from the fact that, at least among his own wide circle, he was held in the highest regard. In this company he saw himself simply as a working musician following his profession and he was unconcerned with matters of mere colour. Perhaps he was a little ingenuous here in not realising how much his path was eased by his wife. Jessie's great–niece Linette Martin asks this pertinent question:

Would he have been received into Edwardian Society in the same way if he had had a black wife? I think not.[131]

This 'adoring, very loyal and very respectable white wife'[132] was, moreover, of appreciably higher social status than her husband; this, too, would have been a telling factor in his acceptance by the middle and upper levels of English society.

But in America a very different perception of him was taking root; a perception which was to stop little short of deification. The American Coleridge–Taylor movement centred on Washington because that city housed many coloured folk whose forbears had gravitated there as freed slaves in the previous forty years or so. However, the first American performances of *Hiawatha* seem to have been given by the Caecilia Musical Society of Boston, who performed the *Wedding Feast* on 12

March 1900 with such success that it had to be repeated two days later.
The composer's cause owed much to the evangelistic efforts of Henry T.
Burleigh (1866–1949), a distinguished black musician who had studied
for a while with Dvorak, and much also to the organisational skills of the
Hilyer family. The Hilyers were a coloured Washington couple who
were amateur singers. Shortly after its publication, Burleigh saw the
score of *Hiawatha's Wedding Feast* and showed it to Mrs M. E. Hilyer.
On the occasion of Coleridge–Taylor's death in 1912, Mamie Hilyer
wrote an 'In Memoriam' in which she described what happened next:

> Having ended a very delightful visit to Paris and the Exposition, I
> was preparing to leave for Oberammergau, where I expected to
> experience the climax of my visit in witnessing that great drama
> 'The Passion Play', which can be seen only at Oberammergau once
> in ten years, when I received a letter from my dear friends in
> England, the Loudins, saying that they would be in London in a
> few days, and wished me to join them there and meet the now
> famous coloured composer, Samuel Coleridge–Taylor. Such was
> the magic of this name, that when I found myself again I was in
> London, having given up without any mental struggle whatever my
> long–cherished purpose to see 'The Passion Play' at Ober-
> ammergau, one of the objects for which I had put three thousand
> miles of ocean between myself and my loved ones.
>
> Mr Coleridge–Taylor regarded Mr. Loudin as the best friend he
> ever had saying, 'He, more than anyone else, helped to make me
> known to our dear American people'. Before going to London I
> knew something of this talented composer's work, thanks to Mr.
> Loudin, who had kept us supplied with English papers from time
> to time containing glowing accounts of this young Anglo–African,
> and to Mr. Harry Burleigh, who had sent me a copy of The
> Wedding Feast shortly after it had made its triumphal appearance
> in 1898.
>
> In due time, Mr. and Mrs. Loudin took Dr. and Mrs. Cabaniss
> and me on the train to the modest suburban house of S. Coleridge–
> Taylor, who, with his charming wife, gave us a hearty welcome to
> their home and hospitality. The simple and unaffected manner, the
> ease and modesty of bearing, the enthusiasm and magnetic
> personality of this remarkable man, his intense interest in his people
> in the States, his high musical standing in England, as the musical
> man of the hour, were qualities calculated not only to awaken our
> admiration, but unconsciously planted within us those seeds of

inspiration, possibility and hope which were destined to grow in virgin soil and to blossom so abundantly, as you have all seen.

I thought it was an unspeakable privilege to have had the opportunity of seeing the world's contributions and triumphs in the arts and sciences as they were so wonderfully portrayed in that great international exhibition at Paris, but when, after my return home, I began to speak of my experiences while in Europe, out of the fullness of my heart my lips would repeat, 'Coleridge–Taylor', and very soon in my little world all were acquainted with his fame and name.

Shortly after my return, Miss Lola Johnson, hearing that I had been quite ill, sent me word that she was coming round to sing for me and talk 'Coleridge–Taylor'. Together we dreamed of the possibility of having a choral society here to sing his works. She volunteered to write Mr. Coleridge–Taylor and ask if he would come over and conduct for us if we should get up a chorus. He wrote her a ready and affirmative reply. This inspiring letter was read to the ladies of 'The Treble Clef', a small band of married women music–lovers, who immediately pledged themselves to promote the cause. A meeting of the prominent musical people was called at my home. Then and there was born the S. Coleridge–Taylor Choral Society, whose achievements and triumphs are of such recent history that it is not necessary to mention them in this presence.

The Washington Coleridge–Taylor Society was founded in 1901, and it consisted entirely of coloured singers. Those whites who applied to join were refused, since it was clearly intended to make a statement of the potential of coloured races. But it was to be some while before the composer for whom they were named would fulfil his promise to conduct them, and the path of negotiations leading to his visit was to be strewn with obstacles.

Shortly after the birth of Hiawatha, Mamie Hilyer's Treble Clef Society sent the baby a present; the proud father responded:

When baby grows old enough to understand I am sure he will be ever so proud of such a remembrance for his coloured friends in Washington ... . When we come to the States we shall make it our first engagement to visit you all, but it is as yet undecided as to when we can undertake the journey ... a photograph of Hiawatha in his mother's arms and one of myself will reach *The Treble Clef* in a week or two, which I hope you will all accept ... [133]

Mr Hilyer then sent Coleridge–Taylor some researches he had been
making into racial origins and achievements, probably with the intention
of igniting a sense of racial responsibility — even duty. Coleridge–
Taylor replied:

> I was keenly interested in reading your remarkable compilation of
> the doing of the coloured race. It makes me wish to be out there
> among you doing my share of the great whole; but perhaps, in
> matters of art, it is better for a coloured individual to live in my
> country than in America as we are so dependent on mood; tho' I
> must say the people I have met from the States have all seemed to
> be extraordinarily cheerful!   Perhaps it is because they are
> philosophical and I am *not* very much so, I'm afraid.
>
> Still, I would like to come over to conduct some of my music,
> especially if a real good coloured chorus were available.[134]

This is a carefully considered reply; Coleridge–Taylor was not going to
be stampeded into the cause. He might visit, but was reluctant to change
domicile.   And, even if he visited, it would be dependent on the
availability of forces satisfactory to him. What might 'doing my share'
be?   Clearly, he would never be militant; he would never man the
barricades as Wagner had done in 1848. His share would always be
musical. His expressed view was that he wanted to do for African music
what Dvorak had done for Bohemian, and certainly this came to fruition
a few years later in the *24 Negro Melodies*. He does not seem to have
seen beyond using African melodies in a European musical context; the
uncompromising path of, say, a Bartok was not for him. Yet something
in Hilyer's letter must have fired him — it would have been around the
Spring and Summer of 1901 that he was working on his overture on the
subject of the coloured revolutionary *Toussaint L'Ouverture*.

One factor in Coleridge–Taylor's reluctance to leave England was
undoubtedly his recent Westmorland appointment, with six hundred
voices to sing and the Hallé Orchestra to play:

> I suppose in your States such a thing would be impossible — and
> yet — why? I cannot but believe that all this real striving and
> earnest work will do something to leaven the prejudice between
> black and white; or am I wrong, and is it a fact that it rather tends
> to increase it, as I was last week informed by a coloured
> American?[135]

Suffering so much at the hands of inadequate choirs and orchestras, he
was loth to commit himself to untried musical circumstances; not, at any

rate, without strong guarantees. Hilyer had probably been worried at the prospect of having to raise an all–black choir of six hundred voices and had very likely written to Coleridge–Taylor seeking guidance; un–fortunately we do not have his prompting letter. Whether or not the following letter by Coleridge–Taylor was actually sent is in doubt, but it is included here because it sets out his musical requirements so precisely:

> Regarding my proposed visit to the States, I had not actually fixed my dates for coming though someone [proposed?] the Fall as being a good time. Regarding [illegible], I don't know how you are situated in Boston.
>
> In our ordinary Northern Choral Societies, from two to three hundred voices is the usual thing — it is only at festivals that very huge forces are employed.
>
> At any rate, three hundred good voices would be ample. My reason for wishing for and suggesting such a chorus be formed was not for the production of Hiawatha so much as to give an impetus for Choral Singing among the Coloured people.
>
> The thing in a nutshell amounts to this — (a) Can a good coloured chorus of three (?) hundred voices be secured? (b) Also a professional orchestra (some amateur I don't mind but the bulk must be professional).
>
> And will this mixed orchestra (for I don't for a moment expect to find many coloured orchestral players yet) play to a black chorus in your strange land of prejudice? It is on this that the whole matter rests, for a piano or makeshift accompaniment is worse than useless!
>
> However, I know so many white musicians in the States, and if the coloured people mean to perform Hiawatha, they must do it *as well* or *better than their white neighbours.*
>
> Perhaps Mr Arthur Gray could tell me about the orchestral matter for he conducted Hiawatha at the Albany May Festival and also the Litchfield Choral Union (of which, by the way, I am Hon. member).
>
> When these points are settled, I can give more detailed inform–ation and in any case I should give one or two recitals while in the States [because the risk?] of trouble connected with such recitals is very small comparatively. Still, I should like to have the oppor–tunity of conducting a Coloured Chorus for the reasons aforesaid [136] ...

At this point, he had foreseen that a white orchestra might not be prepared to accompany a black choir; he had not yet seen the possibility that it might not be prepared to play for a coloured conductor.

Within the next few months, his friends in Washington created a mark of distinction which, if not unique in music up to that time, was nevertheless of remarkable rarity, especially when it is remembered how young the recipient still was. The Samuel Coleridge–Taylor Choral Society of the District of Columbia was formed, and one of its first acts was to issue a formal invitation to the composer to be its guest. The letter, dated 17 December 1901, explained that the society had been formed specifically to perform *Hiawatha* but also had as its general purpose 'the inculcation of higher musical ideals through a better understanding and appreciation of standard musical compositions'. All the conditions made by Coleridge–Taylor could be met; the chorus, consisting entirely of coloured people, was being prepared by Professor John T. Layton, a coloured choir–trainer well known in Washington and lately instructor in vocal music in the city's public schools. The whole project was being enthusiastically welcomed: 'the sentiment in its favour is growing, and only the definite assurance of your coming to America remains to crystallise that sentiment into practical results'.

The February gap in engagements mentioned by Coleridge–Taylor had by now filled up. The months passed by, and in September a post–script to a letter from him to the principal of the Croydon Conservatoire shows that the American visit had been abandoned for 1902. The reason was his reluctance to jeopardise his newly acquired responsibilities in Westmorland (at Kendal) and Rochester; another factor was that Jessie was pregnant with their second child. It is clear, too, that not all his conditions had in fact yet been met.

In the Spring of 1903, the Washington singers went ahead without the composer. On 23 April, in the Metropolitan African Methodist Church, before a very large audience (from which some three thousand would–be listeners had to be turned away), they performed *Hiawatha* with Henry Burleigh as soloist. A few days before the event, Coleridge–Taylor wrote to encourage them:

> No performance has ever interested me half as much as this 'coloured' one, and I would give a great deal to be with you all ... what an immense undertaking it must be for you all, and I feel sure your enthusiasm and hard work will be repaid by great results.[137]

And indeed there was a great result, as the *Boston Herald* made clear, underlining as it did the assumption of close ties and parallels (whether real or imagined) between the black African and American Indian races:

> No white society could interpret it as sympathetically as this coloured choral society. The very genius of the composer is their race–spirit, and the music is as their native voice. There, with the peculiar naturalness of their singing, the depth and richness of many of their voices, and their excellent drilling, the result of patience and enthusiasm, give them special advantages.

But there was no orchestra.

Hilyer wrote with an account of the performance, enclosing press cuttings. Coleridge–Taylor, answering with his thanks, offered some advice on the music they might attempt next. (He suggested Mendelssohn's *Hymn of Praise*.) But the chief interest of the letter is the emphasis he again places on the importance for his work of an orchestra:[138]

> I have never heard *Hiawatha* without orchestra, and can only imagine it to sound fearfully dull without a band; but then you know I live on the orchestra and feel lost without it ... I notice that one paper speaks about the want of a good reliable orchestra for such occasions. It is the same here in England. Only about half–a–dozen towns have really good bands and others have to hire many of their players from the nearest possible centre. And, as you may imagine, this kind of thing is fearfully expensive.

The Society wrote again at the beginning of June, pressing him to come and conduct them. Every argument and persuasion were now used, in a letter couched in such terms as few composers might resist:

> Your coming to this city, and indeed to America generally, would be greeted by an unprecedented outpouring of the people, and would mark an epoch in the history of America.
>
> The S.C.–T.C.S. was born of love of your work, was christened in your honour, and for two years has studied your masterpieces inspired by the hope that you would sooner or later come to America, and personally conduct its presentation. Should you visit us, we can assure you of a thoroughly competent chorus of no less than two hundred voices, all in love with *Hiawatha* and its creator. Your coming will be a great boon to music, and will afford you an opportunity to be introduced to the great American public who are rapidly awaking to the fact that a new star has appeared in the firmament of the world's immortals.[139]

There was in this letter no mention of an orchestra, and Coleridge–Taylor was tenacious on the point. The timid student had become unyielding where he perceived his vital interests to be at stake:

> You see, first of all, it is impossible for me to visit you in a professional way unless I am assured of a first class orchestra.
>
> It is not that I would not come, personally, but I am in touch with so many noted musicians in the States that to conduct a performance without such an orchestra would injure my reputation.
>
> Now, could you negotiate with the management of an orchestra in Washington (or, if there is not one there, in the nearest city where there is one?).
>
> Of course the expenses would be great, perhaps, but orchestras are often sent three or four hundred miles here in England — from London to Scotland — and nothing is thought of it ....
>
> I should require: 1 piccolo, 2 flutes, 2 oboes, 2 clarinets, 2 bassoons, 4 horns, 2 trumpets, 3 trombones, drums, and 8 first violins, 8 seconds, 4 violas, 6 cellos, 4 basses.
>
> Of course, some of the strings might be amateur if very good.
>
> Personally, there is nothing I should like more than to be able to pay you an informal visit and conduct the S.C.T. Society and then return to England. But, as I told you, a first–class orchestra is absolutely imperative, especially as it would be my first visit to the States.
>
> I hope you will understand my reasons for demanding this, and not think I am a difficult person to deal with! I should on no account be permitted to conduct in England unless a band were in attendance, and the same holds good in the States, or more so ...[140]

It was to be some years before Washington was able to sustain an orchestra of the quality of those that matured in Boston, Philadelphia and New York. Coleridge–Taylor had set his friends a problem, for they had set their sights on an all–black presentation, and it would be difficult to find an all–black orchestra. The Society, accepting that they would have to meet the composer's demands, came up with an ingenious solution; they would engage the Marines Band. In the theoretically prejudice–free armed forces the problem could be overcome.

Coleridge–Taylor now committed himself, but he tried to put off a visit until the Spring of 1905. To a chorus that had been practising *Hiawatha* for two years, this seemed understandably a very long way off. Other American societies were performing *Hiawatha* and, on 5 May 1903, The Orpheus Oratorio Society (Eastern Pennsylvania) had given the whole Trilogy. The Washington singers must have feared that the novelty value of their proposal might well evaporate but, after some further correspondence, they managed to pin him down to the Autumn of 1904.

To prepare himself for the visit he read the biography of the escaped slave and black hero Frederick Douglass. Beyond that, Hilyer thought it necessary to give him some background concerning the position of the African in the United States, and sent him a copy of what was to become one of the most influential books in paving the future path of the American coloured man: the newly published *The Souls of Black Folk* by W. E. B. Du Bois.

While they were in no sense personally antagonistic to one another (both were far too civilised and respectful of each other's point of view for that) the standpoints of Booker T. Washington and Du Bois came, during the twentieth century, to represent the twin poles of the American Black Dilemma: whether to accommodate to white domination in a non–violent manner, or to oppose it with militancy.

Washington (1856?–1915), the older man, was the son of a black slave woman and an unknown white father. He suffered much privation in his early years, and had at first to take jobs as a salt–packer, coal miner or house–boy, but he had a yearning for literacy and his persist–ence enabled him to graduate as a trade teacher. At college, his tutors instilled in him the virtues of hard work and thrift; armed with this ethic, he embarked on a teaching career, becoming in due course the first principal of the Tuskegee Institute, Alabama.

His reputation among Whites derived from an influential speech he made at the 1895 Atlanta Exposition, at which Black achievement was strongly featured. The speech, which became known as the Atlanta Compromise, advocated the trading of black civil, social and political rights for low–level economic opportunity and non–violent relations with whites:

> I believe it is the duty of the Negro — as the greater part of the race is already doing — to deport himself modestly in regard to political claims.[141]

This modesty even extended to his tolerance of the 'protected ballot' which set educational and property tests which few Blacks could expect to pass. His philosophy could be summed up in the vivid imagery of his phrase:

> Cast down your bucket where you are.[142]

Lest this philosophy seem unnecessarily craven, it should be considered against its background: some three and a half thousand lynchings of blacks in the U.S.A. between 1885 and 1910. His moderation undoubtedly gave Washington great influence with both white and black; nevertheless, his reception by President Roosevelt in 1901 was greeted in the more extreme regions of the Deep White South as almost treasonable.

Du Bois was at first not averse to Washington's pragmatism. Very much more of an academic, he was educated at Harvard and Berlin Universities, taking as his doctoral thesis aspects of the suppression of the African Slave Trade. But he found the cool scholasticism of his university teaching at Pennsylvania and Atlanta Universities increasingly at loggerheads with the violent, miserable reality of black existence. By the time he came to write *The Souls of Black Folk*, he had reached the point of challenging Washington's 'acceptance' philosophy. 'Mr. Washington,' he wrote, 'represents in Negro thought the old attitude of adjustment and submission'.[143] Du Bois called for 'organised determination and aggressive action'; Washington's followers called him 'Professor of Hysterics'.

Many years later, in his last major speech, Dr Martin Luther King was to acclaim Du Bois as one of the most remarkable men of the century. Yet Dr King himself represented the logical continuation of Washington's approach rather than that of Du Bois. For successors to Du Bois, we would have to look to the Black Power movement, which in fact Du Bois lived to see.

As he read Du Bois, Coleridge–Taylor must have realised for the first time just why his friends were begging him to join them. We have no reason to doubt the sentiment expressed in his letter of thanks to Hilyer; it was his view that the Du Bois work was:

> about the finest book I have ever read by a coloured man and one of the best by any author, white or black.[144]

One wonders if Coleridge–Taylor's modesty allowed him to register the full import of one key sentence in the book:

> The Negro race is going to be saved by its exceptional men.[145]

Hilyer had sent the book with a purpose: it was intended by him that Coleridge–Taylor should join Douglass, Booker T. Washington and Du Bois among role models for their race — models who would be the equal or superior of their white counterparts.

As he made his preparations, he would have been under few illusions about the possibility of his meeting prejudice on a scale he had never experienced in his own country.   But his daughter Avril has pointed out that, as an Englishman, he would have been spared the worst indignities to which he might have been subjected had he been a 'black Yankee'.   His stance as a coloured man was nevertheless robust; Hilyer and his friends would have been delighted by the following:

> I am a great believer in my race, and I never lose an opportunity of letting my white friends here know it.   Please don't make any arrangements to wrap me in cotton wool.   I am not that kind of person at all.   I do a great deal of adjudicating in Wales among a very rough class of people; most adjudicators have had bad eggs and boots thrown at them by the people, but fortunately nothing of the kind has ever happened to me yet.   I mention this so that you may know my life is not spent entirely in drawing rooms and concert halls, but among some of the roughest people in the world, who tell you what they think very plainly.[146]

Throughout 1904, while he mentally prepared himself for the New World, he had also to fulfill his routine but complex pattern of engagements at Croydon (with the Conservatoire Orchestra), Rochester, Westmorland and at the Trinity College of Music, not to speak of teaching, accompanying, adjudicating and conducting up and down the country, often for derisory fees.   On 17 October, for example, he travelled to Staffordshire to conduct *Meg Blane* and, just a few days before sailing to America, he was in London for a general meeting of the Handel Society.

In between all this, in such few gaps as were left, he continued to compose a clutch of short pieces and songs.   Among them were two sets of miniatures for piano; the *Three Cameos* (Augener) and the *Three Silhouettes* (Ashdown), both published in 1904.   They were 'cash–crop' works, all well–crafted but of little individuality.   In the April of that year, Augener brought out the *Moorish Dance*, op. 55, for piano, to be followed in October by the *Four African Dances* for violin and piano (they were dedicated to John Saunders).   The *Moorish Dance* is rather more than a miniature, running to sixteen pages of piano score.   Just as with the early *Moorish Tone Pictures*, it is hard to hear much Moorish–ness in the work; but in its attack and energy it does hark back to the style of the *Ballade in A minor* with which he had scored his earliest success.   *The Moorish Dance* works as a piano piece but is not really piano music; it cries out for orchestral colour.

With the exception of No. 2, the *Four African Dances* are cast in Coleridge–Taylor's favourite ternary form.   The second dance, in which the violin is muted throughout, is based on an idea taken 'from a traditional African melody':

Ex. 71: African Dance No. 2

But what, if any, African connection the other three dances may have is not readily apparent. Indeed, the first dance is in the strong rhythm of a Polish Mazurka:

Ex. 72: African Dance No. 1

The whole set forms an attractive recital item. Compared with it, the *Romance for Violin and Piano,* op. 59 (dedicated to Goldie Baker and published by Augener in 1904), seems lacking in distinctive character. There is an effortless flow of music, but perhaps that very ease of idea has led to a certain blandness about it.

But it is rewarding to turn to the *Six Sorrow Songs*, which also originated in 1904, and find in them a group of songs of the highest quality. The juxtaposition in Coleridge–Taylor of the ordinary and the outstanding can most likely only be explained by chronic overwork and periods of exhaustion which must have sapped his creativity and discrimination. The songs are dedicated to Jessie, and on them he lavished all his vocal skill, with the result that the word–setting is hardly matched elsewhere in his vocal output. The piano writing, moreover, has none of the thickness which is a feature of so much of his solo keyboard work. Above all, his settings of the *Sorrow Songs* are welcome (because rare) instances of Coleridge–Taylor's probing poetry in greater depth than was his habit. One example of these rich songs will have to suffice to show both the subtlety of the phrasing and the complementary nature of the accompaniment:

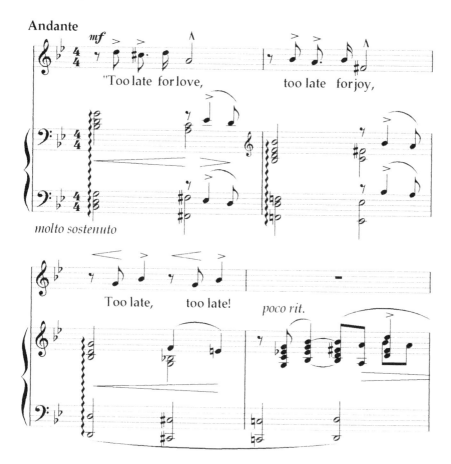

Ex. 73: Sorrow Songs, 'Too late for love'

The *Three Song Poems*, op. 50, settings of words by Thomas Moore, were probably written around the same time as the *Sorrow Songs*. They are slighter in content and lighter in style, but show some unusual phrasing which suggests a growing concern for poetic rhythms. The piano parts, too, maintain a progress towards simplicity. There is not a note too many.

The *Sorrow Songs* were sung by Marie Brema to the composer's accompaniment on 18 May 1904 at the Croydon Public Hall, in a programme which also included much of the other new work mentioned above. He gave concerts in Croydon each year, but never made much money from them; he used them chiefly as a showcase for his recently–written work. Occasionally, he reached back into the past: the concert held in the Public Hall on 31 March 1906, for example, included a revival of his *Clarinet Quintet*.

Reminders of his origins surfaced in the August of 1904 when, on the 25th of that month, his father died in The Gambia. In Bathurst, Dr Taylor had been a much respected man, but in England the circumstances of the birth of his now–famous son would perhaps have tended to make his memory less socially acceptable.

Before the impending American trip, the family managed a short holiday at Worthing in Sussex. They could not be away from home for long, since there were legions of details to be settled: could Hurlstone take the Conservatoire orchestra? Could the Americans send half his fee in advance? Had the publicity photographs arrived there? Had Novello's been given notice to supply the band parts for Hiawatha?

Revealingly, he was still engaged in negotiations to go to Germany. This project, seemingly closer to his heart than fulfilling his destiny in America, was never to be accomplished. For many European and English composers, the New World represented a vast new market for their wares. Mahler, Rachmaninoff and Richard Strauss had little hesitation in going; Dvorak stayed and even found inspiration there; Elgar and Delius went, and Jelka Delius was always seeking perform- ances there of her husband's work. Yet Coleridge–Taylor procrastinated, his gaze eastwards rather than westwards. The fact of this delay, for whatever reason, must weigh in the balance against his often expressed wish to be with his kinsmen and to help 'the cause'.

He was advised not to travel to New York, which was nearer to Washington, but to Boston, which was cheaper. So, on 25 October 1904, four years after the visit was first mooted, he sailed from Liverpool, on the Cunard liner 'Saxonia'.

13 FIRST VISIT TO THE U.S.A.

Whilst, by his own testimony, Lincoln would have sacrificed his anti–slavery position if by so doing he could have preserved the Union, the condition of 'blacks' in the U.S.A. was yet one of the issues over which the Civil War had been fought. In 1904, forty years after the war had been won by the Unionist, anti–slavery North, the position of coloured people was scarcely less lamentable than it had been when it ended. Disenfranchised in many states by educational requirements they were rarely able to meet, they were subject to separate treatment in facilities and services, from education to public transport. Total segregation in the South was tacitly and covertly supported in the North, both by government and by the law courts. Black inferiority was asserted as a matter of scientific fact by white academics, and as a matter of humour by Northern magazines, in which 'Sambo' was the invariable butt of crude jokes. Africans, along with Indians, were consigned to oblivion; where they could not be ignored, they might well be lynched. Within black communities, opinions might differ on how best to advance their cause, but militancy, while still in its infancy, was even in 1904 increasingly evident.

Coleridge–Taylor had not been long in the U.S.A. before he exper-ienced the discrimination all American blacks faced every day of their lives. He boarded a train, and immediately found his presence as a coloured man resented and commented upon. Mustering all the dignity of which he was capable, he retorted:

I am an Englishman![147]

What effect this statement produced is not known; but it is interesting that on this occasion he took his stand not as a coloured man, but rather as an Englishman.

The expedition to America was his first separation for any length of time from Jessie. He hated being parted from her and was desolate. But he joined in all the on–board social activity and fun, and had recovered his normal good humour by the time the 'Saxonia' arrived on 2 November in Boston. His disembarkation gave him a taste of what was to come. Reporters, both black and white, were there in force at the quayside, and his picture was in all the papers next day. Before moving on to Washington, he stayed in Boston for a few days. Genevieve Lee recalled his visit to her parents' house, and she gave a vivid estimate of the reputation he was already enjoying in her country:

> I remember so well at the expected time of his call how we waited in the parlour and library. Think of it! I was to meet one of the greatest musicians living — greater than any in the United States! And then, when Mr Coleridge–Taylor entered the room, and we were introduced, one forgot that he was a great musical genius, and realised that here was a man unassuming and of great personal magnetism.[148]

In Washington, the Choral Society had laid its plans well and had established a guarantee fund to raise the preliminary expenses of three thousand dollars. Its organisation and advance publicity show that it had thoroughly digested Du Bois's insistence on blacks showing at least as much efficiency as whites. On his first Sunday in the capital, Coleridge–Taylor attended church, where it soon became apparent that not all the congregation had come primarily to worship:

> Hundreds seized the opportunity to greet the man whose name is a household word wherever true worth is appreciated.[149]

It was the start of an orgy of hand–shaking which lasted the whole visit.

The first concert took place on 16 November in the Convention Hall, where the two thousand seven hundred seats were sold out and at least one third of the audience was white. It had been hoped that President Theodore Roosevelt would attend, but he had been re–elected only a week before and pressure of work proved too much; he sent his secretary instead. The programme consisted of the *Hiawatha* trilogy. Like the chorus, the chosen soloists (Estella Clough, J. Arthur Freeman and Henry T. Burleigh) were all coloured. The composer was partic–ularly taken with the singing of Burleigh, who was widely credited with having supplied Dvorak with the negro spirituals which in turn suggested ideas for his 'New World' Symphony.

But for both black and white in the audience, the most significant feature was undoubtedly the orchestra. The band of the Marines, aug–mented to fifty–two players, had been prepared by its director (Lieut. William H. Santelmann), and the composer had been accorded a separate rehearsal with them. For the Marines band to play under a coloured conductor had, for the blacks, the force of a moral victory — a force that was not lost on the whites:

the event marked an epoch in the history of the negro race of the world. It was the first time that a man with African blood in his veins ever held a baton over the heads of the members of the great Marine Band, and it appeared to me that the orchestra did its best to respond to every movement of its dark–skinned conductor.[150]

No doubt the black readers of this report relished the ironic image of a baton held over the heads of whites rather than over themselves. But once the gloating had exhausted itself, a valid point had been made:

> The audience and the newpapers stopped little short of delirium in their enthusiasm. To them he was the living realisation of their highest ideal, the indisputable and accepted proof that the more exalted ways of creative art were open to and attainable by the negro.[151]

For those present that evening, Booker T. Washington's acceptance of the lowly utilitarian status of the Black had been refuted, while Du Bois's vision of his high destiny had been endorsed.

The second concert took place on the following night. For this, Coleridge–Taylor had written three settings of Longfellow, at first called *Songs of Slavery*, but subsequently known as the *Choral Ballads*. Three were performed at Washington, and were dedicated to the Society: 'Beside the Ungathered Rice He Lay', 'She Dwells by the Great Kanhawa's Side', and 'Loud He Sang the Psalm of David'. Two other settings were added later, and then the whole set was performed at the Norwich Festival.[152]

On the Friday, 18 November, the performers travelled to nearby Baltimore where, in the Lyric Hall, *Hiawatha* was repeated, together with the three *Songs of Slavery*. On the following Saturday, back in Washington, a concert was given in Coleridge–Taylor's honour by the coloured women musicians who had sent a present to the newly–born baby Hiawatha, The Treble Clef Society. The programme was worlds away from his usual fare in England. What, for example, would he have made of The Aeolian Mandolin, Guitar and Banjo Club playing a medley of melodies from *Tannhauser*? And, strangely, The Treble Clef did not chose to include any of their guest's compositions.

The Choral Society's festival ended on Tuesday 22 November with a public reception held in the Oddfellows' Hall. The formality — the 'comme il faut' — of this event must have been an ordeal for him, for in it there was no conducting in which he could take refuge; no escape from hand–shaking and adulation. The evening began with a reception

of leading dignitaries and citizens, followed by a reception of the choir
members, of which there were two hundred, not counting their husbands
or wives. The main event of the function was the presentation, by Mrs
A. F. Hilyer, of a silver loving cup inscribed with Longfellow's words:

> It is well for us, O brother
> That you come so far to see us.

The ceremony concluded with the singing of an ode specially written by
Arthur S. Gray, set to the music of what the honoured composer knew
as his National Anthem.

Apart from the official programme, other engagements in Washington had included visits to the Howard University (founded for blacks
some thirty years before), to the Washington Normal School and the
Armstrong Training School, from each of which he received tributes and
presents. Theodore Roosevelt handsomely made up for his absence from
the concerts by inviting Coleridge–Taylor to the White House. The
President had, of course, rapidly grasped the significance of the composer
for his black citizens — he presented him with an autographed photograph of himself. Earlier that year, Richard Strauss, on a visit to the
U.S.A. to conduct his music in, among other places, Wanamaker's
department store, had been received by the President; the coloured
community expected no less honourable treatment for their composer.

Although unable to accept his view of the limited position of
coloured folk in society, Coleridge–Taylor was glad to make the
acquaintance of Booker T. Washington, who wrote to him:

> In composing *Hiawatha* you have done the coloured people of the
> United States a service which, I am sure, you never dreamed of
> when composing it. It acts as a source of inspiration to us, not
> only musically but in other lines of endeavour.

Now that the official part of the visit was over, there were other
engagements to fulfil. A concert was given in Chicago with his German
friend Theodore Spiering, who played the *Gypsy Suite* and the newly
published *African Dances*. At the piano, the composer contributed an
'oriental valse' *Zuleika* and three 'symphonically arranged' negro
melodies (from the set of twenty–four). He thought that in many ways
this was the best concert of the tour — 'really musical people'. Chicago
had a large German element in its population. Were any of them so
musical as to recognise an echo in *Zuleika* (oddly placed in what
purported to be an 'oriental waltz') of *The Death of Minnehaha*?:

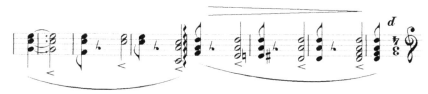

Ex. 74: Zulieka (for comparison, see Ex. 56, bars 3 and 4)

The journey back to Boston included New York and Philadelphia. At Philadelphia, Coleridge–Taylor gave a concert at the Witherspoon Hall, assisted by other soloists. At Boston he was able to attend a rehearsal of the Caecilia Musical Society, whose members had been the first to give *Hiawatha* in the U.S.A. On 13 December, he sailed for home.

It is possible that the events of the month — the heady reception, and the impact of the reality of the Black condition — caused for Coleridge–Taylor what we might today call an identity crisis. Thenceforth he would try to sustain two roles: he would write music of what he perceived to be African character but he would also still try to hold his place in the Anglo–European musical hierarchy. It would be difficult to convey to his English friends just how warm his reception in the U.S.A. had been, let alone the significance of it.

To set it in perspective: in the following year, Elgar would also visit America. He was to be feted by the academics of Yale University — but Coleridge–Taylor had been feted by an entire people.

1. Class photograph, the British School, Tamworth Road, Croydon

2. Samuel Coleridge–Taylor in maturity, studio portrait

3. The composer's mother, Alice Evans, in old age.

4. Gwendolen (Avril) and Hiawatha Coleridge–Taylor with their father, 1905

5. Contemporary cartoon, dating from the early performances of the *Hiawatha* Trilogy: 'A distinguished composer escaping from the autograph fiends'

6. Jessie Coleridge–Taylor, studio portrait

7. The Croydon String–Players' Club, with their conductor

8. Samuel Coleridge–Taylor, writing music at his desk

9. 'Aldwick', St Leonard's Road, Croydon — Coleridge–Taylor's last home;
the 'Music Shed' in which he worked can be seen to the right

10. A page from Coleridge-Taylor's letter to Maud Powell

IN
MEMORY OF
SAMUEL
COLERIDGE-TAYLOR
WHO DIED ON
SEPTEMBER 1ST 1912
AT THE AGE OF THIRTY SEVEN
BEQUEATHING TO THE WORLD
A HERITAGE
OF AN UNDYING BEAUTY.
HIS MUSIC LIVES.

IT PULSED WITH HIS OWN LIFE.
AND NOW IT IS HIS IMMORTALITY.
HE LIVES WHILE MUSIC LIVES.
TOO YOUNG TO DIE —
HIS GREAT SIMPLICITY.
HIS HAPPY COURAGE IN AN ALIEN WORLD.
HIS GENTLENESS.
MADE ALL THAT KNEW HIM LOVE HIM.
SLEEP, CROWNED WITH FAME, FEARLESS OF
CHANGE OR TIME.
SLEEP, LIKE REMEMBERED MUSIC IN THE SOUL.
SILENT, IMMORTAL: WHILE OUR DISCORDS CLIMB
TO THAT GREAT CHORD WHICH SHALL
RESOLVE THE WHOLE.
SILENT, WITH MOZART, ON THAT SOLEMN
SHORE:
SECURE, WHERE NEITHER WAVES NOR HEARTS
CAN BREAK
SLEEP, TILL THE MASTER OF THE WORLD
ONCE MORE
TOUCH THE REMEMBERED STRINGS
AND BID THEE WAKE
TOUCH THE REMEMBERED STRINGS AND BID THEE WAKE.
ALFRED NOYES.

11. Memorial Stone, Bandon Hill Cemetery, Wallington, Surrey;
the verses are by Noyes

12. Cartoon, inscribed by members of the Beecham Orchestra,
among them Albert Sammons and Eugène Goossens

Coleridge–Taylor was back in Britain in time for Christmas. In his absence, the Royal Choral Society had given *Hiawatha* — for the sixth time — in a performance which brought the number of times the work had been heard in England alone to over two hundred. Jessie organised a concert to welcome him home, to which Hurlstone contributed a solo.

The New Year started with a journey to Leeds where he conducted three of the *Choral Ballads*. Throughout 1905, his teaching commitments continued to grow. Among his private pupils was the American coloured musician, Clarence Cameron White, who came over from the U.S.A. to study composition with him and violin with Zacharewitsch. At Trinity College of Music, his position was consolidated when he was 'recognised' as a teacher there by the University of London, and more so when he was elected a member of the College Corporation. The Crystal Palace School of Art and Music had not the prestige of a London institution such as Trinity College, but it was near at hand, and could offer him a teaching room with a view. The Principal (Miss E. M. Prosser) invited him to join her staff; the room's panoramic view of London helped persuade him. She later observed that she never knew a man to be so careless of the value of either time or money. The value of her catch was not lost on her; at four guineas for twelve lessons, the School's prospectus shows him to have been more expensive than any other member of her staff.

In the Spring of 1905, the collection, mentioned above, of *Twenty-four Negro Melodies* was published. With either foresight or hitherto unsuspected business acumen, he had given them to the Boston, U.S.A., publisher Oliver Ditson, no doubt hoping to capitalise on the boost to his growing fame in America resulting from his visit. The following year Ditson brought out a selection of five of them arranged for violin, 'cello and piano. Coleridge–Taylor played some of them on the tour, and even before that took place (and before the two men had met) Booker T. Washington had written a preface for the edition (24 October 1904):

> It is especially gratifying that at this time when interest in the plantation songs seems to be dying out with the generation that gave them birth, when Negro song is in too many minds associated

with the 'rag' music and the more reprehensible 'coon' song, that the most cultivated musician of his race, a man of the highest aesthetic ideals, should seek to give permanence to folksongs of his people by giving them a new interpretation and an added dignity.[153]

These melodies were given a 'symphonic' arrangement, or rather interpretation; before each new interpretation, Coleridge–Taylor set out the unadorned melody. The versions which follow are in each instance cast in the form of a theme with variations. As he said in his foreword:

> What Brahms has done for the Hungarian folk–music, Dvorak for the Bohemian and Grieg for the Norwegian, I have tried to do for these Negro Melodies ...

The collection includes both African and American Negro melodies, together with one from the West Indies. Apart from the intrinsic value of the composer's variations on them, these melodies served as a quarry for ideas for some of his future work. The *Variations on an African Air* (discussed later in this chapter) is based on one, while for a succeeding visit to the U.S.A., he based the Rhapsodic Dance *Bamboula* on the West Indian tune. He sent the set to Stanford — a sure sign of his own satisfaction with them. In his acknowledgement, Stanford suggested a copy be sent to Percy Grainger 'who is greatly interested in folksongs'. His sharp Irish eye noted that two of the tunes were not Negro in origin:

> By the way, one of the tunes 'The angels changed my name' is an Irish tune and also I think The Pilgrim's Song. Like some of the Negro tunes Dvorak got hold of, these have reached the American Negroes thro' the Irish Americans. A curious instance of the transmigration of Folk Singers.[154]

The theme and variations form was particularly appropriate, since some of the tunes — in particular the African ones — were short and not performable in the context of a Western–style concert. One example discussed here is typical of the considerable imaginative treatment which is applied almost without exception to the whole set. 'They Will Not Lend Me a Child'[155] was collected in south–east Africa. The words reflect the plight of a childless woman in those countries where, in Coleridge–Taylor's own words,[156]

> She is considered less than nothing, it is only natural that such a woman should try to borrow a child for adoption ... . Her lament on finding she is unable to discover a child is therefore literal in every sense of the word.

Ex. 75: They will not lend me a child

The African contributions tend to be repetitive phrases as compared with the more formally rounded plantation songs which have been cross–fertilised with popular song and hymn. Coleridge–Taylor's approach is to seize on a musical characteristic of the material and develop that. In this case, the characteristic is the repeated note which descends a step ('a' in Example 75). This may be used as it is or it may be inverted. The result does not sound so much like a 'theme and variations' as a continuous 'rhapsody' or 'fantasy' on the theme.

The music seems to reflect the traditional improvised harmonising of the American coloured people, despite the solo African origin of the theme. Broadly, these principal characteristics are shared by the treat–ment of many of the twenty–four melodies.

1905 proceeded uneventfully as Coleridge–Taylor followed his habitual round of regular teaching and conducting engagements. It seems to have been a relatively quiet year for him, possibly to make up domestically for his inevitably long absence in the previous year. A long summer holiday led into an autumn which found him hard at work on a new orchestral set of variations and more theatre music, while he looked forward to the first complete performance of the *Choral Ballads*. With this work he was evidently well pleased, as a letter to Kilburn makes clear:

> Have you seen the *Whole Set* of my Choral Ballads yet? There are *three* entirely new numbers to be done at Norwich — one for female voices, which is a great favourite there. I wish you could do No. 1 and the one for Female Voices at one of your concerts in Sunderland, Middlesbrough or Bishop Auckland.
>
> I am very busy writing the music to Stephen Phillips' 'Nero' which has appealed to me immensely.[157]

The performance of the complete *Five Choral Ballads* took place in

Norwich under his direction on 25 October 1905; it seems to have gone well, and he was enthusiastic about the singing of the Norwich Festival Chorus.

The Americans wanted him back, and Hilyer sent out the first feelers. But they were clearly troubled in the negotiations by the composer's spidery and often illegible handwriting — so much so that they clubbed together to buy him a typewriter. Years before, Stanford had been so exasperated by his scrawl as to ask Jessie:

Have ye taught him how to write yet?

(To understand the trouble they — and indeed this biographer — had with Coleridge–Taylor's writing, see Plate 10 where a page from a letter to Maud Powell is reproduced.)

Coleridge–Taylor thought he might be able to make another tour in the autumn (which he was now sufficiently Americanised to call 'the Fall') of 1906, and he made his first programme proposals: Handel's *Alexander's Feast* might be possible, or Mendelssohn's *Hymn of Praise*. But in America, they wanted no other music but his own — and, in particular, *Hiawatha*. He was more anxious to advance the fortunes of *The Atonement* and, as in the previous year, his major concern was the orchestra; clearly, despite the efforts of the Washington committee and their success in engaging the Marines Band, much had been left to be desired:

> I must say that the band last year was not a tenth good enough for the chorus, especially in its string department. The wind was not so bad.
>
> So I suggest that a sort of compromise be arranged. That is to say, the strings should be engaged from some other place, and possibly the wind also, but failing the latter, the Marines might supply it. Or another proposition is that a certain number of really fine string players be engaged, and the wind be entirely dispensed with. Of course, this would not be so good in some ways, but much better than a non–capable orchestra, and the wind parts could be filled in on the pianoforte and organ ...[158]

By the time he wrote again (on 17 December) the orchestra matter had been settled; he would have 'no objection to conducting the reduced orchestra ... provided the members are all good'.[159] His tenacity over orchestral standards is striking.

*

Longfellow wrote his *Poems on Slavery* in 1842 when the anti–slavery and pro–slavery forces in the U.S.A. were solidifying into two irreconcilable camps and were drawing up battle lines. Forceful in utterance, even at times lurid, Longfellow's work was a well–calculated choice for a composer to set before an audience of Washington coloured folk. The poems Coleridge–Taylor selected were The Slave's Dream ('Beside the ungathered rice he lay'), The Good Part ('She dwells by great Kenhawa's side'), The Slave Singing at Midnight ('Loud he sang the psalm of David'), The Quadroon Girl ('The slaver in the broad lagoon'), and The Slave in the Dismal Swamp ('In dark fens of dismal swamp'). With the exception of The Quadroon Girl, which is set for S.S.A. and baritone solo, they are written for an S.A.T.B. choir.

It is readily apparent why Coleridge–Taylor did not attempt the last two songs in Washington. Each has its particular difficulty: the need for sensitivity in the fourth and problems of chromatic intonation in the fifth. In both, the present writer hears elusive echoes of early Delius, explicable only in terms of a common (Florida–coloured) ancestry for both idioms. This impression is enhanced by the use, in The Quadroon Girl, of a wordless female chorus.

For the first time in his work, a note of real anger appears. His sympathy for his subjects — the slave dying in the rice fields, hunted in the swamp or singing psalms of praise in his dungeon — is real and tangible. There is also a feeling of profound lamentation, most marked in the first song. The cast of the themes is clear–cut and strong, especially in 'Loud he sang the psalm of David', where they are presented in octave combinations and sung *allegro furioso*. The rhythmic energy of these themes suggest a musical path Coleridge–Taylor might with profit have explored further; as it was, a fellow–pupil, Ralph Vaughan Williams, pursued it in his early work for chorus and orchestra. The *Choral Ballads* were intended for performance with either orchestral or piano accompaniment. They may afford a rare instance where the monochrome piano might be preferable, as it might emphasise the stark qualities of some of the music.

In the seven years that had elapsed since he had hidden in terror from the audience at the first performance of the *Wedding Feast*, in 1898, he had progressed in social confidence to the point that he could be persuaded to stand up and make a formal speech. Such a speech requires far more courage than, say, rehearsing an orchestra (for a musician, that is) or adjudicating a festival (both of which activities had been stages in his progress) for in these activities the mind is too engrossed to feel nervousness. In November 1905, he accepted an invitation to present the prizes at the Streatham School of Music. A minor institution and a minor event, but something of a milestone for Coleridge–Taylor. It provided a forum for some of his ideas on music, the most insistent of which was the need for breadth in the training of musicians, whether they were to be singers or instrumentalists:

> I do not think that the study of what I may term the unpractical side of music — by which I mean harmony, counterpoint, sight reading and extemporisation— can be too strongly insisted upon.[160]

So much for technique; as for the spirit:

> We want to get away from the dull, conventional, respectable and matter–of–fact performances and to go in for something better. We require less of the lady and gentleman, and more of the man and woman.[161]

The memory of the direct emotional response to music that he had experienced among his Washington soul–brothers and –sisters apparently lingered on.

Much of the remainder of 1905 was spent on his new commission from Beerbohm Tree for incidental music for Stephen Phillips's *Nero*. Beerbohm Tree's wife Maud, who played Agrippina in the production, thought the music 'haunting'. Adolph Schmid, the director of music at the theatre, greatly admired it also and, with his vast experience of the theatre, had advised Coleridge–Taylor throughout the preparation of the score. The composer looked in on the rehearsals whenever he could, drinking in the theatre atmosphere. A *Suite* from the music was published which comprised four movements (Prelude, Intermezzo, Eastern Dance and Finale) and concert promoters hurried to programme it. Among others, Godfrey played it at Bournemouth, and Coleridge–Taylor himself conducted it in March at a Halford concert in Birmingham. The next day, the *Birmingham Gazette* praised its

> power, beauty and impressiveness, combined with a high degree of imaginativeness and a technique which seemed to comprise the principal secrets of the orchestra, that unfathomable repository of mysteries.[162]

Today, the music seems to have all this, with the exception of power. It is light music: tuneful and attractive. But how it could have enhanced the effect of a play about one of history's less savoury characters is difficult to see. At the same time as Coleridge–Taylor was working on his incidental music, Richard Strauss was putting the finishing touches to his study in erotic debauchery: *Salome*. Such probing as Strauss indulges in here would have repelled Coleridge–Taylor. Tree and Phillips had to be content with what he had to offer: charming light music.

1905 was also the year in which financial losses brought the Coleridge–Taylor Orchestra to an end. Its place was taken in 1906 by something rather less ambitious: The String Players' Club. The club flourished until 1914, outliving its founder. It had the advantage of a fine leader in Stanton Rees, and its thirty members included some familiar names from the earlier organisations. They were sufficiently accomplished to attempt, for example, Tschaikowsky's *Serenade*, op. 48; an uncompromising test for a semi–amateur string orchestra.[163]

Hurlstone had died in May 1905. As a tribute to his great friend, Coleridge–Taylor included three manuscript pieces by him in his first programmes. The immensely talented Hurlstone had probably been as close to Coleridge–Taylor as anyone — bearing in mind Marjorie's comment on his friendships quoted in chapter 7. He wrote a short tribute for *The Norwood News*, in which he drew attention to Hurlstone's craft: 'I don't suppose he wrote half–a–dozen bars of slipshod stuff in his life'.[164]

His tribute also hints at the value he placed on Hurlstone's critical insight, curiously echoing the similar relationship between Holst and Vaughan Williams:

> (he) had a way of seeing through superficiality ... a shrewd observer ... a scorner of humbug.[165]

But the two composers had not recently managed such close contact as when they had been students together. This was a loss in particular for Coleridge–Taylor, for whom Hurlstone could have been in these later years a surrogate Stanford: someone who provided objective criticism.

Hiawatha was reaching some unlikely audiences. The American Consul–General in Constantinople wrote to tell him of two performances there[166] of *Hiawatha's Wedding Feast* and *The Death of Minnehaha* together with their overture; they were sold out and created a sensation in which the language barrier proved little hindrance for the predom–inantly French audience. His music was heard, too, in Rome. How it fared there is not recorded, but more than likely its tunefulness would have made an immediate appeal to Latin audiences, nurtured as they were on the sturdy melodies of Verdi.

At some point in 1905, Coleridge–Taylor had been introduced to Ernest Hartley Coleridge. A great–nephew of the philosopher–poet

Samuel Taylor Coleridge, he read to the composer his great–uncle's poetic fragment *Kubla Khan*. In chapter 1, the possibility was mooted that the composer's mother might have been the daughter of a dis–tinguished but incognito family who in covert fashion perhaps watched over their unacknowledged child. It must be emphasised that there is no concrete evidence for this attractively romantic legend. And yet ... even if not a household name, the poet Coleridge's work was reasonably well known in the late nineteenth century among those who, like the Evans family, aspired to self–improvement. Did they ever discuss, among the family, the unusual name–relationship? Had indeed Samuel been named after the poet? The young child had been christened Samuel Coleridge; there has been a custom, especially marked in African and Afro–American communities, to name a child after an admired figure, and the possibility of such a tribute cannot be entirely dismissed here. There is at present nothing more substantial than the recollection by Lord Coleridge[167] that his father or grandfather had told him that Daniel Taylor had asked the Coleridge family for permission to incorporate the Coleridge name into that of his son.

Coleridge–Taylor himself told people that he was intentionally named after the poet Samuel Taylor Coleridge.[168] In this connection, it is interesting to note that, at the composer's death, the *Birmingham Daily Post*[169] remarked that the choice of the baptismal name Coleridge was evidence of high culture in the father. It is tempting to build further on this flimsy foundation, given the known musicality of the poet and his family. Samuel Taylor Coleridge learned the violin and was a passionate opera–lover; one grandchild (Arthur Duke Coleridge) was a singer of note and was instrumental in assembling a choir to perform Bach's *B minor Mass*, and this choir became the Bach Choir. And that is all there seems to be. How one would have liked to have been a fly on the wall at that meeting between the composer and Ernest Coleridge, to have heard if the latter urged Coleridge–Taylor to set *Kubla Khan*, and his reasons for pressing it!

All we have of the poem is a 'fragment'; but this fragment is, for its time, of almost unparalleled intensity and splendour of language. When writing it, the poet was deeply addicted to opium, and the poem is said[170] to have come to him in a dream — that is, in a state of opium–induced euphoria. Even so, to achieve such perfection of language, it is likely to have been revised and polished. At the time, Coleridge was living in Somerset, which he would roam on long walks. He knew intimately the Quantocks and the Blackdowns; did he know the Mendip Hills? Were the 'caverns measureless to man' and the 'sunless sea' to be found there, in their gorges and caves?

There would seem to be almost insuperable problems in setting such a poem: where the language itself aspires to the quality of music, little can be added. And indeed, this mystic and erotic vison is quite beyond Coleridge–Taylor's range. Perhaps he should have been warned by the sparsity of other attempts to set it; perhaps it is more suitable as the basis of a tone poem, as Griffes' *The Pleasure Dome of Kubla Khan* bears out.

The composer entrusted his new piece to his Handel Society, who gave the first performance under his direction at The Queen's Hall, London, on 23 May 1906. He then conducted it at the Royal College of Music, and there was a performance at Scarborough. Thenceforth it was scarcely heard. It may be that it had a bad start in print, since its original publisher (Houghton) foundered, and its production was taken on by Novello. The work is a rhapsody lasting about thirty minutes, and is set for contralto soloist, chorus and orchestra. The orchestral prelude takes up about a third of the entire piece; strikingly extensive for such a short work. This prelude could stand as an independent structure, exploring as it does the ideas which are subsequently sung. There are no more than four of these. Inexplicably, Coleridge–Taylor seemed not to see that the principal one, rhythmically inert and lullaby–like in its six–four metre, could not easily accommodate the words of Coleridge's opening line:

Ex. 76: Kubla Kahn, opening phrase

Throughout the work the composer found it necessary to resort to either slur or melisma in order to achieve some kind of marriage between word and tune. Things improve a little with the change of metre at the entry of the solo contralto:

Ex. 77: Kubla Kahn, affettuoso

But the unnatural accenting of the following example may cause the listener reluctantly to wonder if Elgar's jibe about Coleridge–Taylor's 'want of education' was not entirely due to jealousy:

Ex. 78: Kubla Khan, 'Five miles meand'ring'

The poet's convenient repetition of the phrase 'caverns measureless to man' halfway through the piece makes ample justification for the composer to repeat the whole opening lines (of which this phrase is part) to the music of Example 76, and thus provide a structural recapitulation feature. It is followed by Example 79, below — an interesting idea as such and logical in its place in the prelude, but one that does not at all meet the needs of either the prosody or the poet's vision:

Ex. 79: Kubla Khan, 'The shadow of the dome'

A Delius or a Wagner might well have left this idea to the orchestra, over–laying the words set, perhaps, in a quasi–recitative manner.

As always with Coleridge–Taylor, *Kubla Kahn* is superbly orchestrated and finely constructed, using a structure which has some affinities with rondo form. It was simply Coleridge–Taylor's misfortune and perhaps want of wisdom to measure his art against that of one of the most formidable intellects of the early Romantic movement. His daughter Avril never considered it to be a characteristic work; she remembers saying to her brother at an early performance that 'it doesn't sound like father's music'.[171] It is indeed a work beset by problems; it seems that some well–meaning conductors have attempted to alter it, with a view to facilitating its performance. Despite the criticisms above, in sympathetic hands the cantata might well come alive, and certainly the prelude could stand as a concert piece on its own.

On 14 June 1906, Coleridge–Taylor conducted the first performance of a new orchestral work on which he had been working since the previous October. The occasion was a concert of the Philharmonic Society at The Queen's Hall and the work was the *Variations on an African Air*, op. 63. It shared the programme with Tschaikowsky's *Fifth Symphony*, Rachmaninoff's *C Minor Piano Concerto* (both conducted by Dr Frederick Cowen, and with Raoul Pugno as the soloist in the concerto) and a *Ballade* for voice and orchestra by Josef Holbrooke, who also conducted his own work. The reception of Holbrooke's *Ballade* was unenthusiastic: *The Musical Times*[172] found parts of it 'ungrateful' and 'ugly'. In contrast, the journal gave a warm welcome to the *Variations*:

> The theme is said to be an existent African song, *I'm troubled in mind*, a genuine negro tune which presents little attraction by itself. But it has been so cleverly treated, varied in key, time, presentment and orchestral colouring, that it forms quite an attractive piece of

value and deserves re–hearing, and not merely to be put on the shelf and listed as a forgotten opus. The work is replete with life, and strength and ingenuity.[173]

The Daily Telegraph, too, broadly welcomed the new work:

Mr S. Coleridge–Taylor has built a set of beautiful and most interesting variations on a theme of a negro song or hymn ... . As at first presented, it does not seem very promising, but the composer does wonders with it yet preserves its essential character throughout. His work is finely expressive, beautifully scored, and original in design.[174]

Evidently neither reviewer was enthusiastic about the song itself:

Ex. 80: Variations on an African Air, theme

The quality of a melody is in some respects subjective; this one (which was in the repertoire of the Fisk Jubilee Singers) would have much emotional force for Africans, even without taking into account its words. Of more specific importance for a composer is whether or not it offers sufficient opportunities for an imaginative note–smith to exploit. From this standpoint, the theme is potent. It is first heard on soft trombones, accompanied by *tremolando* string chords. The succeeding variations are separate entities but run continuously one into another; in this respect, their starting point is Elgar's *'Enigma' Variations* (1899), while they also point towards the rhapsodically diffuse variation treatment of Delius's *Brigg Fair*, to be completed in 1908. The following succession of examples will show something of the composer's imaginative expertise:

A whimsical variation, with the clarinet leading:

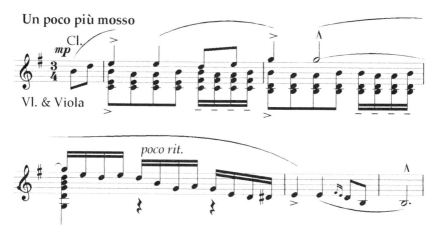

Ex. 81: Variations on an African Air (i)

A playful scherzo for woodwind:

Ex. 82: Variations on an African Air (ii)

which sandwiches an *allegro appassionato* in 2/2 time:

Ex. 83: Variations on an African Air (iii)

(The scherzo derives from the first two bars of the theme; the Allegro from the last two.)

There is two–part counterpoint:

Celli.

Ex. 84: Variations on an African Air (iv)

It will be seen that Ex. 88 below shows Coleridge–Taylor following the example of Brahms in writing a variation not on the theme but on a variation of it. Is there also a parallel with the slow movement of the *Piano Concerto* by Delius which was first heard in London in the following year (1907)? This concerto reflected Delius's period in Florida, when he was in daily contact with his Afro–American workers on his orange–grove.

Ex. 85: Delius, *Piano Concerto*

The *Variations* also include a waltz, with a counterpoint after the manner of Dvorak·

Ex. 86: Variations on an African Air (v)

And a quick march, in the strings:

Ex. 87: Variations on an African Air (vi)

A variation for cor anglais, which turns Example 84 into triple time, creating a Brahms–like lullaby, but with echoes of Dvorak and the *'New World' Symphony*:

Ex. 88: Variations on an African Air (vii)

There is a vigorous triple–time dance:

Ex. 89: Variations on an African Air (viii)

and a Lento of some pathos and intensity:

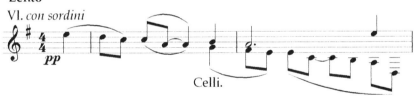

Ex. 90: Variations on an African Air (ix)

The peroration re–states the theme against powerful rhythmic counter–point. These concluding pages re–affirm the influence of Dvorak, specifically that of the *'New World' Symphony*.

There are also some suggestions of his familiarity with the early work of Rachmaninoff. The Russian master's way with building a climax over a pedal point (in, for example, the last movement of the second *Piano Concerto*) is mirrored in the approach to this peroration:

Ex. 91: Variations on an African Air (x)

This lovely work went a long way towards restoring faith in Coleridge–Taylor's genius, which for many had been shaken by some of the uneven work in the years preceding it. Just as with Elgar and the *'Enigma'* *Variations*, he was not here fettered to the choral tradition and was able to give free rein to his fancy.

Whilst these variations have few pretensions to profundity, they are light music of fine quality. Indeed, much of the set of *'Enigma'* *Variations* is also light in style. But where necessary (as, for example, in the 'Nimrod' variation), Elgar has the power to transcend any prevailing cosiness into something of universal profundity. Delius has the same reserve of power. His *Appalachia* (first draft for orchestra only, 1896; revised choral version, 1902) consists for much of its course of pictures of Florida life: the Jacksonville street parade or the elegant ballroom, fondly and nostalgically remembered. But the real intensity of the composer's Florida experience comes when, with overwhelming force, his theme — a commonplace mixture of slave–song 'à la Rigoletto' — is transmuted by the choir and orchestra into a few moments of spine–tingling splendour. Such peak moments were beyond Coleridge–Taylor's range; but in compensation there is an unfailing musical invention and command of structure that had often been obscured in his recent work.

Are the *Variations* a service to his paternal race? It has to be admitted that there seems little difference in approach between the white Delius writing his variations on a slave song and the coloured Coleridge–Taylor writing his on a negro air: both are in the main European stream. For Delius it is the Florida associations that count, rather than the slave ones. One might have expected that the poignant words at least, not to speak of the solemnity of the melody, might have pointed Coleridge–

Taylor to a musical statement of the plight of his kinsfolk. In their book on the Jubilee Singers, Marsh and Loudin have the following note as a preface to the melody:

> The person who furnished this song (Mrs Brown of Nashville, formerly a slave) stated that she first heard it from her old father when she was a child. After he had been whipped he always went and sat upon a certain log near his cabin, and with the tears streaming down his cheeks, sang this song with so much pathos that few could listen without weeping from sympathy; and even his cruel oppressors were not wholly unmoved.[175]

But the theme has for him none of these associations; the intervals and rhythms work on him *musically* rather than polemically and produce not protesting but genial music. The fact, nevertheless, that a coloured man had written so fine an orchestral work for so august a body as the Philharmonic Society, and that it had been so cordially received, was seen by coloured folk as a signal honour and as another bastion breached.

Its neglect today is unaccountable. There seems no reason why it should not become a repertoire concert piece. Even if it is unlikely ever to displace the *'Enigma' Variations* in popularity, it would make a welcome alternative from time to time.

15 SECOND VISIT TO THE U.S.A.

The Autumn of 1906 seems to have been uneventful; that is to say, there was less than usual to interrupt the pattern of teaching and conducting which had become the daily routine of his life. Although the main work of 1905–6 had been the *Variations on an African Air*, a number of smaller works were also completed, including songs, part–songs and the *Scènes de Ballet*, op. 64, for piano.

Amongst the vocal music, *Drake's Drum* (Henry Newbolt) for female voices and piano achieved great success at festivals, but was supplanted in popularity by Stanford's setting. Coleridge–Taylor's version was arranged for men's voices and also for S.A.T.B., in which latter setting it makes its best effect. *A June Rose Bloomed* (Louise Alston Burleigh), for S.S.A. and piano, is a miniature of great beauty, made more widely available in Alex Roloff's piano arrangement under the title *Idyll*.

The *Scènes de Ballet* are in four movements; a suite for piano that could, if necessary, be easily orchestrated. Whether he hoped for a practical use in the theatre for his *Scènes* or whether he simply intended musical pictures of classical ballet language is a matter for conjecture; but a place for the first of them was found in the posthumous dramatised *Hiawatha* performances, when it was occasionally used for a 'Spring' ballet.

In the Autumn of 1906, preparations for his forthcoming visit to the U.S.A. took precedence over composition. This second visit became, in the event, three tours in one. His specific purpose was to conduct a three–day festival in Washington. But this was preceded by a short tour of some of the principal cities, with three fellow coloured musicians: Henry Burleigh, Lola Johnson (soprano) and Felix Fowler Weir (violin), and it was followed by a visit to Norfolk, Connecticut. The cities visited prior to the Washington festival were Pittsburg, St Louis, Chicago, Milwaukee, Detroit and Toronto, commencing at the Mendelssohn Hall, New York on 16 November 1906.

The basis of their programme, given with minor variations, is shown below. All the pieces are by Coleridge–Taylor:

183

Nero Incidental Music: Intermezzo & First Entracte
Soprano songs: 'The Young Indian Maid'
                   'Beauty and Song'
Baritone songs: 'Love's Passing'
                   'A Corn song'
Piano pieces: Two Oriental Waltzes
Violin: Romance (probably that dating from 1904)
Soprano songs: 'Spring had come' (from *Hiawatha's Departure*)
                   'Minguillo'
Baritone songs: 'She rested by the broken brook'
                   'Beat, Beat, Drums'
Violin: Four African Dances.

He had picked the songs carefully to appeal to his audience; he included one — 'She rested by the broken brook' — from a group of new songs he had sold to his Boston publisher Oliver Ditson as part of his continuing policy of extending his American representation.[176]

Reviewing the New York performance next day, Richard Aldrich wrote:[177]

> Mr Coleridge–Taylor himself plays the piano with the skill of a composer, not of a virtuoso, but he gave an admirable account of his piano pieces and played the accompaniments of his other works with taste and skill.
>
> His songs show a fine gift of melody and distinction in the harmonic treatment of the accompaniment. Most characteristic and most valuable from a musical point of view is his setting of Paul Laurance [*sic*] Dunbar's *Corn Song*, a reminder of antebellum days on a plantation in the South, with a negro refrain ... Mr Coleridge–Taylor played two of his 'symphonic arrangements' of Negro songs for the piano ... *I'm Troubled in my Mind* and the West Indian *Bamboula* ... a most interesting attempt to use the Negro folk–song material in artistic music ...

Coleridge–Taylor had added these two to the published programme; they were favourites of his and, in a few years, *Bamboula* would be expanded into a brilliant orchestral piece.

The New York audience numbered many coloured folk, but it was the whites who applauded most vociferously. The *New York Herald* critic wondered if the coloured members were anxious not to appear conspicuous. But no such restraint was needed five days later in Washington, where on 21 November, the Coleridge–Taylor Festival commenced with performances of *The Atonement* and *The Quadroon Girl*. These two works had achieved little success in England, but he thought highly of them; he no doubt hoped that the strong emotional impact of *The Atonement* in particular would prompt a response from a black American audience, whereas it had apparently violated the reserve of an English one. The following night the festival continued with *Hiawatha*; it appears to have been the thirteenth performance of the *Feast* in Washington. The final night (23 November 1906) was devoted to a performance of miscellaneous items, in which Coleridge–Taylor was again joined by the artists who had accompanied him on the preceding tour.

There were just two engagements left to fulfil, in Philadelphia and Boston on the 6 and 13 December respectively, after which he intended to return to England. But he now received an invitation to visit Norfolk, Connecticut. On the face of it, there was little incentive for him to accept — no fee would be payable — but he had been elected as honorary member of the Litchfield County Choral Union whose centre was at Norfolk. Taking with him Reed Miller, Henry Burleigh and Felix Fowler Weir, he gave a free recital on 17 December in the Norfolk Village Hall. The inspirational figure in Litchfield County was Carl Stoeckel (1858–1925) and, as in some ways Stoeckel was to influence much of Coleridge–Taylor's remaining life, it will be fitting to say something of him here.

He was the son of Gustav Stoeckel, a Bavarian musician who fled from Germany to the United States in 1848 in the wake of revolutionary troubles. Gustav Stoeckel prospered in his new country, becoming Professor of Music at Yale and first Head of the Yale School of Music. His son Carl was sufficiently well endowed financially (thanks to his parent and to his wife) to follow his inclination as a patron of music and musicians. In 1906, he built The Music Shed on his Norfolk estate as a home for choral and orchestral music in Litchfield County, and in 1899 he established the Norfolk Festival as a memorial to Mrs Stoeckel's father. Prominent musicians were invited to Norfolk to enjoy Stoeckel's lavish hospitality with all expenses paid. Rachmaninoff and Kreisler played there. Sibelius went in 1914, taking with him the score of *The Oceanides*, which received its first performance there. In 1915, Stanford took his new *Piano Concerto* and in 1923 Vaughan Williams and his wife were invited. They enjoyed the white colonial house with its high pillared portico and lovely garden, and Adeline Vaughan Williams sketched something of the way of life Stoeckel offered his guests:

> The Stoeckels are very dear people — only we have to do just what
> Mr Stoeckel plans for us ... . Mrs Stoeckel is good company ... she
> is the heiress of the estate here. Meals are too rich, and wine flows
> all the time.[178]

The Festival was endowed with ten thousand dollars each year, to which
Stoeckel usually added a further twenty thousand dollars.

Coleridge–Taylor's subsequent and last visit to the States would be
under the aegis of Stoeckel, who could command the presence of a fully
professional orchestra. But he did not neglect his Washington friends.
Indeed, he obliged them by placing on record his condemnation of the
ever–popular 'coon' songs and the growing fancy for ragtime, which
respectable black Americans were seeing as a corruption of their efforts
to emulate white culture. Neither he nor they could have been expected
to anticipate the force and energy of the new idioms which, in a mere
decade or so, would influence the work of those white composers, such
as Stravinsky, Lambert and Walton, who were striving to escape German
artistic domination.

But music, not the politics of race, was his mainspring. For music,
Stoeckel's resources were infinitely greater than those of the Washington
coloured community. Stoekel, too, was German. Coleridge–Taylor still
gravitated to German musicians, and was indeed taking German lessons,
so successfully that he was able to write to his German friends in their
own language.

The visit to the U.S.A. for Stoeckel's Litchfield Festival was to take
place four years later in 1910, and will be considered in chapter 18. The
Coleridge–Taylor Choral Society of Washington did not long survive the
composer's second visit: it was dissolved at some point towards the end
of the first decade of this century, to be revived briefly for one performance in the 1920s before disappearing for good.[179] Few references to any
musical activity by the Society appear in the Washington press in the
years following 1906, although it seems to have continued for a while
with its social programme and its old members organised a Testimonial
Concert as a tribute on the occasion of the composer's death. The
conjecture may be made that there may have been a relationship between
Coleridge–Taylor's visit to the white Litchfield Festival and the
dissolution of the black Washington Society. If the Black Race were to
be 'saved by its exceptional men', had Coleridge–Taylor, in the Society's
perception, perhaps failed the test? Betrayal would be too strong a word;
disappointment would not.

A contrary view is expressed by Dr Doris McGinty, who is an

acknowledged authority on music in Washington. She speculates[180] that the coloured citizens would have perceived the invitation to Coleridge–Taylor from Stoeckel as an indication of his importance and a sign that their introduction of the composer to the U.S.A. had borne important fruit.

She points out that the Howard University Choir came into prominence around 1907 and took on the tradition of performing Coleridge–Taylor's music, giving its first performance of the 'Trilogy' in 1919. The Treble Clef Society lived on, and for many years it devoted an annual meeting to remembrances and tributes to him.

> Ensembles were named after him and theatres frequented by black citizens were named *The Hiawatha* and *The Minnehaha*, presumably in reference to the works of Coleridge–Taylor.[181]

He returned to England in time for Christmas but, after a short break, he was off on his travels again, to start the New Year (1907) in Wales, adjudicating the Dolgellau Festival. (His acceptance in Wales and his affinity with the Welsh is worth remarking upon; a large number of his adjudication engagements occurred in that country.) The end of January found him conducting another String Players' Club concert in Croydon (26 January 1907) and, in the following month, an estimated 4500 people were present in Liverpool to hear him conduct the *Variations on an African Air*. He noted that the greatest enthusiasm seemed to come from the cheapest seats:

> It is to the great masses that I feel that we owe it here in England today that music stands on the high level it undoubtedly does ...

Three months later, in April, the work was heard in Bournemouth, where the doughty Dan Godfrey was continuing to be a staunch ally.

Coleridge–Taylor had made little money from the second American trip and financial necessity made it essential for him to resume his pattern of engagements as soon as he could. His own nature did not help:

> My husband had an unfortunate weakness for giving money to all who asked for it.[182]

Nor was his generosity limited only to fellow coloureds:

> There was one white fellow who often asked Coleridge for a financial tip, as it were. He would start his begging by saying, 'I was just about going to ask you', and Coleridge always called him

that: he would tell mother that he'd just seen 'Just about going to ask you'. It tickled him.[183]

The distances involved in getting to engagements were often tiring and always time consuming; this circumstance reminds one of the actor–manager Sir Donald Wolfit's sad comment that, while Sir Laurence Olivier was a tour–de–force, he himself was forced to tour. Coleridge–Taylor was admittedly on his home ground on 16 March 1907 with the String Players' Club in Croydon, but that same night he had to journey to Cornwall for an engagement next day in the small town of Liskeard.

The Club continued to attract good audiences, and was self–supporting even with ticket prices at only sixpence or a shilling. And it was more enterprising in its programmes than the Croydon Orchestral Society or the Coleridge–Taylor Orchestra could afford to be. Its fifth concert (given in the Large Public Hall, Croydon) included the *Suite in G*, op. 35, by Glazounow, a composer little known in this country at that time, and a manuscript *Ballade* by the young Julius Harrison.

On 7 July, he was invited to New Brighton to conduct a concert of his work. Here Granville Bantock was in charge, and had craftily by–passed his function of providing popular music for the trippers in favour of exploring the early twentieth century repertoire. Coleridge–Taylor had benefitted from this policy the previous year when a concert was held there devoted mainly to his music, including *Kubla Khan*, the *Variations on an African Air* and the *Nero* Suite. For this 1907 concert, Coleridge–Taylor included the first performance of his *Fantasiestücke in A* for 'cello and orchestra in which the soloist was Mary McCullagh. At present, all efforts to trace this work have failed. Berwick Sayers heard the work and thought highly of it:

> The work is in the form of variations upon a theme, but has greater homogeneity of treatment than is usual in such works, and is marked by the restraint with which the orchestral accompaniment is scored and the consequent effective prominence given to the solo instrument ...
>
> ... Few even of Coleridge–Taylor's instrumental works are marked by a finer sense of proportion.[184]

One of the German friends with whom he was corresponding in 1907 was the violinist Theodore Spiering. Writing to him in September 1907, he mentioned 'a new piece (a ballade) for violin and piano, and I hope you will soon play it if you like it enough'.[185] The reference is probably to the *Ballade in C minor*, op. 73. Spiering did take the work into his repertoire, and played it frequently in Germany, but the first performance was given by Zacharewitsch (to whom it is dedicated) accompanied by the composer, at a concert in Leeds on 29 October 1907. It might be expected that such a work would be idiomatically written for the violin, and indeed this is so. What is perhaps unexpected is the equally fine writing for the piano, and this quality makes it an attractive recital piece in which the two instruments complement one another.

This second *Ballade* is cast very freely in the form of a set of variations, although it might not be recognised as such in performance since ideas which appear to be newly minted yet have their origin in the theme:

Ex. 92: Ballade no.2, theme and derivation

New influences are apparent; there is less of Dvorak, but something of Grieg,[186] while the sequences of falling sixths suggest he has, at the last, found Elgar impossible to ignore. While not a major work, the second *Ballade* is rather more than a salon piece, and would justify a hearing from time to time. In 1910 his old friend, William Read, asked him to orchestrate the work but, so far as is known, this task was never completed.

That October (in 1907), the family moved house to Norbury. Their new home, called 'Hillcrest', was in the London Road. This was the main London to Brighton road and was subject to rapidly growing motor traffic. Coleridge–Taylor was not accustomed to so much noise, but the family stayed there for three years.

Few requests for his presence at local musical functions were turned down, whether it was to present prizes at the Beckenham and Bromley School of Music or to attend the concerts of the Blackheath, Brockley and Lewisham Orchestral Society. He was President of the latter; all such occasions, of course, meant speeches — and speech–preparation stole time from composing. The leading light of the Orchestral Society was really angling for him to conduct them.[187] First, she persuaded him to direct his *Nero* Suite; thence it was but a short step to taking on the directorship, especially as it could be pointed out that the London, Brighton and South Coast Railway ran a convenient service from Waddon to New Cross. He was easy game: Florence Montgomery later remarked to Berwick Sayers that he 'retained much of the child's beautiful nature'.[188]

Another new set of variations appeared on 30 November 1907 when, at a String Players' Club concert, the cellist A. E. Crabbe played the *Variations on an Original Theme* for 'cello and piano. The work was played from manuscript; subsequently it was mislaid but it re-appeared a few years later, to be published posthumously by Augener in 1918. Clearly, in this period, beginning with the *African Variations*, Coleridge–Taylor found the form stimulating. It is sad to have to say that, in the new work, the 'Original Theme' itself is sterile, with the result that the 'cello *Variations* seem rather obvious and even common-place.

Ex. 93: Variations on an Original Theme, theme

All the technical assurance is there, but the work is little more than a 'cello showpiece, one whose style is very reminiscent of similar examples by Saint–Saëns. It is possible that it was not so much lost as suppressed by the composer after its first performance.

Much more rewarding is an eight–part *a cappella* setting of *Sea Drift*. This is a setting of a poem by T. B. Aldrich, so the result is not in any way comparable with the setting by Delius of Whitman's poem of the same title. Coleridge–Taylor's work was completed by March 1908, at which date he assigned it outright to Novello for £20. The problem with so much of his choral music is that it is the victim of changing fashion; of no work is this more true than *Sea Drift*. The poem depicts a frail sorrowing woman silhouetted against a wild seascape. It would have struck a chord at the time, when the horror of ship–wreck was more common around the coasts than it is today:

> See where she stands
> On the wet sea sands,
> Looking across the water:
> Wild is the night, but wilder still
> The face of the fisher's daughter.
>
> What does she there
> In the lightning's glare,
> What does she there, I wonder?
> What dread demon drags her forth
> In the night and wind and thunder?

Few would dare to set such lines today. But the unsophisticated Coleridge–Taylor did set them, and in so doing he produced a four–minute musical seascape arguably of greater imaginative power than his *Meg Blane* cantata. In style, the work reaches back to the *Ballade in A minor* written nearly ten years before for the Gloucester Three Choirs Festival; indeed, the work is orchestral rather than choral in style. The description of it as a rhapsody — a word with orchestral rather than choral connotations — gives a clue to the composer's thinking. Only embrace the fashions of 1908 and you have a miniature masterpiece which, while it might cause a trembling lip in sophisticated circles, still has some potency:

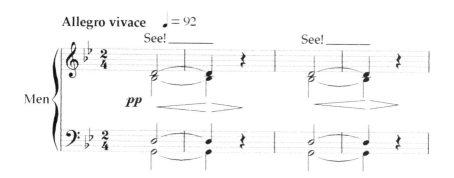

Ex. 94: Sea Drift, 'See where she stands'

By chance, March 1908 found him for the first, and probably only, time of his life in association with Delius when he, Delius and Ernest Walker acted as judges in a composition competition organised by the Norwich Festival. All the entries were submitted under pseudonyms, but Coleridge–Taylor recognised the handwriting of one entry: that of Julius Harrison, whose *Ballade* for strings he had conducted from a manuscript score less than a year earlier. It was Harrison who won the competition with his setting of the given text on the subject of Cleopatra; but, as a letter from Delius to Granville Bantock shows,[189] it was a close decision:

> To my great astonishment, I see from a paper that the 'Holy Pabrun' was Havergal Brian — I am sorry he did not get the prize — if Coleridge–Taylor had only mentioned the 'Holy Pabrun' he would have tied with the other and they would have been obliged to pay them both and divide the prize.

It is remarkable that one so young[190] (Coleridge–Taylor was thirty–three) should have been adjudicating such a prestigious competition; but then it is perhaps even more remarkable that anyone should have persuaded the autocratic Delius to join the panel.

16 OPERA AND DRAMA: *THELMA* AND *FAUST*

The early months of 1908 saw Coleridge–Taylor engaged in much other adjudication. In January and February it was in London, with The Queen's Hall and People's Palaces Festivals respectively; also in February was that at Horbury, and in June came the Gwent Eisteddfod at Rhymney in South Wales. On 5 April he was in Bournemouth to conduct *Hiawatha's Vision* and the *Ballade in A minor*, dashing thence to Wolverhampton, to take part in a recital there the following night with the singer Frank Mullings and the violinist W. J. Read. Later that month, 25 April 1908, he was back on home ground with the String Players' Club, conducting a programme of Bach and Handel.[191]

These were distractions from what had become his major composition project which was occupying many months of work. A letter, written in October 1908 to his American friend Andrew Hilyer, is the principal source for the pathetically little which is known of this project:

> I am in the middle of my first opera ... getting it well in hand now, and it probably will be produced here next June. It is, of course, grand opera and on a Norwegian subject.

The score is lost and the work was never produced; the few known facts about it are sparse. The opera's original title was *The Amulet*, but this was changed later to *Thelma*. The composer told Berwick Sayers that his libretto was based on a 'Norse–saga legend'.

After much revision, he completed the work in 1909, hoping for a production that year by the Carl Rosa Opera Company. But when he showed his score to Van Noorden, the director of the Carl Rosa Company, it was pointed out to him that his opera would pose in–superable problems to stage. We must assume that the fault lay in the libretto: this was certainly Avril's understanding. It is not known who wrote it, but again the assumption must be that it was the work of the composer himself and that, due to his inexperience and failure to consult theatrical experts in the early stages, problems were built in from the start. Only its Prelude seems ever to have been played: in March 1910 by Landon Ronald and the New Symphony Orchestra.

The Musical Times critic heard it and applauded the 'virile music, highly characteristic of the composer in its rhythms, and effectively scored'.[192] Why would he have been prepared to make such a huge commitment of time and energy for a project which in its failure left him still financially insecure? Why undertake a task for which the market was so uncertain? Could he not have secured a commission for it, which would have at least ensured some return?

There are no satisfactory answers to these questions, but he must have felt, as one of the composers most in demand, that there would be no problem in getting his work staged. Moreover, it is not strictly true to say, as is often asserted, that, after Handel, British opera was moribund until the advent of Benjamin Britten. This view ignores the efforts of Arne, Dibdin, Balfe, Wallace, Sullivan and Coleridge–Taylor's own teacher, Stanford. There were plenty of composers; the problem was that there were too few companies and those few were of variable standard. Outside London, there were only the travelling opera companies such as Carl Rosa or Moody–Manners, for opera had not yet become for the British a natural means of entertainment. By the closing years of the nineteenth century, such a prolific opera composer as Delius thought entirely (and not very successfully) in terms of production on the continent; in the early twentieth century, the intrepid Ethel Smyth was storming the stage doors of Dresden and Leipzig with *Der Wald* and *The Wreckers*. Even such a prestigious figure as Stanford looked to the continent.

The weak British dramatic instinct had been channelled into the great Provincial Festivals and thence into the 'dramatic' cantata, from which there seemed little alternative. Elgar found salvation from it only when he was sufficiently well known and could develop as an orchestral composer. A white knight would later appear in the shape of Thomas Beecham, but his time was still a few years away. Sir Henry Wood indicated the musical standards among the travelling operatic companies:

> The orchestra — as usual — was hopeless. I fear I became sarcastic and upset things a little by asking the violins whether they were sure they were playing on the right string. The woodwind played so out of tune that I begged them not to transpose — a remark that did not go down very well.[193]

All of which makes one wonder why composers persisted in trying to scale the frustrating challenge of the operatic salmon–leap.

For Coleridge–Taylor, a partial answer to this question must have been the continuing aim of success in Europe, and the possibility of making an escape from the drudgery of Festival commissions. *Hiawatha* was being performed by everyone everywhere, but little else among his Festival cantatas had so far established itself as a repertoire piece.

His failure to secure a staging for *Thelma* was a severe blow. As Hubert Foss wrote later,[194] Coleridge–Taylor was 'another man who was stifled by English lack of operatic opportunity'. He seems, however, to have absorbed the disappointment with his usual equanimity. His character was distinguished by endurance, but not by forcefulness. Those who did succeed in getting their operas staged — Ethel Smyth or Josef Holbrooke, for example — exhibited a forcefulness amounting almost to pugnaciousness. But, just as he did when Stanford condemned the last movement of the *Symphony* years before, he seems to have abandoned *Thelma* without a fight. Indeed, only in the case of *The Atonement* does he seem to have persisted in cherishing a work which had been heavily criticised. The possibility that *Thelma* may have been destroyed by its creator cannot be entirely dismissed; certainly, its manuscript has not yet been found.

He did not abandon his operatic ambitions, and indeed others thought he might yet produce The Great Opera. At the very end of his life, he entered into correspondence with Reginald Buckley, who pressed him hard to try again. Buckley had heard that Clara Butt and her husband Kennerley Rumford were looking for an opera; he thought that Boadicea might make a suitable subject. One look at photos of the majestic Clara Butt shows why. Alternately, he suggested *Kate Meredith* (a novel set in West Africa) or even Cleopatra. This third alternative seems unlikely to have been within Clara Butts's range. Buckley had no doubt that Coleridge–Taylor was his man, but nothing came of the project; he was too late.

Throughout 1908 there were encouragements to compensate for *Thelma*, even if few of them were financially rewarding.

> I suppose, of course, that you have heard of the many Samuel Coleridge–Taylor societies being organised all over the country?[195]

wrote Andrew Hilyer from Washington, who added

> Your compositions are often rendered by prominent white orchestras and musicians.[196]

This was progress indeed in race–troubled America. Hilyer added:

> When we are going to have a Hiawatha concert here, for at least one month we seem, as it were, to be lifted above the clouds of American colour–prejudice?[197]

Hilyer and his colleagues, too, had experienced the therapeutic choir-
reviving properties of *Hiawatha*, which could be matched by numerous
English choral societies:

> We were plodding along with The Messiah and when the time came
> to make arrangements for our Spring concert, it was evident that the
> Society did not know The Messiah well enough to attempt it,
> especially since the white choral society had rendered it every year
> for twenty–five years. Besides, something was needed to rally the
> chorus. We decided that Hiawatha would do it, went out, blew the
> bugle call 'Hiawatha, Hiawatha' and they came.[198]

Perhaps nearer Coleridge–Taylor's heart, the Washington singers planned
also to do *The Atonement* again and to repeat the performance for the
Y.M.C.A. in Baltimore.

At home, another commission from Beerbohm Tree not only kept
open the stage door but was, as usual from this source, well paid. The
production of *Faust* (written by Stephen Phillips and J. Comyns Carr)
opened at His Majesty's Theatre on 7 September. In his letter to
Andrew Hilyer, Coleridge–Taylor clearly appears to be taken with the
young actress playing the female lead:[199]

> Just fancy, the principal woman part (Margaret) is taken by a Miss
> Marie Lohr, only seventeen and a half years old, in London's
> greatest and most artistic theatre.

Tree's *Faust* was immensely successful; Coleridge–Taylor told Hilyer
that it would be difficult to get a ticket for weeks. Not all the music was
his (some by Berlioz was used), but his contribution was extensive, com-
prising as it did a Prelude, two Entractes, a male voice Chorus, a Dance
of the Apes and a setting of 'A King there Lived in Thule'. From all
this he subsequently made an orchestral *Suite* of three movements, well
boiled–down from the large amount of music actually written for the
production. From the mass of Coleridge–Taylor's working sketches for
Faust, something of the complexity of Beerbohm Tree's demands may
be gathered. They show, for instance, the composer adding and sub-
tracting passages to meet alterations in Tree's timing requirements. The
Walpurgis Night music had some choral passages and its dialogue was
spoken against an orchestral background. At least one idea, a theme for
the love–music in the garden scene, was vintage Coleridge–Taylor.

With *Faust* established, Coleridge–Taylor's year gently ran down, but
not before he had crossed the Severn to adjudicate the Newport and
Monmouth Total Abstinence Society Semi–National Eisteddfod.[200]

The time and effort necessarily taken by the opera must have meant much financial hardship for the family over the years 1907 and 1908. Faced with continuing low funds, Coleridge–Taylor was probably hoping to write a work which would stand a chance of matching the popularity of *Hiawatha*. A commission from the Brighton Festival offered an opportunity, and lyric poems by Thomas Moore suggested a choral suite.

The *'Bon–Bon' Suite* initiated a period of renewed inspiration for Coleridge–Taylor which was to last until his death four years later. In this last period, commencing with this work and continuing through such works as *Bamboula, Petite Suite de Concert, A Tale of Old Japan* and the *Violin Concerto*, he recovered the quality and élan of his earlier successes. No longer aspiring to the high ground of his youthful chamber music, the drama of *Meg Blane* or the spiritual world of *The Atonement*, he was now content to settle for entertainment. Perhaps, although he would still stray from it from time to time, light music really was his true path and vocation.

The *'Bon–Bon' Suite* includes a substantial part for baritone, and here the composer was fortunate in his soloist. He had met the young Julien Henry, a singer he came to admire deeply and one who became a close friend. The solo part was tailored to Henry's voice, as indeed would be that in the subsequent *A Tale of Old Japan*. The style of the work is light and frankly popular; even so, his publishers were loth to accept it. Neither they nor he had made money from *Meg Blane, Kubla Khan* or *The Atonement*. He had hoped for a £50 advance on royalties; Novellos offered him £10.

The *Suite* was first performed on 14 January 1909, at Brighton, under the composer's direction.[201] It shared the programme with the third act of *Lohengrin* and other 'bleeding chunks' of Wagner. It was to have come last, but the organisers changed the order of the programme so that the composer could catch the last train back to Croydon that night.

This première gained for Coleridge–Taylor some of the most enthusiastic reviews he had received in years. It was 'hailed with shouts of delight', enthused the *Sussex Daily News*.[202] The composer, 'looking like the victor just emerged from some fierce battle, was recalled again and again', wrote the *Herald*.[203] Coleridge–Taylor had indicated, perhaps without giving too much thought to it, that his title *'Bon–Bon'* was selected because he had written the work for children. It is true that it is dedicated to 'Miss Sunshine' (Doris), a child he and Jessie had met on holiday in Worthing with whom they became friendly, and who they would take with them on their walks; yet, while it is innocent and even child–like in places, the *Suite* is hardly for children. But the suggestion coloured the perception of the *Daily Telegraph* reviewer:

> If the music seems on a first hearing to be a little more complex than necessary, a little more heavily scored than would seem to fit its purpose, if the purpose is indeed that stated, it certainly possesses not a little charm ... .
>
> Moreover, the hand of Mr Coleridge–Taylor is clearly to be observed in several numbers, as in Hiawatha, so far its composer's masterpiece.[204]

(The 'so far' cannot have been very welcome to the composer.)

The *'Bon–Bon' Suite* represents a fairly radical departure from the dramatic story cantatas which, along with so many contemporaries, he had regularly offered. Light as air, and frothy, sentimental and brilliant by turns, these songs demand considerable virtuosity from the chorus. The settings are: 'The Magic Mirror', 'The Fairy Boat', 'To Rosa', 'Love and Hymen', 'The Watchman', and 'Say, what shall we dance?'

'The Magic Mirror', driven onwards by its rhythm, is built on sequence:

Ex. 95: 'The Magic Mirror'

There is a new freedom here, through which the occasionally obvious nature of some of his recent music is avoided — a freedom which shows itself in the unexpected exits at phrase–endings to unusual keys.

While too much ought not to be made of the point, there is a striking resemblance in the sequence quoted above to a similar one in Elgar's first *Organ Sonata*, a work he probably did not know. Whatever the genesis of this specific instance, the fact remains that the influence generally of Elgar, noted earlier, is still present:

Ex. 96: 'To Rosa'

The second song, 'The Fairy Boat', is set as a kind of fast minuet, to create a picture of porcelain delicacy:

Ex. 97: 'The Fairy Boat'

Sequence is important in this song too; not so Elgarian, perhaps, but marked again by resourcefulness in avoiding obvious phrase endings.

The heart of the *'Bon–Bon' Suite* is the setting of 'To Rosa'. Arguably one of the composer's finest single movements, 'To Rosa' manages to keep just the right side of the line between sentiment and sentimentality. The voice placing is that of a master, as is the use of silence. In the following example, there are two bars silence before the voices deliver their final phrases; the feeling for effect is unerring:

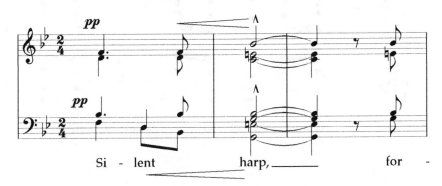

got - ten lo - ver_____

Ex. 98: 'To Rosa'

Moore's embarrassingly arch verse would probably preclude performance today of the fourth song, 'Love and Hymen'; in the fifth, 'The Watchman', the accompaniment consists of little more than a bell to mark the passing hours as the baritone lover, loth to depart, inveighs against the remorseless intoning of the choir:

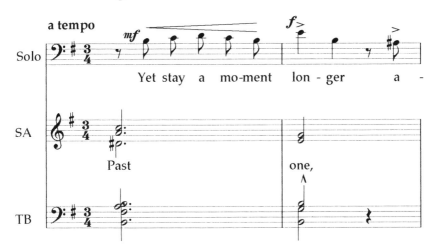

Ex. 99: 'The Watchman'

'Say, what shall we dance?' asks the sixth and last song; mostly it is set as a kind of tarantella, with occasional lapses into waltz or quick march time, as the words dictate. The composer achieves a brilliant effect by the most simple means:

plain,   a - long   the   moon - light   plain

Ex. 100: 'Say, what shall we dance?'

The *'Bon–Bon' Suite* is a masterly exposition of choral styles as they would have been understood by English composers from Elgar to Stanford. No racial overtones are apparent; all is English and open.

Having said that, Mahler might have admired at least the second song, 'The Fairy Boat'. But had he set it he would have been alive to the possibilities of darker irony, whereas Coleridge–Taylor, true to his uncomplicated and sunny nature, was content not to probe too deeply.

As the composer had hoped, the *'Bon–Bon' Suite* did achieve a popularity surpassed only by the *Hiawatha* trilogy and the as yet unwritten *A Tale of Old Japan*. As a result, the Brighton connection prospered, leading to a second commission and further conducting engagements.

One of Coleridge–Taylor's more remarkable qualities was his capacity for concentration; his ability to write music in odd moments and in uncongenial places. This he was forced to cultivate because of his constant travelling and the pressures of his life style — a thread which has been running through our story. And then there was the family, which he loved but which could at times be tumultuous. Marjorie thought that

> his family responsibilities restricted him. Jessie's bad temper would upset the children and that made it difficult to settle down to compose. I know he didn't like that sort of thing ...[205]

If anything, 1909 proved an even more frenetic year than those it followed, in which, with the exception of *Endymion's Dream*, a work in progress for the Brighton Festival in 1910, composition was limited to the smaller forms. At the beginning of the year, he was anticipating with some pleasure a conducting engagement in Guernsey. In February there was the Handel Society's performance of *Acis and Galatea* at the People's Palace, to be followed shortly after by the String Players' Club in Croydon. In April, Bournemouth heard him direct the *Faust* music, which in the summer also formed part of an entire Coleridge–Taylor concert given at the Dome by the Brighton Municipal Orchestra. Even Christmas brought little respite; the day before New Year's Eve found him back at the Winter Gardens in Bournemouth, conducting the *Faust* music again, together with the *Variations on an African Air*.

These were but high points in the year: punctuation marks in the paragraphs of weekly work with the Handel Society, The String Players' Club, the Central Croydon Choral Society and the Rochester Choral Society, not to speak of the endless teaching and adjudicating. In 1909, he adjudicated, among others, the Festivals at Warrington and Southport, and the Eisteddfodau of Cardigan and Newport. Anyone who has done it will know that adjudication is perhaps the most exhausting work available to the music profession. Nor were matters helped when domestic harmony was shattered by a burglary at 'Hillcrest', in which jewellery was stolen and some presentation batons broken.

Most of the work described above was with amateurs; but now, in his thirty–fourth year, professional orchestras were increasingly engaging him to conduct them: an interesting parallel with Elgar, who about this time was touring as conductor of the London Symphony Orchestra. Both men tended to be engaged initially to present their own works but, in the course of time, both were asked to conduct the work of others. As a conductor, Coleridge–Taylor had not the brilliance of Beecham nor the vast and intimidating experience of Richter, but he was efficient, thorough and probably a 'natural'. At the Brighton Dome concert noted above, the local music critic was as impressed with his conducting as he was with his music (the *'Nero'* Suite):

> Mr Coleridge–Taylor carried the orchestra up the heights of sound to a triumphant climax. It was in this majestic finale that the composer's vigorous personality as a conductor, his urgent stimulus upon all the forces under his control, had its complete manifestation.

Stoeckel noted his grace of movement and demeanour on mounting the rostrum: like a 'well–restrained warhorse panting for the fray'.[206]

There was a marked contrast at recitals, where:

He seemed to shrink within himself.[207]

The Brighton Dome concert also included the *Variations on an African Air*. Writing of them, the local critic was loth to allow Coleridge–Taylor's aspirations as a civilised European:

> The music of Mr Coleridge–Taylor represents the apotheosis of the barbaric ... . His temperament has magnificent expression in the barbaric, which [has] to have a compelling call for his genius. The cult of the barbaric, like a subtle current, runs through nearly all his music, giving it a wonderful individual colour ...
>
> Yet by his supreme talent, the composer brings just enough of the refining [ambience] of the West to give artistic form to the glamour of the South ...

No doubt such criticism — clearly favourably meant — amused a man of such cultivated finesse as Coleridge–Taylor. For, in it, 'coloured' equalled 'African', and equalled 'uncivilised' and therefore 'barbaric'. There is nothing remotely barbaric about the *Variations*; nevertheless, some will hear what they want to hear, and the perception of barbarism in his work was something the composer, as a coloured man in a white country, was resigned to living with.

Whether as conductor or performer, he was proving a magnet for audiences; of the Bournemouth performance of the *Variations* he himself wrote that the 'band played magnificently, and they had the biggest audience of the season'. Where he was the director of a society, the programmes of that society very soon reflected his musical tastes. This tended to mean large helpings of Dvorak. The Central Croydon Society were given the *Stabat Mater* to learn. 'This work', he wrote to the Society's Secretary, 'impresses me more than any other religious work I know'.[208] As for the Handel Society (after due tribute to the composer after whom they were named: the performance of *Acis and Galatea* in February 1909), they were given Dvorak's *Te Deum*. These directorships were taken very seriously; he busied himself with the trivia of their routine to an extent which must have encroached on composition time: letters solicitous of the health of backsliders, letters dealing with choir seating, letters seeking subscriptions, and dozens of other details. Nothing seemed too small for his attention.

In May 1909, after years of wasting illness, August Jaeger died. On 24 January 1910, a memorial concert for the benefit of his widow and children was held in The Queen's Hall. Coleridge–Taylor was probably

never aware how in recent years Jaeger had turned against him; with the
London Symphony Orchestra in attendance, he took part in the tribute.
Elgar contributed his new songs to words by Sir Gilbert Parker, Richter
conducted the *'Enigma' Variations*, and Coleridge–Taylor gave his
Ballade in A minor.

He now turned his mind to the forthcoming first performance of
Endymion's Dream. As it stands, the work is a cantata for soprano and
tenor soloists, chorus and orchestra.   It was commissioned by the
Brighton Festival, well pleased as they were with the success of the
'Bon–Bon' Suite.   But Coleridge–Taylor had hopes that it might be
staged by Beerbohm Tree as a one–act opera, a hope shared by his
librettist, C. R. B. Barrett, who took the precaution of reserving to
himself the stage rights of his book. The work had been completed by
the autumn of 1909. Novello's published it, but were loth to part with
any higher sum in advance royalties than they had for the *'Bon–Bon'
Suite*. The first performance was given on 3 February 1910 in Brighton,
but there were few performances therafter.

The story concerns the love of the Moon–goddess Selene for the
somnolent Endymion — a love forbidden by Jove, whose anger at their
refusal to obey him causes worlds to fall.   For this mini–*Gotter-
damerung*, Coleridge–Taylor's resources are slight. The opening chorus,
'Hail, Crescent–Queen', finds him limping along in vacuous six–eight
time. With Endymion's aria, 'Who Calls?', the interest quickens:

Tranquillo

Tenor

When in soft arms   of sleep_ em-braced,   'Twas

Orch.

mp

Ex. 101: Endymion's Dream, 'When in soft arms'

Avril considered this aria to be almost as good as 'Onaway, Awake, Beloved'; the composer himself thought it better. Certainly there is much melody and it is all finely written for the voice, but there is little of the freshness of the earlier aria. Selene's aria provides a counter–balance, and the relationship is enhanced by thematic links which make these two arias the best things in the score. But the cantata as a whole fails because of the uninspired chorus work; in particular, such a portentous utterance as 'See the universe totters to its fall', calls for something more imaginative than the stock phrases offered by Coleridge–Taylor.

The fact that he thought there were stage possibilities in *Endymion's Dream* may cast doubt on his aspirations as a man of the theatre. While the proportions and balance of the work suggest that both poet and musician had Greek drama in mind (in the first version, the chorus — female only, and having the functions of both comment and narrative, was to be hidden), it is unlikely that even the most imaginative producer could do much with it.

Immediately after the performance, Coleridge–Taylor travelled north to Lancashire for two days of adjudicating in Warrington.[209] Shortly before, he thought he had reason to hope that his European ambitions might be advanced by the eminent Russian conductor Safonoff. In London to conduct Elgar's (first) *Symphony*, Safonoff had been present at Jaeger's memorial concert and had been impressed by the *Ballade*.

The composer spied a chance and wrote to him to try to interest him in the *Variations on an African Air*. Safonoff was cordial enough but could only offer him half–an–hour at the Langham Hotel: 'Please call on me with your score ... promptly'.[210] A minor incident, but one which shows Coleridge–Taylor still pushing hard towards the continent. Perhaps it also shows the growing power of the international conductor, now hierarchically a step above the cap–in–hand composer. But, now that he was a conductor himself, he was also discussed among, and ranked with, the great names:

> Mr Coleridge–Taylor himself comes to the Town Hall to conduct the Birmingham Symphony Orchestra and to praise it, after the manner of Richter and Safonoff and Sir Charles Stanford and other distin–guished conductors.[211]

This Birmingham concert (on 26 February 1910) was the culmination of a week of performances of Coleridge–Taylor's music, during which the *Hiawatha* trilogy was given twice in the district: once by the Midland Music Society and once by the Festival Choral Society. Coleridge–Taylor's own concert included works by other composers: predictably those by the European nationalists. It seems that in Smetana's overture to *The Bartered Bride*, three of Dvorak's *Slavonic Dances* and Sibelius's *Finlandia*

> the Birmingham Orchestra fully merited the high opinion of their talent expressed to us by Mr Coleridge–Taylor, who is familiar with all the best orchestras, and whose emphasis as to the capability of the forces he had just conducted was unmistakeable. All the improve–ment he could suggest related to numbers, not quality.[212]

'Numbers' meant strings; lamentations over tight–fistedness when it came to providing an adequate string–band were to be echoed by suc–ceeding generations of composers.

Before he finished his account of this concert, one further comment by the *Gazette and Express* reviewer illuminated a widening gap in perception of Coleridge–Taylor's music between the 'cognoscenti' (represented, for example, by Jaeger) and the general public:

> Though it must be admitted that the musical prigs are against him, he may take comfort from the assurance that the people are on his side, as they always were and are, with Grieg, another composer reviled by the 'superior'.[213]

Against a period of such sustained conducting and rehearsing, and in the little time left from work on *Endymion's Dream*, the creation of music was, for much of 1909 and the first months of 1910, limited to piano pieces and songs which could be sold outright for immediate cash.

Although slightly earlier (it was published in 1908), *Papillon*, for piano, is a good example of these short pieces. *Forest Scenes* is another; its very title gives some indication that the composer's mind was directed towards Schumann. This unpretentious piece is a simple study in *presto* broken chords, with a waltz for contrast at its centre. The *Forest Scenes* consist of five movements, each of which has a title:

1 The Lone Forest Maiden.
2 The Phantom Lover Arrives.
3 The Phantom tells his tale of longing.
4 Erstwhile they ride. The Forest Maiden acknowledges her love.
5 Now proudly they journey together towards the great city.

Schumann's *Forest Scenes*, too, are named; but in the Coleridge–Taylor work, there is a skeletal suggestion of narrative. The work appeared in 1907. The year before, he had produced the set of four *Scènes de Ballet*; possibly some kind of ballet scenario was also envisaged for the *Forest Scenes*. Neither work is idiomatically written for the piano, and both seem to cry out for orchestral colour. Quite often when writing for the piano, he seems not to take into account the piano's overtones, with the result that the harmony sometimes sounds thick:

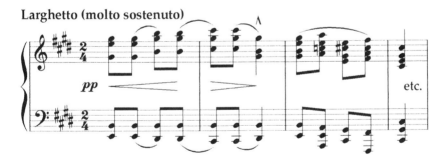

Ex. 102: Forest Scenes, no. 3

In these suites, drastic thinning out of the piano textures might be beneficial, but the ethics of such treatment are questionable. Neither work should be dismissed, however, and the *Forest Scenes* are certainly worth attention; the movement quoted above has a quiet intensity and, in several passages, the composer shows a striking freedom in his phrase structures:

Allegro maestoso

Ex. 103: Forest Scenes, no. 5

The suite of six waltzes for solo piano, *Three Fours*, appeared in 1909. It is dedicated to Myrtle Meggie, an Australian pianist with whom the composer worked occasionally at this period. In common with much of his other music, the publisher (Augener) also issued it in other versions; in this case for piano duet, violin and piano and piano trio. Some years after the composer's death, an orchestration of it by Norman O'Neill appeared. The suite continues the exploration of unusual phrase–structures, and in this respect, these waltzes are a considerable advance on the earlier *Four Characteristic Waltzes*. In the first waltz, for example, the composer divides sixteen bars thus:

Allegro molto

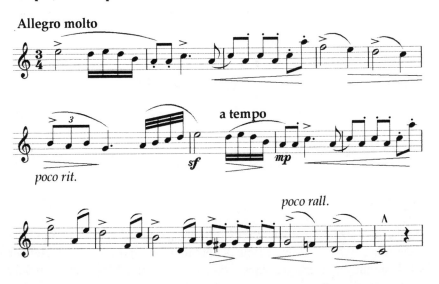

Ex. 104: Three Fours, no. 1

while in the second, the principal idea is of an irregular nine bars:

Ex. 105: Three Fours, no. 2

The predominant waltz rhythms of the Schumann piano suites are again a prime influence, but sometimes a phrase seems oddly reminiscent of very early music by Delius which he could not possibly have heard:

Ex. 106: Three Fours

The common ancestor of these pieces was Grieg, with whose work he was very familiar. Their light touch, whimsicality and even wistfulness would be tapped again in the *Petite Suite de Concert* and beyond that would influence a whole generation of light orchestral suites from later composers, including Eric Coates, Frederick Curzon and Armstrong Gibbs.

Throughout his life, Coleridge–Taylor produced liberal quantities of songs. Few, if any, aspire higher than the pleasantries of the drawing–room; the dramatic intensity of Schubert or the psychological penetration of Schumann were not within his range. This is not intended as a criticism; along with many others, he was simply meeting a market demand. But it must be admitted that few of his songs achieved the success of the early Coates songs or even of, say, Landon Ronald's 'Down in the Forest'.

Among Coleridge–Taylor's favoured poets at this time was his friend, Kathleen Easmon:

> a coloured girl from Africa who studied in London. She was slightly coloured. She wrote the Fairy Ballads and he set them to music.[214]

The five *Fairy Ballads* are children's songs — trouble–free, sunny, and without ambiguous, adult, sub–texts. They are, therefore, the reflection of an open, uncomplicated nature with (apparently) no psychological hang–ups. The last point is confirmed by a letter he wrote to one of his amateurs:

> [I] want both you and Mrs Carr to believe me when I tell you that my 'outlook' in life is just as wholesome and beautiful as it was when I first knew you years ago.[215]

With the possible exception of Haydn, wholesome and beautiful natures have not necessarily produced great art. It is the reaction of the distorted soul to nature, to circumstance or to words which so often is the catalyst for the creation of something memorable. Had Elgar set these *Fairy Ballads*, they would have reflected all the regrets of a melancholy, self–absorbed being seeking to recover his own childhood, and to that degree they would have engaged the adult listener in an identity of nostalgic interest. But Coleridge–Taylor takes Kathleen Easmon's poetry at face value: a child's view of butterflies, the moon and a rose. Even the poet's pseudo–negroid patois in 'The Stars' has no power to embarrass the composer.

And so we, too, must take these songs at their face value, whereupon they reveal themselves as miniatures of great charm, such as might even today be sung as festival items by a child of appropriate age. As the composer is writing for children, his accompaniments are light in style, and correspondingly much more pianistic than is usual with him. The five as a whole make an effective group, although one of them, 'Big Lady Moon', achieved an independent popularity.

The *Fairy Ballads*, together with other recently–written songs, were first heard at a benefit concert for the composer held on 6 April in the Croydon Public Hall. Various friends helped in this — Effie Martyn, Julien Henry, Myrtle Meggie and his old college friend William Read — and Coleridge–Taylor himself played the piano. According to his letter to Read dated April 1st, the programme included the *Ballade in C minor* and *Three Dances for Violin and Piano* in manuscript; it is probable that these latter were three movements of the *Three Fours* suite in their violin and piano arrangement.

In October of the previous year (1909), Carl Stoeckel had been in London. Coleridge–Taylor called on him at Claridge's Hotel and Stoeckel gave him presents for the children: an Indian suit for Hiawatha and a jewelled pin for Gwendolen (Avril). The outcome of this meeting was an agreement for the composer to visit the U.S.A. in the spring of 1910. It was to be the twentieth anniversary of the foundation of the Litchfield Choral Union, and for it Stoeckel had ballotted the members to find the most popular work performed in those two decades, promising to repeat the chosen work with its composer to conduct it. Two works came out on top: Verdi's *Requiem* and Coleridge–Taylor's *Hiawatha*. Verdi was dead but Coleridge–Taylor was thriving and available. He was engaged to conduct the *Wedding Feast* and *The Death of Minne-haha*, together with an as yet unwritten orchestral work.

For this new orchestral work, he went back to the *Twenty–Four Negro Melodies* and from them extracted *The Bamboula*. Work on it was in hand in the early spring of 1910:

> I am dreadfully busy with a new orchestral work for the Connecticut Musical Festival ...[216]

A 'bamboula' is an African form of tambourine, taken by slaves to the West Indies, and to the Southern States of the U.S.A.; in particular, to Louisiana and the city of New Orleans, where it gave its name to a dance. In the early years of the nineteenth century the dance could be seen in the Congo Square district of the city; in the late nineteenth century, an eye–witness[217] wrote of the

> booming of African drums and blast of huge wooden horns, the use of triangles, jews' harps, rattles, banjo and the slap of bare feet on earth.

The tune is Creole in origin, with the words 'Quand potate la cuite na va mangé li'.[218] There was at least one earlier setting: one for piano by Louis Moreau Gottschalk (1829–1869). The tune is short, and Gott–schalk does little more than repeat it with elaborations. Coleridge–Taylor overcomes the problem of its brevity by using thematic extensions:

Ex. 107: Bamboula, basic dance idea

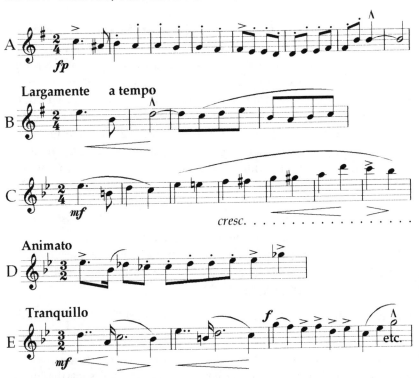

Ex. 108: Bamboula, variants

The result is typical of Coleridge–Taylor: a mixture of variation and ternary forms. (In the ideas shown in Example 108, E constitutes the centre of the ternary form; the basic tune and its other variants form the outer sections.)

The piano version in *Twenty–Four Negro Melodies*, it should be pointed out, has little beyond its snippet of tune in common with this orchestral rhapsody, and any departures from the snippet are quite different in each version.   But one counter–subject features in both versions.

The *Bamboula* is brilliant, colourful and gay, depending to a great extent for its effect on its orchestration, which derives more from Tschaikowsky than from the dominant school of Wagner, Strauss and Elgar. It celebrates a mature and confident composer who is now sure of his way forward.

18 CARL STOECKEL AND THE THIRD VISIT TO THE U.S.A.

On 7 May 1910, Coleridge–Taylor embarked on the Leyland liner 'Cestrian', bound for Boston, to begin his third and last trip to the United States. There he boarded the steamer 'Harvard' which arrived in New York on 26 May. Although as usual he joined in the on–board fun, *Bamboula* was still unfinished. Certainly most of the orchestration and perhaps some of the composition were done at sea. Avril had no doubt that the sheer joyousness and energy of the work owes much to his enforced but trouble–free holiday from the distractions of teaching, adjudicating and conducting.

No expense was spared for the Litchfield Festival. Stoeckel engaged an orchestra which consisted mostly of members of the New York Philharmonic Orchestra, having previously taken the precaution of asking if anyone objected to performing under a coloured conductor. He did the same with the singers; out of all the forces taking part, only one person dropped out for this reason. The New York Philharmonic was currently directed by Gustav Mahler, although his troubles with the wealthy committee of formidable matrons who controlled the orchestra's finances would shortly bring his rule to an end.

Coleridge–Taylor met the orchestra for a first rehearsal of *Bamboula*, and the other music he was to conduct, in the Carnegie Hall on 27 May. The musicians were impressed, dubbing him 'the African Mahler'. For his part, the composer–conductor was overwhelmed by their prowess. Meeting Stoeckel in the hall, he said:

This is a wonderful orchestra. I never directed anything like it.[219]

At Litchfield, there was to be a week of rehearsals: there were two rehearsals with the choir, one with orchestra only, and two full rehearsals with all the forces. In all, Stoeckel records that a total of 450 performers took part.

The Music Shed has already been mentioned. It held an audience of 1650 persons, all invited guests of the Stoeckels, and its fine acoustics derived from the unvarnished Californian Redwood from which it was built. At the first concert, Richard Paine (the conductor of the Litchfield Choral Union) directed a performance of the other work which had been voted for: Verdi's *Requiem*. Coleridge–Taylor attended as a member of

217

the audience. Paine's programme also included Tschaikowsky's *Second Piano Concerto* and Liszt's *Les Preludes*. On the following night, Coleridge–Taylor conducted the first two parts of the *Hiawatha* trilogy. Some idea of the status he held can be gathered from the reverential programme note:

> The composer has accepted an invitation to be present, and is coming from England to conduct his masterpiece.

After the performance, he told Stoeckel that he did not think that there had ever been a better one:

> I know that I have never directed it so well before, because I felt that everybody, the chorus, the orchestra and audience were with me. This is one of the happiest days of my life.[220]

The programme had continued that evening with Tschaikowsky's *'Nutcracker' Suite* and Lalo's *Symphonie Espagnole* (with Fritz Kreisler), and it had concluded with Coleridge–Taylor returning to the rostrum to give the first performance of *Bamboula*. At a supper party afterwards, he summoned the courage to rise and volunteer a few words of heartfelt thanks to the assembled guests. It had been the time of his life. The triumph when the audience rose to him was perhaps the greater because, unlike the earlier Washington visits, he was the solitary coloured man in an entirely white musical event. He was used to this situation in England; but this was the north–eastern seaboard of the U.S.A.

Before leaving Litchfield, he was taken for a car ride through the surrounding countryside, then in the first floral blossoming of early summer. Nothing was ever wasted with him. Inspired by these idyllic scenes, he made some musical sketches, which were to find a place a few months later in a new choral work, *A Tale of Old Japan*. Well content with his reception, and with Stoeckel's substantial fee in his pocket, he returned to England to take Jessie for a short holiday in Eastbourne, whence he wrote to his choir secretary, still relishing

> the greatest delight of my life — the orchestra was simply superb — 18 first fiddles, 16 seconds, 12 violas, 12 cellos and 8 basses — the pick of America.[221]

Soon he was deep in work on *A Tale of Old Japan*, which was to occupy him during most of the summer of 1910. This second work for Stoeckel was a setting of words by Alfred Noyes. But the work was interrupted by a commission from Beerbohm Tree; by chance, it was for another work by Noyes, a drama entitled *The Forest of Wild Thyme*. For it,

Coleridge–Taylor produced an enormous quantity of music, none of which was to serve its intended purpose since, after much rehearsal, the production never materialised; time wasted from his point of view.

The commissioning and abandoning of *The Forest of Wild Thyme* was a lamentable exercise which benefitted neither poet nor composer. It was in 1909 that Beerbohm Tree had asked Noyes to adapt his poetic fantasy into a prose drama set in enchanted forest through which children, magically shrunk to the size of ladybirds, wandered and encountered terrifying hazards. Beerbohm Tree, who had recently played Caliban, would take the role of the hideous hermit — half human, half spider — who lured the children into his web. Over a period of three years, Tree procrastinated; he returned from time to time to work on it in a desultory fashion, while falsely encouraging first Noyes and then Coleridge–Taylor to hope that it might actually be staged.

In addition to these major assignments, Coleridge–Taylor was also setting down his first thoughts on a new orchestral work: the *Petite Suite de Concert*. Towards the end of the year came yet another commission from Tree, this time for his new production of *Othello*; a letter to Hilyer in Washington reveals that Stoeckel, too, wanted a further work:

> Mr and Mrs Stoeckel, for whom I came to Norfolk last June, have commissioned me to write a work for Madame Maud Powell to play there for the first time.[222]

Maud Powell, the distinguished American violinist virtuoso, had been present as a guest at Litchfield, but she and Coleridge–Taylor had already met some years before in London. She was familiar with his style, having in her repertoire the *Gypsy Suite*, op. 20. She had also arranged for violin and piano his *Deep River*, and had recorded it. The work commissioned by the Stoeckels was to be a *Violin Concerto*.

Despite this mass of work, he found time to respond to an appeal for help from his old friend William Read, on behalf of the Duke of Devon–shire's orchestra, which performed regularly in Eastbourne and was under threat of disbandment. In October 1910, he joined Edward German in conducting a concert intended to benefit the orchestra and to show the esteem in which it was held by distinguished musicians. Despite this, the Devonshire Park Orchestra eventually became a musical football kicked between the Eastbourne Town Council and the Devonshire Park Company; it struggled on but was finally dispersed in 1922.

Coleridge–Taylor's family had been unsettled by the burglary the previous year. They looked to move and, in the summer of 1910, they found a house in St Leonard's Road, Croydon. This house, named

'Aldwick', was to be the composer's home for the remaining years of his life. One advantage was its quiet situation; another was the substantial shed adjoining the house, in which the composer soon installed an old upright piano and a plain table. Outside grew roses — the 'Dorothy Perkins' and (naturally) 'Hiawatha' varieties. Here, in his music shed, he could escape the attentions of naughty children and work in peace.

In 1910, the Guildhall School of Music appointed a new Principal. The choice of Landon Ronald was seen as something of an affront to musical academics, for Ronald was a practical man rather than a scholar. He was ambitious for his School:

> I want to make it equal to any establishment for musical education, English or Foreign, that can be named. For this purpose, I shall surround myself with the finest staff of professors it is possible to obtain.[223]

He much admired Coleridge–Taylor's work and, as we have seen, earlier in the year he had salvaged the Prelude from the wreck of the opera *Thelma* and had performed it with his New Symphony Orchestra. Perhaps, too, he felt an affinity with the composer as a fellow outsider. Coleridge–Taylor was coloured in a white world; Ronald was a Jew in an anti–semitic one.

One of his first acts as Principal was to recruit Coleridge–Taylor, who then wrote to A. F. Hilyer:

> I have just been appointed professor of composition and sub–conductor of the orchestra. Mr Landon Ronald ... takes the orchestra, being Principal of the whole concern, but he'll be often away, and I feel greatly honoured by being deputy as he is perhaps our finest English conductor.[224]

Thus pressure of work in London continued to be unrelenting, exacer–bated as it was by the occasional foray into the provinces. In December, for example, he was in Birmingham to conduct the Birmingham Symphony Orchestra in a popular concert whose programme included Landon Ronald's *Birthday Overture*, Chabrier's rhapsody *Espana*, and Grieg's first *'Peer Gynt' Suite*. Of his own work, he performed *Bamboula*, the *'Nero'* Suite ('repeated by general request'), and two recently–written songs in which he accompanied James Coleman at the piano.

The New Year of 1911 dawned, with trips to Woking to conduct *Kubla Khan*, to Bristol for the Ladies' Night of the Bristol Madrigal Society, where he conducted part–songs,[225] and back to London for the

Handel Society's performance of the *'Bon–Bon' Suite*. It was Coronation Year, and in May his work was represented in royal concerts at the Drury Lane Theatre and the Royal Albert Hall. In June, he conducted at Brighton, and at the Crystal Palace when he took part in the Festival of the Empire. There were just too many commitments to juggle with, and he was forced during this year to relinquish a labour of love: his work with the Croydon String Players' Club. It was taken on by his and Elgar's friend, W. H. Reed.

By April, the music for *The Forest of Wild Thyme*, the *Petite Suite de Concert* and *A Tale of Old Japan* were somehow finished. The first night of Tree's production of *Othello* took place on 11 April; then the Bournemouth Municipal Orchestra, under the composer's direction, performed the *Petite Suite*, together with *Bamboula*, on the 20th of that same month in what was certainly one of the earliest performances of the *Suite*, and may even have been the first.

The remarkable thing is that much of this outpouring was to rank among his finest work. But the music for the aborted production of *The Forest of Wild Thyme* is variable in quality. As published, it stands as follows (op. 74):

1 Scenes from an Imaginary Ballet (five pieces), Schirmer 1911
2 Three Dream Dances, Ascherberg 1911
3 Intermezzo, Ascherberg 1911
4 Songs and Part–Songs:
    a. 'Your Heart's Desire', Boosey 1920
    b. 'Little Boy Blue' (unison female voices), Boosey 1923
    c. 'Come In', Boosey 1920
    d. 'Dreams, Dreams' (unison children's voices), Boosey 1923
5 Christmas Overture, Boosey 1925

The first three items were published by Coleridge–Taylor (the last two appeared posthumously), from which it might be deduced that the composer himself did not consider the songs and the overture to be sufficiently worthy. Certainly, the Christmas Overture may strike the listener as one of his most banal works; yet in performance, even this has the potency of trite popular music. But the Scenes from an Imaginary Ballet, the Three Dream Dances and Intermezzo are light music of high quality. The influence of Schumann on at least the fifth number of the Scenes, with its strong syncopation, is very evident; moreover, some of the moods in the suite might have been recognised by his contemporary Elgar as characteristic of his own preserve:

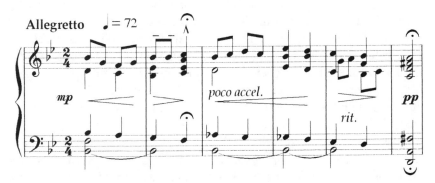

Ex. 109: Scenes from an Imaginary Ballet, no.2

And if, as he had mentioned to Jaeger years before, Elgar had found difficulty in 'sequentiating' parts of Coleridge–Taylor's *Solemn Prelude*, he would have had no such problems with *Wild Thyme*; many of its ideas are sequential.

The *Three Dream Dances* achieved a great and well–deserved popularity in the repertoire of spa and resort ensembles. At this period of his life, the spring of memorable ideas seemed inexhaustible:

Ex. 110: Three Dream Dances, no. 3

But his work stands or falls by its melody, and the second dance ('Intermezzo') is less striking to the extent that its melody is not so memorable; its turns of phrase are a little too obvious.

While much of *The Forest of Wild Thyme* is good light music, the *Petite Suite de Concert* shows Coleridge–Taylor at his very considerable best. The work is a masterpiece of light music which will make its effect with almost any combination of instruments. It is to be heard to best effect in the composer's splendid orchestral version, but he himself played the piano in a performance for violin and piano[226] and there is, at the time of writing, a very acceptable version on compact disc for piano solo.[227] The first movement, La Caprice de Nannette, explores further some of the ways of Schumann; here are the syncopations and here, too, are Schumann's structural concepts. It is quite usual in Coleridge–Taylor's music for there to be little or no development; it proceeds in a procession of melodies. But even he has rarely produced such a succession of tunes as are found in this movement. There are five of them, tumbling over one another, very much as they do in the early Schumann piano suites — especially in *Carnaval*, which Coleridge–Taylor had learned to play as a student:

Ex. 111a: Petite Suite de Concert, first movement (1)

Ex. 111b: Schumann, *Symphony in E♭*

Ex. 111c: Petite Suite de Concert, first movement (2)

Other, and specific, responses are suggested: in Example 111 to Schumann's 'Rhenish' *Symphony* and, in Example 112, to Edward German's *Welsh Rhapsody*. With regard to the Edward German, it is likely that in the course of his work as an adjudicator he would have heard many versions of this beautiful tune on his trips to Wales:

Ex. 112a: Petite Suite de Concert, first movement (3)

Ex. 112b: German, *Welsh Rhapsody (1904)*

Ex. 112c: *Petite Suite de Concert, first movement (4)*

Ex. 112c: *Petite Suite de Concert, first movement (5)*

The second movement, a slow waltz entitled 'Demande et Réponse', achieved huge popularity in innumerable drawing rooms throughout the world:

Ex. 113: *Petite Suite de Concert, second movement*

This melody was resurrected from an early unpublished work for piano trio and reciter called *The Clown and Columbine*, based on Hans Christian Andersen's story 'What the Moon Saw'. In Coleridge–Taylor's version, the melody in Example 113 accompanies the first mention of the lovely Columbine who, while kind to the disfigured clown Punchinello, prefers the attractive Harlequin. The second idea:

Ex. 114: *Petite Suite de Concert, second movement (second idea)*

also appeared in the earlier work as funeral music for the deceased Columbine:

Molto moderato

(Vn. & cello in 8ves).

Ex. 115: The Clown and Columbine, funeral music

From the handwriting and the appearance of the manuscript, it is likely that *The Clown and Columbine* was written within a short while of Coleridge–Taylor's discovery of Schumann's *Carnaval*; the links are tenuous, but the Schumann work also features Harlequin and Columbine figures and, while Schumann has no 'Question', he does have a 'Réplique'. The *Petite Suite* has musically Schumannesque features, where the earlier work does not, and in it faint echoes of Harlequinade are still audible.

The third movement, 'Un Sonnet D'Amour', is a delicate miniature and, like the first movement, is balletic in style:

Ex. 116: Petite Suite de Concert, third movement

In the final movement, 'La Tarantelle Fretillante', there is once more almost a surfeit of material, much of it sequential in style:

Ex. 117: Petite Suite de Concert, final movement

Even here, Coleridge–Taylor had not finished with *The Clown and Columbine* idea; in Example 117 above, (ii) was also salvaged from the earlier work, where it had been used for Punchinello's dancing.

It is in this work that his characteristic orchestration can best be heard. There is hardly a redundant note; its clarity illuminates a comment he made on the music of some of the Russians; 'all orchestration'. Yet there are many touches of colour, such as the use of the glockenspiel in the last movement.

Taking *Bamboula, Wild Thyme* and the *Petite Suite de Concert* together, one thing is striking: that the composer has found his path again. The light touch of *The Wedding Feast* has returned.

The point is confirmed by the quality of the two sets of *Impromptus* published in 1911: two for piano in A major and B minor, and three for organ in F major, C major and A minor. Those for piano, in particular, display the range of fanciful invention one might expect from the title 'impromptu' but which had been sadly missing in some of his miniatures in the few years up to that time.

Also published in 1911 was the set of five *Songs of Sun and Shade*, to poems by Marguerite Radclyffe–Hall; these songs, too, are of high quality. Two in particular, 'The Rainbow Child' and 'Thou art Risen, my Beloved', are striking for the simplicity of their melodies; their very simplicity imparts to them an element of nobility not often heard in his work:

Ex. 118: Songs of Sun and Shade, 'Thou art Risen'

The music for Beerbohm Tree's production of *Othello* consisted of at least seven pieces: a Prelude, Entracte, a Dance in the second act, a Prelude to act three, the Willow Song, an Introduction to the fourth act and a Part–song. *The Musical Times* observed that there was more than enough material to fashion a suite 'which should last long after Sir Herbert's production has become historical'.[228] With some pieces re–named, the published suite consists of: Dance, Children's Intermezzo, Funeral March, Willow Song and Military March.

Metzler, the publisher, thought sufficiently highly of it to engrave the full score — a signal honour for this type of work — and for a decade

or two it did indeed fulfil the prophecy of *The Musical Times*. The
opening dance is savage; he had long been saddled with this attribute but
here, at least, it has substance. The music makes much of the following
energetic motif:

Ex. 119: Othello, opening dance

In the key (D minor) this is a decoration of the dominant note of the
scale, a favourite trait of Coleridge–Taylor's melodies, which often centre
on the dominant.

The Children's Intermezzo has survived not only in its orchestral
version but also as an attractive part–song. As Percy Young has pointed
out, it has an element of faded grace and wistfulness worthy of Elgar.
But its attractive melody gives no hint of the trouble it caused the
composer. A number of attempts at this behind–the–scenes chorus for
Act III were made, none of which satisfied either Tree or Coleridge–
Taylor. The final inspiration, which was used, came to the composer on
the train as he travelled to Bath for a conducting engagement.

Ex. 120a: Othello, Children's Intermezzo

The fine Funeral March and Willow Song (the latter providing in its
vocal version an opportunity for the singing of the actress Phyllis
Neilson–Terry) are succeeded by the concluding Military March which,
in its orchestration, has much of Elgar's boldness and, in the cast of its
ideas, even more of the same composer's 'Pomp and Circumstance'
manner:

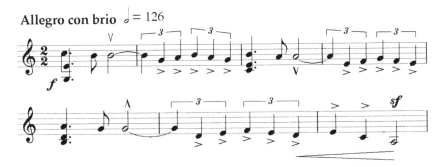

Allegro con brio ♩= 126

Ex. 120b: Othello, Military March

(The melody is a variant of that of the Children's Intermezzo, Example 120a; towards the end of the march, the relationship of the two is made even clearer, with an explicit appearance of Example 120a.)

The second of the works dedicated to Mr and Mrs Stoeckel, the cantata *A Tale of Old Japan*, was said by both Jessie and Avril to have been preferred by the composer to *The Song of Hiawatha*. The imagery of flowers is a fundamental aspect of Alfred Noyes's poem 'The Two Painters', and while Coleridge–Taylor had stored up the idea of setting it ever since his friend J. H. Smither Jackson had shown it to him, there is no doubt that his experience of Connecticut in bloom had been the catalyst to fire his imagination.[229] For there was apparently — unusually — no immediate commission for the work. This was something he wanted to write, despite being already committed with demands for other already bespoke music.

He worked on it intermittently throughout the summer of 1910; the short score was probably complete by the time the family moved to 'Aldwick', for Jessie says[230] that he orchestrated it there in his music shed and that he was indeed working on the orchestration even on the moving day. The work would have been completed by April 1911.

In much of his music, Coleridge–Taylor continually sought the exotic. Not for him a response to his actual environment, such as inspired his contemporary Vaughan Williams and, to an extent, his elders Elgar and Delius. But then, his environment was not idyllic Gloucester-shire, Worcestershire or Grez, but suburban Croydon. Given this, what else would he do but create his own microcosm? There was, perhaps, another factor in his choice of a Japanese subject; after an uncertain start, Puccini's *Madame Butterfly* had travelled successfully around Europe, reaching Covent Garden in July 1905, with Destinn and Caruso.

The parallel was not lost on the critic of the *Morning Post*:

> Mr Coleridge–Taylor provides the Japanese story with a very charm–
> ing musical colouring. Like Puccini, he has his own conception as
> to how local colour is best represented, and carries it out in a way of
> his own.[231]

There are, moreover, coincidences of narrative between the two works.
A short orchestral introduction, scored lightly and delicately, is descrip–
tive of the heroine Kimi:

Ex. 121: A Tale of Old Japan, introduction

As an orphan, she has been brought up by the renowned artist Tenko,
who paints the Peacock Islands:

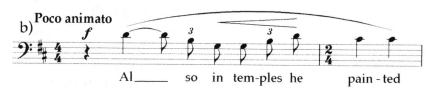

Ex. 122: A Tale of Old Japan, 'Also in temples'

The second stanza introduces the young student artist Sawara, who has
come to study with Tenko:

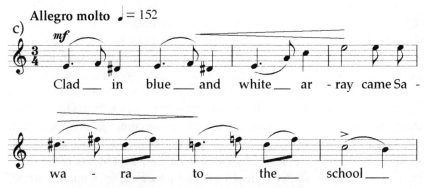

Ex. 123: A Tale of Old Japan, 'Clad in blue and white'

with whom Kimi soon falls in love. This section is set for the chorus, which is joined by the soprano soloist to describe, in the first of a number of ensemble 'purple patches', Tenko's wonder at, and admiration for, the growing mastery of his pupil:

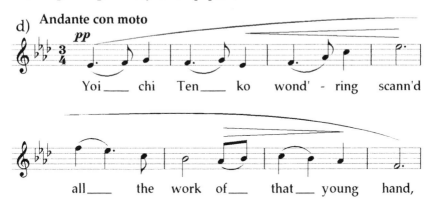

Ex. 124: A Tale of Old Japan, 'Yoichi Tenko wond'ring scann'd'

Tenko (baritone solo) tells Sawara that he can teach him no more; Sawara must go to seek his fortune. In despair on hearing this:

Ex. 125: A Tale of Old Japan, 'Lying on the golden sand'

The whole of this passage is harmonised in the most sumptuous style, with the three soloists adding their own counterpoint, to fashion a second 'purple patch'. In the third stanza, Kimi tries to persuade Sawara to take her with him:

Ex. 126: A Tale of Old Japan, 'You are my king'

This section demonstrates anew the composer's skill in variation; the ideas, however much they are disguised, derive from Examples 122 and 125 above. Beyond this, the section also shows how far he had pro–gressed from traditional cantata towards opera.

At this half–way point, the balance of Noyes's poem now helps the composer, for it rewinds, yo–yo fashion, enabling the music to re–capitulate and thus to make wry comment on itself. The second half begins with an orchestral Interlude, impassioned and turbulent, and musically based on Examples 121 and 122 above:

Ex. 127: A Tale of Old Japan, Interlude

Although this interlude is un–named, it could perhaps depict the one night of love of Kimi and Sarawa — but the poem suggests no justifi–cation for this. Certainly, this Interlude has considerable power, with quite spectacular brass writing, for which Elgar had again pointed the way.

The fourth section describes Kimi's long wait as the years roll by. Sometimes she prays in the temple; always she scans the sea for her

lover's return.   Coleridge–Taylor's fine unaccompanied choral writing
here derives once more from Example 121 above, and continues:

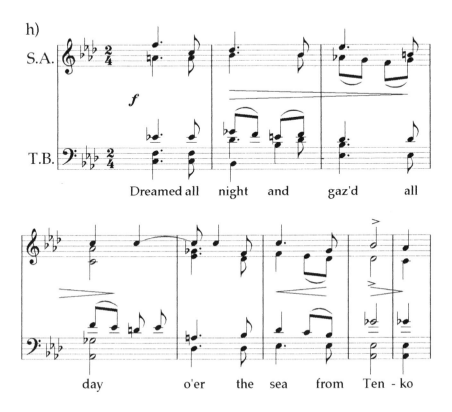

Ex. 128: A Tale of Old Japan, 'Dreamed all night'

But, instead of the long–awaited Sarawa, a rich young merchant appears
and offers gold to Tenko for the hand of Kimi. The merchant's theme
is loud and coarse in its trombone orchestration, all but crushing Kimi's
pathetic wisp of a tune:

Ex. 129: A Tale of Old Japan, merchant's theme

In order to persuade her, Tenko lies to her that Sawara has married. Distraught, she runs away 'where she had watch'd him of old painting the rose–red islands'.

But, in the sixth section, Sawara returns; his reappearance permits the composer further musical recapitulations to match the music of the young man's first appearance. Tenko tells him of Kimi's departure; Sawara has forgotten her, but the orchestra has not:

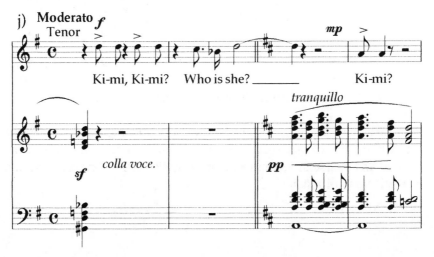

Ex. 130: A Tale of Old Japan, 'Kimi, kimi'

Sawara has come to paint again the scenes he had loved as a student. 'Under the silvery willow tree' he meets and weds another young maid to the music of Example 124 above. At this point, Coleridge–Taylor omits some lines of Noyes, where Tenko suggests that Sawara's new love is more attractive than Kimi, who:

> Had a twistful nose
> And a foot too small for me
> And her face was dull as lead.

In the final section, Sawara's search for a setting to paint 'worthy of Ho–Kusai' unwittingly leads him to the Peacock Islands, where Kimi has exiled herself. She sees him, and now he remembers her. He tells her he is wed, against the background of the music of Example 130, which now makes ironic comment on her hopes. She relinquishes him to the music of Example 126:

Ex. 131: A Tale of Old Japan, 'Be happy'

She begs a final kiss and, to solemn orchestral chords, dies in his embrace. The chords for this fatalistic ending recall those which open Rachmaninoff's equally fatalistic C minor *Piano Concerto*. The music rewinds further to a reprise of the material of the orchestral prelude with which it had begun.

Puccini's Cho–Sho–San suffered from the callousness and faithless-ness of Pinkerton; Kimi (and to an extent, Sawara) from the cunning and avarice of Tenko. While these parallels with Puccini's opera are obvious, there appears to be no musical correspondence. Nor in Coleridge–Taylor is there any attempt at Japanese local colour, such as Sullivan tried in *The Mikado*. As it happens, there may be some of the influence of Sullivan himself in, for example, the 'Peonies' chorus:

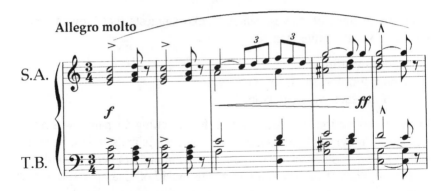

Ex. 132: A Tale of Old Japan, 'Peonies' chorus

But, as in *Bamboula*, the major influences appear to be Russian: the
fatalistic moods of Tschaikowsky or Rachmaninoff.

For his setting, Coleridge–Taylor omitted the end of Noyes's poem.
For the poet, the conclusion had enshrined its whole point. In it, the
great painter Sawara, with artistic objectivity or, perhaps, callous in–
difference, paints a picture of the girl who had loved him, lying before
him in death. This act wins the admiration of Tenko, his master:

> Ho–Kusai is not so great.
> This is art, said Tenko.

It may be that Coleridge–Taylor chooses deliberately to ignore the
cynical overtones of the poem, and for this reason the work may not
appeal in the unsentimental climate prevailing today. If so, this would
be our loss for, in *A Tale of Old Japan*, Coleridge–Taylor produced if
not his most popular choral work, certainly his most perfectly–fashioned
one. In structure, balance, word–setting, orchestration and varied choral
writing nothing in his output excels it.

Its first performance was given by the London Choral Society under
its director Arthur Fagge at The Queen's Hall on 6 December 1911. The
programme contained other new music, by Margaret Meredith and
Charles Speer, which posterity has forgotten altogether. Coleridge–
Taylor would have liked to conduct his work (he did in fact conduct the
second performance at Birmingham, by the Birmingham Choral Union)
but Fagge even requested that he keep away from the practices until they
were fairly advanced. When in the final stages he did appear, he seemed
happy enough with what Fagge and the choir were doing; afterwards,
though, he said the speeds were too fast. With the London Symphony
Orchestra in attendance, the soloists were Leah Felissa, Effie Martyn,

Maurice D'Oisby and Dalton Baker; he was pleased with Leah Felissa as Kimi, but regretted that Julien Henry, for whom he wrote the part of Tenko, had not been engaged.

The press was favourable: 'The new work made an instant appeal',[232] said the *Morning Post*, while *The Musical Times* critic wrote of its 'astounding fluency of invention, much grace and occasional poignancy'.[233]   Coleridge–Taylor thought his own performance at Birmingham had been 'wonderful' and 'the orchestra was really magnificent'.[234] The London Choral Society did the work again in the following year (on 18 April 1912) and two months later, in June, it was given in the U.S.A. at Carl Stoeckel's Connecticut Festival. He cabled the composer: 'Great Success — congratulations'.

Thence it travelled the world and *A Tale of Old Japan* became, for a short while, together with Sullivan's *Golden Legend* and Coleridge–Taylor's own *Song of Hiawatha*, one of the most popular choral works to have been written by an Englishman.

19 THE *VIOLIN CONCERTO*

At least three of the leading English composers of the early twentieth century — Elgar, Delius and Coleridge–Taylor — were violinists; each of the three wrote a violin concerto. Coleridge–Taylor's *Violin Concerto in G minor* was commissioned by Stoeckel during the 1910 visit, and it received its first performance at the same concert in Norfolk, Connect–icut, at which *A Tale of Old Japan* was first heard in the U.S.A. It was played by Maud Powell, to whom it was dedicated. This third work written for Mr and Mrs Stoeckel had a complex genesis.

Stoeckel had suggested that the composer might use some of the old negro songs and hymns from the Deep South as a basis for his work. Incongruously, since it is not a negro song, he also asked if 'Yankee Doodle' might be used. During his visit, Coleridge–Taylor had over–heard Mrs Stoeckel playing the negro hymn 'Keep me from sinking down, good Lord':

Ex. 133: 'Keep me from sinking down'

Impressed with its beauty, he thought he had found a subject for his slow movement. It was a tune Mrs Stoeckel had learned from her father, to whom it had been passed down by a slave. In the event, Coleridge–Taylor found it impracticable to use this tune. Instead, he wrote a slow movement based on another negro hymn, 'Many thousand gone'.

But he did write a finale which used 'Yankee Doodle'. The score was despatched to the U.S.A. but, after playing it over, the Stoeckels found themselves very much in the position of Jaeger with *Hiawatha's Departure* and, before him, of Stanford with the last movement of the

Symphony. The *Violin Concerto*, as Stanford might have said, plainly 'wouldn't do'.

Maud Powell had also received a copy, and perhaps Coleridge–Taylor detected in her letter of thanks something less than enthusiasm. They were all three spared the embarrassment of having to tell him their verdict, for he himself wrote and asked them to destroy it; he had written a new *Concerto* 'a hundred times better'. Stoeckel did not destroy it entirely, for 'it seemed a pity to lose the second movement', and he returned it to the composer. Both he and Maud Powell pressed for an arrangement of 'Keep me from sinking down, good Lord' to be made for violin and orchestra, 'as we have no room for a piano on the stage',[235] and this was sent by Coleridge–Taylor in time for it to be used as an encore in a performance of the rewritten *Concerto*, which was given in June 1912 at the Norfolk, Connecticut, Festival.

These bare facts can now be subject to a little conjecture. The first version would have been completed in short score by the early spring of 1911. What factors influenced him to withdraw it? All that he retained was the opening subject of the first movement; this was an original theme with no apparent Afro–American associations:

Ex. 134: first version of Violin Concerto, first subject

Apart from this subject, the original first movement seems not to have survived. But the original second movement is extant in manuscript in short score for violin and piano. So, too, is much of the original 'Yankee Doodle' finale,[236] and it has to be admitted that this finale is a movement of appalling banality. The problem with this movement, as other composers have found, and as Coleridge–Taylor conceded, is that ready–made tunes will not as a rule readily yield satisfactory large–scale structures. And the tune 'Yankee Doodle' proved to be particularly sterile, even though the composer relieved it with a reprise of Example 134 from the first movement.

But the original second movement, 'Many thousand gone', is a jewel of quiet, intense beauty, the tune itself having some affinity with that well–known today as 'We shall overcome':

Ex. 135: first version of Violin Concerto, second movement

This movement is certainly one of Coleridge–Taylor's finest for instru–ments, and it must have caused much heart–searching before he dropped it from the rewritten *Violin Concerto*. Is it possible that, with his eye as ever on Europe, he came to the conclusion that a work based on Afro–American themes might have restricted appeal? He was obviously sufficiently self–critical in this instance to realise the failings of the outer movements, and he may also have realised that they were just too light–weight. Another factor here might well have been the cordial reception accorded the first performance, on 10 November 1910, of Elgar's *Violin Concerto*. There is no direct evidence that Coleridge–Taylor heard this profound work, but a survey of prominent musicians carried out by the *Musical Herald* found that, for a very substantial majority, Elgar's concerto was their strongest musical impression of that year. Coleridge–Taylor would then have been working on the first version of his *Concerto*; at the very least, he would have been told by his violinist friends of the quality and beauty of the Elgar. He would have realised that his embryo work would be unlikely to stand comparison.

Well into his second version by the autumn of 1911, he was able to write to his friend Julien Henry, 30 November, that it was 'an absolutely different work'. A few weeks later he was asking his violinist friend William Read to have a look at it: it was 'ten thousand times better than the other — those native melodies rather tied me down'.[237] By March, he had sent the short score to Maud Powell and was busy with the orchestration.

Once she had overcome the problems of reading the manuscript ('almost impossible to read ... the writing is so fine'), Miss Powell liked the work, suggesting only a few minor adjustments to the solo part, with which Coleridge–Taylor agreed. He wrote again to her on 4 May giving precise metronome speeds and a suggestion for the number of violin desks to be used in the orchestra. (A page from this letter is reproduced as Plate 10.)

The full score and orchestral parts were then sent over — but they were sent on the 'Titanic'. A further set was hastily produced, which arrived only just in time for the first performance at Norfolk on the 4th of June.

The work of Maud Powell is not well known outside the U.S.A. She was a veritable Brünnhilde of a violinist, and was the first to introduce the Tschaikowsky, Sibelius and Max Bruch concertos to America. She toured indefatigably, even on one occasion defying doctors and peri–tonitis to play, with a nervous nurse in attendance. This is how she appeared to one prominent New York critic, Richard Aldrich:

> Maud Powell stands for the sincerest art, and what she does is all for music and not at all for the exploitation of self. She is today at the height of her powers and her recital yesterday afternoon once more attested her ... profound musical feeling and insight, her fine taste,

her high technical accomplishment and especially her vigorous and robust style.

While she played Coleridge–Taylor's concerto, a portrait of the absent composer looked down from the stage onto the assembled company. At its conclusion, she gracefully shared the warm applause with the portrait. The day after, back in England, William Read and the composer gave the necessary copyright performance in the Croydon Public Hall. It was, said Coleridge–Taylor, 'just sight–read'.

Henry Wood was planning a Promenade Concert performance with Arthur Catterall as soloist, and there was now a rush to get the parts back to London for the composer to make some revisions in time for Catterall's performance. The eminent violinist John Dunn enquired for it, and other performances were beginning to line up on the continent:

> I am to conduct my Violin Concerto for a Miss Whitman in Berlin and Dresden in November next, and Maud Powell has been requested to play it at the New York Philharmonic concerts, and at Chicago, also November. Metzlers, and not Novellos, are doing it, because the latter insisted on the performing fee business ...[238]

From this letter, it appears that the hoped–for continental début was nearer reality than it had ever been. His letter to Metzler, who had also brought out the *Othello* music, gives a little more detail to illuminate 'the performing fee business':

> I could, if you thought favourably of it, hand you the full score and a large set of parts in M.S., and a fee of £6 is to be paid to me for each of the American performances, part of which would, of course, go to you in the event of your doing it.
>
> But I do not wish any performing fee to be charged in England, as I am sure it will hurt rather than help.
>
> The work is not very long and not very difficult ...[239]

If he seemed to be selling his work too cheaply, it may be that he had heard of Elgar's troubles the year before with the violinist Eugène Ysaye, who had cancelled his projected English performances of Elgar's con–certo when he had been told that a hire charge would be made. The point is highlighted by an interview given by Maud Powell herself to the *New York Times*:[240]

> I had a bitter experience in regard to the Elgar concerto ... I offered him $600 for the first performing rights ... the letter was answered by his publishers, who demanded $1000 ... . I told Mr Stoeckel ...

> by no means to consider it ... . It is an empty, pompous work, the
> Elgar concerto in my opinion ...

The element of sour grapes here cannot disguise the growing tension
which very shortly would lead to an attempt at fair settlement of the
performing fees question, and in due course to the establishment in the
U.K. of the Performing Right Society.

As it stands, the final version of the Coleridge–Taylor *Violin
Concerto* is a three movement work in which, as in the earlier version,
the principal idea (Example 134) of the first movement is recalled in the
last. The Elgar concerto had featured a strikingly original cadenza,
accompanied by 'thrummed' strings; Coleridge–Taylor's first movement
also has an accompanied cadenza, the accompaniment being provided by
a timpani roll. This may or may not be a response to Elgar's idea, but
there are other Elgar responses, together with responses to Mendelssohn
and Dvorak. Certainly, the opening subject (Example 134) has the spirit
of the Bohemian master in it, enhanced as it is by the dark glow of its
orchestration. From it, Coleridge–Taylor proceeds to fashion a loose
sonata–form movement. Loose, because one rather striking idea, heard
after both orchestra and soloist have played the opening subject, appears
to have no structural purpose and is not heard again:

Ex. 136: Violin Concerto, first movement

In these matters, Coleridge–Taylor can be as wayward as his model. But
it does not seem to matter. The second idea is as capricious as the first
was solemn; a model for this is not hard to find, given his early and
enduring love of Schubert:

Ex. 137: Violin Concerto, first movement's second theme

Development of ideas had not featured in his music a great deal since the early chamber music and the symphony; variation had tended to take its place. But, in the *Concerto*, the first movement's development is one of the more striking passages, as the soloist plays an expressive 'cantilena' as a bass to a light orchestral synthesis of both first and second subjects:

Ex. 138: Violin Concerto, first movement 'cantilena'

The cadenza is, unusually, placed immediately after the recapitulation of the first subject; there it acts as a preamble to an Allegro Molto coda, into which is slipped only the most perfunctory reference to the second subject.

The new slow movement is lighter in weight than 'Many thousands gone'. Mendelssohn supplants Dvorak as the role model — although Mendelssohn would have been unlikely to have indulged in such chrom-aticism as the seventh bar of Example 139 (overleaf). The movement is quite as fine as its discarded predecessor. It is a serene little tone poem, the mood of which is hardly disturbed by the gentle easing into duple time for a contrasting idea (Example 140, p. 247).

The solo writing here is finely idiomatic. Nowhere, though, does the soloist play the principal idea (Example 139) in its entirety.

Ex. 139: Violin Concerto, slow movement

Ex. 140: Violin Concerto, slow movement (contrasting idea)

The finale rejects the trivialities of 'Yankee Doodle' in favour of a
nonchalant dance tune whose syncopations have some affinity with the
corresponding movement of the Dvorak *Violin Concerto*:[241]

Ex. 141: Violin Concerto, finale dance tune

The movement is fashioned as a rondo, although the treatment is loose.
The rondo episodes seem to darken the music to an extent that carries the
music worlds away from the finale originally written:

Ex. 142: Violin Concerto, rondo episode

While this idea in itself may not be Elgarian, it does seem possible that
it is a response to the seriousness of Elgar's concerto in its sombre
expressiveness. Just as it was in the 'Yankee Doodle' movement, the
central episode is a reprise of the introductory idea from the first
movement (Example 134) followed by the secondary one (Example 140)
from the slow movement. The rondo stereotype is not formally completed since, in place of the restatement of Example 141 which might
have been expected, a further recurrence is preferred of the first
movement's introductory idea. The re–use of ideas from earlier movements has more affinity with César Franck than with Tschaikowsky's
motto theme usage. In Coleridge–Taylor's hands, these reprises occur
quite naturally and seamlessly, following along in the flow of the music.

The American critics liked the lyricism of the new work, but some
saw contradictions in it; contradictions to what they had come to expect
in a work called a concerto:

> How limited was the ability of even so well and favourably known
> a composer as Coleridge–Taylor to develop themes in sonata form
> [242]
> ...

Shrewdly, they estimated its future:

> I believe it will have a decade of popularity, possibly more, should

it have the good fortune of being played by those rare artists who can make a work seem much greater than it is.[243]

It certainly had good fortune in Maud Powell, who continued to play it wherever she went, whether with orchestral or only piano accompaniment. She, too, was worried that it had to be called a concerto:

I wish somebody would suggest some name besides that of 'concerto' to be attached to a composition which is not too serious in its nature ... it is not quite a full-grown concerto, nor is it yet a suite.[244]

20 OVERWORK AND DEATH

While Coleridge–Taylor hardly paraded his pride in his father's race, it was always quietly evident in his dignified approach to every aspect of his life. But his measure of success would always be the extent to which he could succeed in the acknowledged preserves of the White Man. Just occasionally, however, he would encounter such unreasoning prejudice as would penetrate even his habitual equanimity. Something of the kind happened in February 1912; it was too near at hand to be ignored. A debating group in Purley (just south of Croydon), presided over by the local vicar and addressed by a barrister, discussed 'The Negro Problem in North America'. According to a report of the meeting in the *Croydon Guardian*, it was asserted that black men, in the Darwinian hierarchy, were a lower order of human, and therefore nearer to the primate ape; that their skulls were more ape–like; that they exuded a different smell to other humans, and that they had never managed to improve them–selves.

When his attention was drawn to this report, Coleridge–Taylor happened to be in Birmingham to conduct the Choral Union in the second performance of *A Tale of Old Japan*, and he wrote thence to the paper.[245] His letter is worth quoting in full because it displays the unique flavour of his caustic and biting wit, and it may to an extent correct any impression given so far that his humanity and restraint left no room for a cutting edge when it was necessary:

> I hear that the next subject for discussion at the 'Purley Circle' is to be 'God and his great mistake in creating Black Men', with Jack Johnson in the chair.[246]
>
> This meeting will be almost as interesting as the last meeting, at which, (as I gather from your report) a clergyman–Chairman actually thanked a lecturer for expressing not only un–Christian but unmanly sentiments about the race in question. Doubtless the 'Purley Circle' is working up for a lynching in the near future. I hope I shall be a mere spectator and not the victim! Shame on the lecturer and a thousand times on the clergyman! And yet there was a vast amount of humour in some of the things that were said at that meeting. The smell of the negro for instance. All uncivilised

people smell for a very obvious reason — they do not wash. But what about the smell of the lecturer's own ancestors who ran about half naked some centuries ago? Was it that of a June rose? I wonder!

It is amazing that grown–up, and presumably educated, people can listen to such primitive and ignorant nonsense–mongers, who are men without vision, utterly incapable of penetrating beneath the surface of things.

No one realises more than I that coloured people have not yet taken their place in the scheme of things, but to say that they never will is arrogant rubbish, and an insult to the God in Whom they profess to believe. Why, I personally know hundreds of men and women of negro blood who have already made their mark in the great world, and this is only the beginning. I might suggest that the 'Purley Circle' engage someone to lecture on one Alexandre Dumas, a rather well–known author, I fancy, who had more than a drop of negro blood in him. Who is there who has not read and loved his Dumas? And what about Poushkin, the poet? And Du Bois, whose 'Souls of Black Folk' was hailed by James Payn as the greatest book that had come out of the United States for fifty years? I mention these three because not only are they distinguished men, but men of colossal genius. And will the lecturer refer to a chapter in H. G. Wells's 'The Future of America', called 'The Tragedy of Colour'? — this, because Wells is undoubtedly possessed of the heaven–born gift of insight to a greater degree than any other living Englishman — not even excluding G. B. S.

The fact is that there is an appalling amount of ignorance amongst English people regarding the negro and his doings. If the Purley lecturer (I forget his name, and am away from home, the Birmingham people having engaged me to direct something that has come out of my ill–formed skull) — I say, if he is right, then let us at once and for ever stop the humbug of missions to darkest Africa, and let the clergy stop calling their congregation 'dear brethren', at any rate whenever a black man happens to be in the church. Let us change our prayer–books, our Bibles, and everything pertaining to Christianity, and be honest.

Personally, I consider myself the equal of any white man who ever lived, and no–one could ever change me in that respect; on the other hand, no man reverences worth more than I, irrespective of colour and creed. May I further remind the lecturer that really great people always see the best in others? It is the little man who looks for the worst — and finds it. It is a peculiar thing that almost without exception all distinguished white men have been favourably disposed towards their black brethren. No woman has ever been more courteous to me than a certain member of our own English Royal Family, and no man more so than President Roosevelt.

It was an arrogant 'little' white man who dared to say to the great Dumas: 'And I hear you actually have negro blood in you.'

'Yes', said the witty writer, 'my father was a mulatto, his father a negro, and his father a monkey. My ancestry began where yours ends.'

Somehow, I always manage to remember that wonderful answer when I meet a certain type of white man (a type, thank goodness, as far removed from the best as the poles from each other), and the remembrance makes me feel quite happy — wickedly happy, in fact!

In this letter, he seems to have retained the dignity required by Booker T. Washington, yet to have moved even more strongly towards the position of Du Bois. The letter was noticed by some of the London newspapers, who quoted from it. The vicar–chairman wrote to Coleridge–Taylor and disassociated himself from some of the offensive views expressed, but others wrote to the *Croydon Guardian* justifying lynching as the only protection of white man and women from the savagery of coloureds, suggesting that Coleridge–Taylor might have inherited his talents from his mother, amplifying the point about the smell of negroes, and questioning Dumas's African ancestry. They provoked a final salvo:[247]

Dumas was not a creole. The dark side of him was West–Indian and the dark West–Indians hailed from Africa. Therefore Dumas' own summing up of his nationality was correct.

Secondly, there is no reason for adopting an aggressive tone when discussing the coloured people of America. It must be remembered that they did not go to that country of their own accord; on the contrary, it was very much 'by desire' of their white brothers.

A careful study of condition between black and white in America during the past hundred years will throw a lurid and unexpected light on the subject. It is obvious, therefore, that had not the white Americans made the great mistake (shall we call it?) of forcing the blacks to pay them a long visit there would be today no colour question at all in America.

As for South Africa, after all, the blacks were born there, and Africa is their own country in many ways. White people who go there must expect 'occasionally' to meet a half–clothed native. And if these people will persist in employing these native men as 'chambermaids', there is sure to be a little trouble now and again. I wonder there is not more.

This exchange seems to have served to bring his consciousness of race to the fore again, so that he was in receptive mood when, later in the year, he was approached by the editor of the new *African Times and Orient Review* for an occasional article. The periodical was aimed at coloured British people; a sign of a growing element in the population. As a response to the first issue, however, a letter from Coleridge–Taylor revealed scepticism. The issue prompted a somewhat non–commital 'interesting' from him:[248]

Whether or not it will be appreciated by the British public is, however, a point on which I am not so certain.

There is, of course, a larger section of the British people interested in coloured races; but it is, generally speaking, a commercial interest only. Some of these may possibly be interested in the aims and desires of the coloured peoples; but taking them as a whole, I fancy one accomplished fact carries more weight than a thousand aims and desires, regrettable though it may be.

It seems that the different section of the whites are not interested in the aims of each other (excepting, perhaps, financially), and I doubt if more than a few will be inclined to study the aspirations of those of another race.

There is a hard realism about this. Coleridge–Taylor had, during the spring and summer of 1912, accomplished many 'facts', both as composer and conductor.

A further letter from the editor (Duse Mohamed) to Coleridge–Taylor dated 29 August 1912 reveals the composer desperately trying to reduce his work–load by putting forward his wife to write the *Review*'s monthly musical column. A sentence in the same letter reveals another undertaking which never materialised, probably for the same reason:

What have you done in regard to 'A Daughter of the Pharaohs' and what do you propose doing with regard to my Cleopatra ballet?

In June, 1912, The Keats–Shelley Memorial Association organised a festival with the aim of raising enough money to purchase the house in

Piazza di Spagna, Rome, where Keats had died in 1821. Two memorial matinees were held at the Haymarket Theatre where the director of music was Norman O'Neill. O'Neill contributed his own setting of *La Belle Dame sans Merci* for baritone and orchestra (1908) and asked Parry, Bax and Coleridge–Taylor for works. Bax produced *Prelude to Adonais*[249]; Coleridge–Taylor wrote *The Eve of St Agnes* to accompany a series of tableaux. Three movements were subsequently arranged and adapted by Adolph Lotter and published posthumously in 1922 by Hawkes. They seem to confirm that Coleridge–Taylor was not responsive to the atmosphere of poetry of the English Romantic Revival. Just as he had not matched the extravagant fantasy of *Kubla Khan*, here his music seems prosaic:

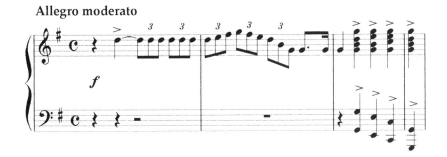

Ex. 143: The Eve of St Agnes, fanfare

This fanfare hardly matches the imagery of Keats's line:

> The silver, snarling trumpets 'gan to chide

The whole undertaking nevertheless shows Coleridge–Taylor still hankering after the world of the theatre. Opera as such may have been closed to him, but there were still tableaux, ballet and even music hall. He had, according to Berwick Sayers, conducted some 'dances of oriental character'[250] at a music hall, and he would have been alive to Elgar's success at the London Coliseum with the masque *Crown of India*, first performed 11 March 1912. There certainly was a trend for impresarios to attempt to interest their audiences in something more sophisticated than their usual fare; only a year later would see Henry Coward's Sheffield Choir appearing nightly at the Coliseum, while Oswald Stoll prevailed on Sir Henry Wood to conduct boiled–down Wagner for some *Parsifal* tableaux in the same theatre.

In the summer of 1912, Coleridge–Taylor met a young theatrical producer, T. C. Fairbairn. At their meeting, Fairbairn outlined to the composer his ideas for producing a dramatised version of the first part of the *Hiawatha* 'Trilogy' at the Coliseum:

> We discussed every possible detail, and reviewed the poem, and music from every angle. It is a joy to remember how pleased he was with the scheme and how he helped with his suggestions. He was so enthusiastic, so fearless, and so anxious to help and please.[251]

At the time it came to nothing. But he was engaged on a *Hiawatha* ballet and, following the *Thelma* debacle, he became almost Handelian in his tireless search for whatever might appeal to the theatre–going public; like other composers, he had registered the impact made in London by the first visit (in 1911) of the Diaghilev Russian Ballet. Arnold Bax, overwhelmed by the Russian dancers, sought to write for them. Coleridge–Taylor seems to have been led to believe that his *Hiawatha* ballet might be produced at the Alhambra Theatre under the direction of Thomas Beecham. It was another project that came to nothing; although he wrote a considerable quantity of music for it in short score, it does not seem to have been orchestrated by him. It was published posthumously by Hawkes in 1919 as a *Suite from the Hiawatha Ballet Music*; this was followed in 1925 by a further selection entitled *Minnehaha Suite*. Both suites were orchestrated by Percy Fletcher.

Neither suite has any connection with the *Hiawatha* 'Trilogy'. Nor is it possible to say whether or not the published items represent the entire ballet as Coleridge–Taylor conceived it. The ballet has never been staged, although some items were occasionally used for the dances in the dramatised *Hiawatha* which was produced in the 1920s and 1930s. In all, there are five movements in the *Hiawatha Suite* and four in that for the *Minnehaha Suite*. Avril considered that both misrepresented her father's intentions, and had hoped to prepare a new score. The music is certainly balletic in the clarity and variety of its rhythms and the simplicity of its melody. But with the coming of the Russians, bringing with them the early Stravinsky ballets, its time had passed. A little of the savagery some critics thought they heard in his earlier music might now have served him well against the onslaught of *The Firebird* and *Petrouchka*.

The tone of his correspondence now began to take an ominous turn as chronic overwork piled up and made a trap from which ultimately he was unable to escape. We have to read between the lines. On 23

February (a few days after returning from the Birmingham performance of *A Tale of Old Japan* and after the trauma of the correspondence concerning racialism) he missed a Handel Society practice. In his place, Basil Hindenburg[252] took it. A short while later, he wrote to Julien Henry:[253]

> I had to give up yesterday's Guildhall rehearsal again because of that 'tired feeling'.

More revealing still was a letter some weeks later to William Read:[254]

> I am afraid I have been doing too much conducting lately (some–times nine rehearsals a week) and have had to knock off a bit, so [I] really don't think I should consider any proposal to conduct again at Eastbourne.

But he didn't 'knock off' very much, for March concluded with him conducting the Guildhall Operatic Department's production of Sullivan's *The Gondoliers*. Francesco Berger congratulated him:[255]

> It is by no means every musician, nor every gifted composer, who can control a body of the amateur class, however good and reliable they may be; but you seem to have them and the orchestra so entirely in your hand that the result was quite remarkable and stamped you as cut out to make a career as a conductor.

Here was the dilemma of the composer in the days before the establish–ment of the Performing Right Society. The temptation was to take on more and more conducting; composition of large–scale works would be justified financially by the fees concert promoters paid to a composer to conduct his own work.

The screw on him was tightened further in the early summer months by the illness of Landon Ronald which lead to an even heavier load of Guildhall work. To this was added the Stock Exchange Orchestra, which on 16 April performed under his direction a programme at The Queen's Hall. *The Musical Times*[256] commented on 'an excellent performance of Dvorak's picturesque Fourth Symphony'. Two days later he was in the Hall again to hear the London Choral Society repeat *A Tale of Old Japan*. On 4 May, he was at the Blackheath Concert Hall to conduct the Brockley and Lewisham Society in *Hiawatha*. When they came to it, they found that the trombone parts for *The Death of Minnehaha* had been mislaid. Coleridge–Taylor handed the players his score and conducted the remainder from memory.

Nine days later (on 13 May) he was back in The Queen's Hall again with the Handel Society. Its programme included Beethoven's *Egmont* overture and *Mount of Olives* oratorio together with works by Humper-dinck, Bizet, Mozart and Schumann.

The core of his problem was the difference between working with amateurs and working with professionals. A conductor such as Beecham, for example, was conducting more concerts, but most of his work was with professionals who needed far less rehearsal than Coleridge–Taylor's amateurs. And the conductor of professionals would have his 'fixer' (in Beecham's case, the formidable Donald Baylis) who would take care of the mass of detail involved in a concert. Each group with which Coleridge–Taylor worked had weekly rehearsals, and was committee-ridden. Secretaries still tended to refer every query to him, just as they had in the days of the Croydon Orchestra at the start of his conducting career:

> Let me know if you think Miss Martin's voice is high enough for in the Beethoven — it has a high C, with the option of a high E flat.[257]

May ended and June began with a few days' work of adjudicating and conducting at the Rhyl and Leamington festivals. Some scribbled notes on the back of a letter from the secretary at Leamington were clearly made by Coleridge–Taylor for his concluding remarks to that Festival, and they give some idea of the seriousness with which he took this work:

> 1 Competitive Festival good for audience — hearing things several times helps them to discriminate.
> 2 Also promotes good feeling between competitors — splendid to see those who lose so good tempered.
> 3 Sight–singing for all — instrumental and vocal — ought to be the most important part of the Festival.
> 3a An accompanying test now needed.
> 4 Instrumentally Leamington very high — there certainly ought to be a string quartet competition and a string orchestra ditto.
> 5 [illegible]

June continued with the copyright performance of the *Violin Concerto* already noted in chapter 19 (page 243); then to Brighton for a symphony concert. A letter to Julien Henry reporting this shows further signs of growing pressure:[258]

> I've had to get all my next week's work in somehow in two days, and, as Ronald is away, I'm at the Guildhall a good deal.

He had planned a holiday but it had to be postponed because Beerbohm Tree had commissioned more incidental music from him — to be ready by the beginning of September. The family went to Eastbourne for a few days in July but it was no holiday for Coleridge–Taylor. His corres–pondence was becoming mountainous:

> This makes my eighteenth letter — hence the writing ...[259]

and a note of desperation creeps in:

> I don't know what you'll think of me [—] I've simply been working against time.[260]

By August, many of the worst tensions were behind him. The amateur societies and the Guildhall School of Music had closed for the Summer, and most of the commissioned work was either completed or well advanced. He was now looking forward to the postponed holiday, for which he and his family hoped to rent a house at Hastings in Sussex. There were minor worries — Hiawatha was ill with tonsilitis, and the weather that year had been depressing — but Coleridge–Taylor was relaxed and enjoying the rare freedom to walk the Beddington lanes. On 28 August, he walked to West Croydon station, intending to take a train to Crystal Palace. He collapsed at the station, but managed to struggle home.

Even during what was to prove a fatal illness he worked, checking the parts of the *Violin Concerto* in preparation for Arthur Catterall's performance at Wood's 'Prom' in October.

Acute pneumonia was diagnosed. As so often happens, the illness had struck after the tensions were over and when the composer, having overworked for years, had no physical resources left with which to fight it. Marjorie remembered his last hours:

> I was at home when Watha came in with the news that his father was ill. We lived at 18 Whitehorse Rd then, not too far from Coleridge. Watha came in and said 'Daddy's ill' and mother said 'I'll come along in a minute, Watha', and he said 'Mother said you're to come back with me'. No more than a couple of hours later Coleridge passed away. 1 September 1912 — Pneumonia.[261]

In her book[262] Jessie wrote that he died 'in the presence of his mother, a West African friend, two nurses and myself'.

Coleridge–Taylor's funeral service was held on 5 September at St Michael and All Angels church, West Croydon, and was conducted by Canon Hoare. The church was packed; among the hundreds of mourners

were many representatives of the British black community. Also present
was Alice Evans. Many thought she was dead, and few outside the
family would have recognised her as the great man's mother. One of the
last friends he had met on his walks around the district had been H. L.
Balfour, the organist of the Royal Albert Hall. Balfour was at the
console for the service; he played the funeral music from *The Death of
Minnehaha* and accompanied Julien Henry who sang 'When I am Dead,
My Dearest' from the *Sorrow Songs*. Years later, Marjorie recalled the
interment, which was at Bandon Hill cemetery, Wallington, past which
he had often walked:

> Crowds in the streets and at the church. On both sides of the road,
> three or four deep. That shows you just how famous and respected
> my brother was.[263]

Flowers were sent from the Royal Choral Society, The Royal Academy
of Music, The Guildhall School of Music, Trinity College of Music, The
London Symphony Orchestra, the New Symphony Orchestra, The Stock
Exchange Musical Society, The Alexandra Palace Choral Society, the
String Players' Club, The Bournemouth Orchestra and Messrs Novello
and Co., among numerous others. One particularly striking wreath
showed a representation of Africa, all in white except for a red Sierra
Leone. It was from 'the sons and daughters of West Africa resident in
London'. One funeral card, unsigned, simply said, 'Sent on behalf of
unknown relatives in distant Sierra Leone, who wished him well in life
— and Peace in death'.

Tributes poured in from all sides. Landon Ronald's concentrated on
Coleridge–Taylor's personal qualities:

> his exceptionally courteous and lovable nature made him beloved
> by everyone that came across his path ... he was in every sense a
> gentleman, and was ever ready to give a helping hand, and had a
> kindly word for everybody. He was inclined to exaggerate the few
> kindnesses that were extended to him, and, considering his great
> gifts, he was one of the most modest men it has been my lot to
> meet.[264]

(This letter, written to the *Daily Telegraph*, was reprinted in the Sierra
Leone *Daily Mail* and subsequently in the Sierra Leone *Weekly News*.)

The Times discussed his music from the point of view of his mixed
race:

His mixed descent cannot be forgotten in any study of his music, since he makes his work an interesting example to all who are concerned with the appearance of racial characteristics in music. For in any of his work which one may take up it is obvious at once that it has certain features in its melody, style of treatment and use of orchestral colour which distinguish it from the music of English composers.[265]

Sir Hubert Parry, writing a tribute in *The Musical Times*, went a little further into the perceived effects of mixed race:[266]

He did not thirst for intellectual analysis, for recondite problems, or for odd and self–conscious effects. He wanted to put down what welled up in him quite simply and straightforwardly. Like his half–brothers of primitive race he loved plenty of sound, plenty of colour, simple and definite rhythms, and above all things, plenty of tune. Tune pours out in passage after passage, genial and kindly and apt to the subject, and, in an emotional way, often warmly and touchingly expressive. The pure occidental composer would have gone wrong trying to do something subtle and uncanny to show the fineness of his insight — and details would have got out of gear. But Coleridge–Taylor had no such temptations. The musical activity was so prompt in him that he had no occasion for research-fulness. The balance of style is perfectly maintained. It is in this that the inwardness of a very interesting situation may be recog-nised. It was the very simplicity and unconsciousness of his character which caused racial motives and impulses to be revealed so clearly. He had no occasion to conceal them; and the niche which he made for himself in musical history derives its individ-uality from the frankness with which he revealed the qualities which were the inevitable outcome of an exceptional and interesting combination of influences.

The Musical Times's own obituary was revealing about Coleridge–Taylor's composition methods:[267]

although the fluency of his writing suggests spontaneity, we have his word that he had almost a mania for revising. At the first inspiration he wrote his music very rapidly, and then, as he has told us, he would rewrite and revise perhaps twenty times ... the cantata *A Tale of Old Japan*, brimful, as it seems, of loving spontaneity, was in many places written several times before it satisfied him.

The obituary then seemed to countermand the force of this point:

> Yet it could hardly be said that he had a supreme gift of self–criticism.[268]

The Manchester Guardian, speaking from what had been deep Hans Richter country, concentrated on *Hiawatha*:[269]

> No other English cantata has ever gained so rapid a success. Its charm, like that of Elgar's and Bantock's works for chorus and orchestra, was more instrumental than vocal, and historically his importance will be that, like these composers, he has helped to establish instrumental modes of musical thought in the country.

But the *Guardian*'s critic (probably Samuel Langford) was one of those who perceived a decline in his work after the *Hiawatha* trilogy:

> Once only had he spoken in an inspired way, when the enchantment of youth was upon him. He became, afterwards, no more than the successful practitioner, ready to turn his hand skilfully to the opportune task, and not apparently galled by it.[270]

In conclusion, the *Guardian* touched again on the effect of his mixed racial origin:

> In a sense, he may be called a colonial composer, and his adaptability to European standards must, considering the racial ad–mixture of his blood, be considered in itself a unique triumph.[271]

Whilst later generations of critics might well question some of the judgements contained in them, these tributes represented a broad consensus of informed musical opinion at the time. But no–one seems to have observed that a man of such distinction and achievement, not to speak of his service as an unofficial ambassador of his country, should in his lifetime have been accorded no royal honour or decoration.

21 AFTERMATH: THE HIAWATHA MAN?

Two months after the composer's death, *The Times* reported:

> Colonel A. Walters, V. D., formerly commanding the 4th battalion
> of the Queen's Regiment who was guardian to the late Mr Samuel
> Coleridge–Taylor, has received a letter from Lord Stamfordham,
> Private Secretary to the King, expressing 'their Majesties' deep
> regret at the early death of this talented composer'.[272]

Not unnaturally, Jessie wondered why the letter had not been written to
her, and Colonel Walters had to explain to her the etiquette involved.
More important than the hierarchical ritual is the use of the word
'guardian', which immediately suggests a more formal relationship
between Walters and Coleridge–Taylor than has so far appeared. But
there are no facts to support the suggestion.

Down in the less exalted region of the family, the immediate
situation was, as Marjorie tells us, desperate:

> Well, we were in a bit of a tight spot after Coleridge died, because
> we had no money. Coleridge used to help out with a weekly
> cheque for seven shillings, which was worth a lot in those days. He
> was never a rich man because he sold the rights to his successful
> works and that's why Jessie and the children had a tough time.
> There was a charity concert in aid of them; no one thought of
> mother. I think most people thought she was dead then.[273]

The 'charity concert' was the Coleridge–Taylor Memorial Concert
organised by Colonel Walters for St Cecilia's Day, 22 November 1912,
at the Royal Albert Hall. The choir of about 1100 voices was formed by
the Royal Choral Society (Sir Frederick Bridge), The Alexandra Palace
Choral Society (Allen Gill), The London Choral Society (Arthur Fagge)
and the Crystal Palace Choir (W. Hedgcock). In addition, the following
orchestras were represented: The London Symphony, the New
Symphony, the Royal Amateur, the Stock Exchange and the Handel
Society. The solo artists were Miss Carrie Tubb, Miss Esta D'Argo,
Madame Ada Crossley, Mr Ben Davies, Mr Gervase Elwes, Mr Julien
Henry and Mr Robert Radford. The conductors were Sir Frederick
Bridge, Sir Charles Stanford, Adolph Schmid and Landon Ronald. The

following was the full programme:

> *Hiawatha's Wedding Feast*
> *The Death of Minnehaha*
> *Ballade in A minor* for orchestra
> Songs: 'Unmindful of the roses'   Ada Crossley
>   'Big Lady Moon'   Ada Crossley
>   'My Love'   Gervase Elwes
>   'Over the Hills'   Gervase Elwes
> 'Valse de la Reine' and 'Valse Bohemienne'
>   (from *Four Characteristic Waltzes*, op. 22)
> Air: 'Spring had come' (from *Hiawatha*)   Esta D'Argo
> Song: 'Thou art risen, my beloved'   Robert Radford
> *Bamboula* (Rhapsodic Dance)

The audience for it was immense:

> such an audience as carried one back to the never–to–be–forgotten
> days of the Patti concerts ... chief among those present were
> Princess Louise and the Duke of Argyll ... and in the audience were
> to be seen many faces well known both in the social and in the
> musical worlds.[274]

The concert raised a net amount, including donations, of £1440 for the
family. Messrs Novello & Co. headed the list of over eighty donors with
a gift of a hundred guineas (£105). Other contributors included Nellie
Melba, Carl Stoeckel, Beerbohm Tree and a number of choral societies.
The money raised was held in trust for the two children, Hiawatha and
Gwendoline (Avril), both of whom were by now receiving free tuition
at the Guildhall School of Music. Jessie, however, received the interest.

There were a number of other memorial concerts, including one by
the Central Croydon Choral Society[275] and one overseas in Boston
U.S.A., where a memorial committee had been formed. For this Boston
concert, Henry Burleigh came to sing. Instrumental items were provided
by members of the Boston Symphony Orchestra, and an address was
given by W. E. B. Du Bois.

The Samuel Coleridge–Taylor Choral Society of Washington had
been moribund, but it now came together again to sponsor a Testimonial
Concert on 13 May 1913. The Society sang *Hiawatha's Wedding Feast*
and *The Death of Minnehaha*, and Mamie Hilyer contributed a spoken
eulogy. The proceeds from the testimonials and subscription lists of
Coleridge–Taylor's coloured friends in the U.S.A. were sufficient for the
house 'Aldwick' to be presented to his widow.

Early in the following year, the Prime Minister's Secretary wrote to Jessie:[276]

> The King has been pleased to award you a Civil List Pension of £100, in recognition of the eminence of your husband, the late Mr Samuel Coleridge–Taylor, as a composer of music.

Two American friends resident in London, Mr and Mrs Henry Downing, took up the plight of his mother with the result that she, too, received a small annuity:

> ... she got £30: I can picture mother drawing fifteen pounds at a time from the post office. The pension lasted right until she died in 1953.[277]

About this time, a firm of accountants produced a statement for Jessie summarising Coleridge–Taylor's royalties over the period from 1905 until his death. It showed an average annual royalty (on sales of sheet music where the work had not been sold outright) of £119. The need for the funds raised by the concert, the award of the pension and the knowledge of the composer's poverty despite exhausting work now filtered into the public consciousness and some controversy in the press ensued. Only a year later (1914) would see the establishment of the Performing Right Society; this controversy may well have been in the minds of those active in its creation. For, as Dan Godfrey said:

> He practically sacrificed himself to his work. His energy and toil were unremitting, and his death was the direct result of his insisting on working when he was really very ill.

The pertinent correspondence began in *The Times* with a letter from the Society of Authors having in mind *Hiawatha's Wedding Feast* and urging composers to insist on royalties rather than receiving a lump–sum payment. The firm of Novello rose to the bait. They admitted that all the rights to the *Ballade in A minor* had been made over to them in return for twenty copies of the score, but denied that Coleridge–Taylor had been refused a royalty for *Hiawatha's Wedding Feast*. Novello's insisted, in a letter to *The Times* dated 28 November 1912, that they always gave a composer a choice between selling his work outright, or of a royalty–earning contract. Many composers, they wrote, preferred to sell their work. They could not, however, be drawn any further on the details of the *Hiawatha* transaction; they regarded their business arrange–ments as private. To this, Sir Charles Stanford replied that the public would draw its own conclusions from the fact that an appeal on behalf of the family had been needed. Walford Davies joined in to ask Novello's to put *Hiawatha*, even at that late stage, on a royalty basis; but he did not succeed. In defence of Novello's, it was pointed out that a number of cantatas and other works by Coleridge–Taylor published by them had shown a net loss.

The Society of Authors returned to the attack with an article by its representative Dr Squire Sprigge in the *English Review*,[278] having as its subject 'the author's due'. *The Musical Times* thought the whole controversy 'unnecessary and barren' (as well it might, since it was published by Novello). The editor of the rival *Musical Herald*, published by Curwen, attempted to conclude the matter in his editorial of the March issue of 1913:

> Dr Squire Sprigge's article in the *English Review* deals with the admitted facts: 1. of the death of Coleridge–Taylor in comparative poverty; 2. the admitted popularity of certain of his work; 3. the outright sale of much of his property as a musical composer. Coleridge–Taylor is allowed on all hands to have been a hard-working simple–living man. It appears that he received £250 in all for *Hiawatha*, £50 for each of the three parts, and £100 as a bonus, a sort of reward for being a good boy. How many thousands *Hiawatha* has earned one may never know, as Messrs Novellos state that they do not intend to disclose the secrets of their business to anyone. But we know enough to see that when Coleridge–Taylor transferred the copyright of *Hiawatha* to Messrs Novellos he made a lamentable bargain. Dr Sprigge admits that the plan of outright sale gives the composer a sum down, but he urges composers to prefer a royalty, so that the publisher may partly recoup himself for his outlay. It is, says Dr Sprigge, an excellent omen for the future that Messrs Novello should have stated publicly, in the course of the correspondence in *The Times*, their general habit of publishing on whatever footing the composer prefers.

In the years immediately following Coleridge–Taylor's death, the popularity of his music continued undiminished. An advertisement by the publishers Curwen in 1914, for example, showed that works by Coleridge–Taylor had been chosen for eleven major music festivals. Those who remember that Sir Adrian Boult included an Eric Coates march in his 80th birthday concert would not be surprised to know that, as a young man of 26, he included some of Coleridge–Taylor's music in his first concerts as a conductor in Liverpool. In the same year (1915), the composer's work received further impetus with the publication of his first biography, by Berwick Sayers. In addition, *A Tale of Old Japan* seemed set to rival *Hiawatha*, and Arthur Catterall's performance of the *Violin Concerto* on 8 October 1912, under Sir Henry Wood, was well received. The *Concerto*, said *The Musical Times*:

> was originally produced in America, as recorded in our columns. Since that occasion, the composer is understood to have made considerable revisions which were completed only shortly before his death. It is before all things genial; bold rhythms abound, the construction is always logical and effective, and much of the orchestration has an aplomb that could only be paralleled in Tschaikowsky. Although the work belongs more largely to the downright type of *Hiawatha* and *Nero* than to the subtler *Tale of Old Japan* there are moments which point more definitely to the future than any of Coleridge–Taylor's previous music.[279]

Always among the first in the provinces to offer the London novelties, Dan Godfrey and his Bournemouth Orchestra included the *Concerto* in their programme on 13 February 1913, and in the October of the following year they included *Bamboula*.

Novelties were what musicians, publishers and public alike seemed to want and, over the next few years, there appeared a trickle of posthumous publications (some no more than sweepings from the composer's workshop) which are difficult to date. Some of them show a considerable degree of arranging and alteration, and some are of questionable quality.

One work, little discussion of which seems to have appeared in print while he was alive, was the Rhapsody, *From the Prairie*. It was performed by Sir Henry Wood at a Queen's Hall 'Prom' on 26 August 1914 and repeated by the indefatigable Godfrey two years later at Bournemouth. It was then put into Boosey and Hawkes' hire library, whence it seems to have made few if any reappearances. Of Wood's performance, *The Musical Times* reported starkly:

> a straightforward Rhapsody *From the Prairie* by Coleridge–Taylor was well received.[280]

The cast of the two principal themes is simple and strong:

Ex. 144: From the Prairie, principal themes

However, the themes do not suggest that the composer's genius responded to scenery as readily as it did to words. It is not known when the work was written, but it is likely to have been prompted by the last of his visits to the U.S.A. It never established itself in the repertoire; but then, three weeks after the start of the First World War, was hardly a propitious time to launch any new work.

There was a flurry of interest in the *Clarinet Quintet* in 1917 when the London String Quartet revived it at the Aeolian Hall.[281] 'Native chamber music is too rarely heard', commented *The Musical Herald*, apparently ingenuously. That same year, Hawkes brought out a *Sonata in D minor* for violin and piano, in an edition by Albert Sammons. It had been given an opus number (op. 28), but the publisher did not include an explanatory note which might have suggested the date of its composition. In a note on her own score, Avril suggested the work originated in 1898, at the same period as *Hiawatha's Wedding Feast*.

The principal idea of the second movement is also that of the *Romance in G* for violin and orchestra, which dates from 1894–5:

Ex. 145: Violin Sonata in D minor, second movement

Since the *Romance* was published at the time of its composition, it is likely that the *Sonata*, in manuscript until 1917, was written first and then 'cannibalised' for the *Romance*.

On the surface, this three–movement sonata is simplistic to the point of crudity, and the piano writing is in many places ineffective and in others starkly attenuated; it nevertheless repays study and is notable for the clarity of its design. Its ideas themselves are heavily indebted to Dvorak; the following, for example, from the first movement:

Ex. 146: Violin Sonata in D minor, first movement

The last movement is a fierce *allegro vivo con fuoco* which embraces the cyclic principle to the extent that the two ideas in Example 145 and Example 146 recur to form a coda. He does not seem to have taken part in a performance of it either as pianist or violinist, nor does he seem to have pressed his violinist friends Zacharewitsch or Read to play it. It is possible, therefore, that he did not consider it as a whole to be up to standard. Like so much of Coleridge–Taylor's music, it may well make an effect in performance not apparent from the printed page and it would be good to experience an occasional performance of it. The infringement of copyright when Hawkes brought out the *Sonata* would hardly matter now.

At the time of the composer's death, some works were in the process of publication. Among these was the scena to words by Alfred Noyes, *Waiting* (op. 81, no. 1). This quite extensive melodrama is a setting of the lament of a woman who has lost both husband and son at sea, and it inhabits a similar sound–world to *Meg Blane*. The reality of the perils of the ocean had been reinforced in April 1912 by the news of the loss of the 'Titanic'. Dramatic the setting certainly is but, along with its predecessor, *Waiting* would probably have little appeal today.

Two songs appeared in 1914: *An Explanation* (Walter Learned) and *Life and Death* (Jessie Adelaide Middleton). The former is a trifle, possibly intended as an encore piece; the latter, described by Augener as 'Coleridge–Taylor's last song', was taken up by Marchesi, Ada Crossley, Caruso, John McCormack and other leading singers of the day. Although the title belies the setting — 'Death and Life' would be more suitable — it is fitting that this song, if it was indeed his last, should maintain the effortless melodic line which had been the hallmark of so much of his work.

As discussed in chapter 20, the *Hiawatha* and *Minnehaha* ballet suites were published in 1919 and 1925 respectively, in Percy Fletcher's orchestration. In 1920, Augener brought out Norman O'Neill's orchest–ration of the *Three Fours* suite. Then the remaining unpublished pieces from *The Forest of Wild Thyme* appeared: the songs 'Your Heart's Desire' and 'Come In' in 1920, the two children's songs 'Little Boy Blue' and 'Dreams, Dreams' in 1923, and the Christmas Overture in 1925. The Overture achieved popularity and was soon recorded, in versions by Percy Pitt and Malcolm Sargent, but it hardly does its composer credit. Of the songs, 'Come In' again demonstrates an effort–less melodic flow, set this time against the simplest of accompaniments.

In 1924, T. C. Fairbairn realised the dream he had discussed with Coleridge–Taylor in the last year of the composer's life, when he pro–duced *Hiawatha* 'in operatic form with scenery and costumes'. Fairbairn came from a family of Lincolnshire engineers; advised to take up singing as an aid to his delicate constitution and chest weakness, Charles Manners noticed his work and took him on — not as a singer but as a stage manager. Later in his career, he worked with Sarah Bernhardt; he also spent a short time as a producer for Sir Thomas Beecham.

The *Hiawatha* performances took place in the Royal Albert Hall, and *The Musical Times* reviewer was there to record the scene:

> To claim the whole vast arena as well as the platform for stage, and to place at a remote distance, and masking the organ, the back–scene of snow–clad mountains, pine forest and wigwam, was at one stroke to bring the drama to close quarters. Subtly the surrounding audience — or at all events those in the stalls and adjacent — were made to feel [part] of the stage crowd, bound up with their fate.
>
> To this, largely, was the success of the spectacle due; but also to the skilful and artistic management of the lighting, of which the singularly complete illusion of falling snow at the opening of the second act is a happy instance; part also to the grouping. The sea of hundreds of faces, of braves and squaws, with waving arms by way of foam crests, raised to greet Hiawatha and Minnehaha, was a sight not soon to be forgotten.[282]

In the first year, 1924, six performances of *Hiawatha* were given, using the Royal Choral Society and the Royal Philharmonic Orchestra.[283] The conductor was Eugène Goossens III, assisted by Coleridge–Taylor's old friend H. L. Balfour, while the composer's son Hiawatha conducted the ballet music.[284] Profits from the performances were distributed among charities for the blind. The following year came Malcolm Sargent's first appearance as conductor of the dramatised *Hiawatha* performances and, with the exception of 1933 and 1934 when he was ill and Geoffrey Toye and Albert Coates took his place, he returned each year until 1940 for the event. Over the period of fifteen years prominent singers of the day took part: Stiles Allen, Miriam Licette, Harold Williams, Elsie Suddaby, Frank Titterton, Parry Jones, and many others. Among the dancers were Lydia Lopokova, Leighton Lucas (who later was to distinguish himself as a conductor) and a very young Wendy Toye, who later achieved prominence as a choreographer. One of the few surviving members of the cast, she remembers the scale and brilliance of the production. She also recalls[285] that some members of the chorus never became used to the requirements of theatre. Spectacles and wristwatches were not always dispensed with, while on some nights a dress suit might be seen, inadequately hidden under an 'Indian' costume, as friends who had been unsuccessful in buying a ticket were smuggled in.

From 1925 onwards, Fairbairn enhanced his production with the introduction of a chief of the Mohawks, Chief Os–Ke–Nan–Ton, to play the Medicine Man, and the Royal Choral Society grew in size from 600 to 800. The work which had done so little for its composer's well–being but which had made a fortune for its publisher now proved a money–spinner for the Royal Choral Society and the Royal Albert Hall corporation, between whom each year the proceeds were now divided; an irony, when it is remembered that the Hall was the scene and the Society the perpetrator of that first complete performance which had caused the composer such grief.

Similar presentations spread into the provinces and then to the extremes of the Empire. In 1932, for example, it was done, with Fairbairn's advisory help, in Wellington, New Zealand. For the perform–ances held at the City Hall, Sheffield, in the winter of 1934, the music for the ballet sequences was conducted by the composer's daughter Gwendolen, now called Avril. In the previous year she had founded the Coleridge–Taylor Symphony Orchestra to give employment to musicians made redundant either through the slump or through the ravages caused by the disbanding of the cinema orchestras.

The advent of these dramatised performances in 1924 co–incided with a flickering re–kindling of the embers of Empire; the programmes featured full–length portraits of royalty and aristocracy from King and Emperor George V downwards, while the synopsis of the story managed, with dubious logic, to suggest that 'Hiawatha played a great part in the history of our Empire'.[286]

The work was presented in dramatic form, after the 1939–1945 war, in celebration of the crowning of the young Queen Elizabeth II in 1953. The conductor Colin Ratcliffe created the London Coronation Choir specially for the event, and the soloists were from a new generation: William Herbert, Elsie Morison and Kenneth McKellar were among them. But by then _Hiawatha_'s time had passed and little else of Coleridge–Taylor's work was being performed.

His training as a composer, under Stanford, had equipped him with a technique that others, most notably Elgar, had to acquire painfully and slowly. Which is the better way: to apply technique to music, or to let the music within find its own technique? This question is ever a matter for argument, but what no teacher can do is to invest his charge with an individual voice or an individual message. And in Coleridge–Taylor's case, the question must be asked: did he have an individual voice and message?

No experienced musician, or music–loving listener for that matter, would often fail to identify the work of Vaughan Williams, of Elgar, of Delius or, in light music, of Eric Coates. Coleridge–Taylor's music might present them with more problems. He had his models which included Dvorak, Schumann and Tschaikowsky. So, of course, did the others: Parry for early Vaughan Williams, Brahms and Schumann for Elgar, Grieg and Strauss for Delius and Elgar, and German for Coates. But certainly in the cases of Vaughan Williams, Elgar and Delius their models were but a starting point for a journey in which an individual message was increasingly refined. Elgar and Delius were additionally provided with a necessary irritant (on the analogy of that needed to create a fine pearl): for Elgar, it was the hurt and accompanying insecurity which was expressed in the prevalent melancholy of his music, coupled with a driving need to achieve 'something great'. For Delius, it was the need to re–experience the ecstasies of his youth spent in Yorkshire, Florida, Norway and Paris.

Coleridge–Taylor was only too normal, too balanced, to have an equivalent irritant. Which is not to say that he had no stimulus for the creation of music. Rather, it was one of his problems that the spring of music bubbled up effortlessly with seemingly little need of control from him. Because of this, there is an inconsistency of quality and an unevenness, in which a masterpiece might be followed by a bland failure. And even when a work is a masterpiece, it may yet not be as moving as some of the more imperfectly–realised works of the other great masters of English music. The situation was exacerbated by a faulty self–critical faculty which caused Coleridge–Taylor not to discriminate between his varied inspirations as successfully as he should have done.

The fact of his mixed racial origin led eventually to a division of aim in his work, as he tried to reconcile the two worlds into which he had been born. And, because he was coloured, that aspect of his work which related to the expression of his paternal side has been accorded in the past more than its due weight in critical appraisal. He was, after all, an Englishman.

The ambivalence arose because from the beginning he aspired to succeed in the music to which, by his upbringing, education and training, he was naturally drawn: that is to say, European instrumental and vocal music. But as he matured, and especially after meeting Dunbar, he became conscious of the importance of his paternal inheritance. Whether through genuine desire or mere duty, he certainly tried thereafter in work after work to express the spirit of his father's race. He saw this task in terms of arranging African songs and dances, or setting words by coloured authors — but always within the context of European harmony, European textures and European vocal and instrumental usage.

It was in the U.S.A. that black corporate consciousness was maturing faster than elsewhere; faster than in Africa, in fact. Its authentic musical voice, overwhelming that of Booker T. Washington as he protested, was to be found in the syncopated styles spreading from New Orleans. European academicism was of no use to it. Improvised close–harmony was preferred to classical written–down harmony. The small close–knit jazz group was more practical use than the huge symphony orchestra. Its musical heroes in a very short while would be Bechet or Armstrong and, where it felt the need for permanence, it would turn to Duke Ellington for its Classicism.

Coleridge–Taylor had little musical influence either in America or in Europe, even though so percipient a critic as Hubert Foss professed to hear echoes of him in the last movement of Vaughan Williams's *Sea Symphony*. But when we consider him as a man, it is an entirely different matter.

With many artists, it is only the art which matters, for there is not necessarily a correlation between the significance of the art and the nature, and character, of the artist. But whatever view is taken of his music, there can be little doubting the significance of Coleridge–Taylor himself. At the Royal College of Music he was blazing a trail and, as a model student, he was universally admired. Thereafter, by his dignity, hard work, good humour and sheer technical excellence at his job, he showed how a coloured man might rise to the very top of a profession which at the time would hardly have seemed to have been even open to him. He was modest, but not unduly so; he knew his worth. And his achievement was seized on hungrily by his fellow–coloureds — not so much in his own country as in the U.S.A., where his career pointed the way to his brothers even though he himself would probably never have fully grasped his significance for them. Some did now follow as serious composers, for example William Grant Still, Cecil Burleigh and Robert Dett. Others, such as Dean Dixon and Rudolph Dunbar, emulated him as conductors. Among singers, such artists as Paul Robeson, Marian Anderson and even Jessye Norman benefitted from passage through a door which he had pushed open. His real importance was his example, the impact of which was not limited to musicians alone.

Two questions remain: was he the musical genius who would in his work express the aspirations and spirit of the West African people? Was he in fact a musical genius at all, or was he, as the obituary of the *Manchester Guardian* suggested, just a successful 'practitioner' who 'spoke once only ... in an inspired way'? Just 'The Hiawatha Man', in fact?

With regard to the first question, he certainly did what was expected of him. Whenever contact with his coloured friends pushed racial con-sciousness to the fore, he responded. But it was a response rather than an elemental need, and what he did was always and inevitably to be within the framework of his European culture, where his own training and experience lay. More than that, whenever the immediacy of coloured contact receded, so too did his African commitment, for his instincts were English and his musical surroundings, those of the English rehearsal room and concert hall, were too congenial for him to renounce them in any pioneering endeavour.

As for the question of his musical stature, the initial judgement of the *Manchester Guardian* now seems harsh; *Bamboula*, *A Tale of Old Japan*, the *Violin Concerto*, the *Petite Suite de Concert* and the *Clarinet Quintet* — to name just a few of the finer works — suggest otherwise. The problem of making a fair assessment is compounded, first, by the fact that there is little evidence of growth of stature in his work (in general the early work seems hardly less accomplished than the later; nor is it much different in style and content) and, second, by the uneven quality of so much of it. But the English were generally indifferent to the material circumstances of their musical men of genius, until their attention was focused too late on them; they neglected their well–being. These circumstances, in the case of Coleridge–Taylor, exhausted him from time to time and they blunted his cutting edge. His true diamonds are all too often lost among the semi–precious stones and paste.

At the time of writing, a gratifying trickle of new recordings of Coleridge–Taylor's music suggests that, after a period of neglect, a new generation of listeners is prepared to explore the creative legacy of this distinguished man, whose music touched greatness rather more often than has yet been recognised.

NOTES

Chapter 1, **Parentage:**

1 W. C. Berwick Sayers, p. 3
2 Director of Medical Services, The Gambia, to Sidney Butterworth, 2
   November 1982. If this age is correct, Daniel Taylor's date of birth,
   as given to Wesley College, must have been wrong; he would have
   been born not in 1849 but in 1847, making him in reality twenty–three
   on entry to the College; Avril opted for 'circa 1848'.
3, 4, 5 Avril Coleridge–Taylor's MS notes on her grandfather
6 His name is given thus, inaccurately.
7, 8, 9 *I Remember Coleridge: Recollections of Samuel Coleridge–Taylor*
   (1875–1912), p. 31
10 Nigel Dashwood, in conversation with the author

Chapter 2, **Childhood in Croydon:**

11 Avril Coleridge–Taylor's MS notes on her grandfather
12 Marjorie Evans, *I Remember Coleridge*, p. 37
13 These villages have now merged into a large built–up suburban area, of
   which Croydon is the 'capital'.
14 Marjorie Evans, loc. cit.
15 Marjorie Evans, op. cit., p. 40
16 Jessie Coleridge–Taylor, *Samuel Coleridge–Taylor; Genius and
   Musician*, p. 14: 'a lady who knew my husband'.
17 Avril Coleridge–Taylor, *The Heritage of Samuel Coleridge–Taylor*
18 Once the headquarters of the Y.M.C.A., it was demolished in 1907
   to make way for the Strand Palace Hotel. The date of the meeting was
   18 June 1888, and their attendance here suggests that Walters and his
   protégé were then still at St George's Church.
19 Avril Coleridge–Taylor, op. cit.
20 W. Berwick Sayers, op. cit., p. 15
21 Percy Young, *George Grove 1820–1900* (Macmillan, 1980), p. 147

Chapter 3, **At The Royal College of Music:**

22 Percy Young, *George Grove 1820–1900* (Macmillan, 1980), p. 238
23 ibid.

24 His own copy of the work is dated February 1894. Other piano works he possessed included Schubert's *Impromptus* and the op. 42 *Sonata*, and Beethoven's op. 2 no. 3 C major *Sonata*.

Chapter 4, Stanford's teaching:

25 The six manuscript songs comprise: 1. 'Ah! Tell me Gentle Zephyrs' (poet untraced; MS in poor condition), 2. 'Keep those Eyes' (Thomas Moore), 3. 'We Watched her Breathing through the Night' (Thomas Hood), 4. 'She Dwelt Amid the Untrodden Ways' (William Words–worth), 5. 'The Arrow and the Song' (Longfellow), 6. 'Why Does the Azure Deck the Skies?' (poet untraced).
26 Marjorie Evans, *I Remember Coleridge*, p. 39
27 For 5 September 1896; he took the College orchestra through the *Prelude* and *Liebestod*.

Chapter 5, Elgar, Gloucester and the Ballade:

28 *Radio Times*, 20 November 1925
29 Linette Martin to G.R.S., November 1993
30 24 December 1898

Chapter 6, Hiawatha's Wedding Feast:

31 By George Strong (1832–1912) and Lewis Carroll (Charles Dodgson, 1832–1898), for example.
32 James Hepokoski, 'The Culture Clash', *The Musical Times* (December 1993), pp. 685–8
33 *The Musical Times*
34 Coleridge–Taylor to Walter Hayson, quoted by Sayers, op. cit., p. 57
35 Dan Godfrey, *Memories and Music* (Hutchinson, 1924)
36 Elgar's *Minuet*, op. 21, is dedicated to Paul Kilburn.
37 Coleridge–Taylor to Kilburn; date illegible
38 Coleridge–Taylor to Kilburn, 17 November 1898

Chapter 7, The Death of Minneheha:

39 *Memories and Music* (London, 1924)
40 Writing in the *Musical Quarterly*, 1922, p. 182
41 *Brighton Herald*, 16 January 1909
42 *Sussex Daily News,* 15 January 1909
43 Marjorie Evans, *I Remember Coleridge*, p. 35
44 Coleridge–Taylor to Kilburn, April 1899 [date partly illegible]
45 Coleridge–Taylor to Kilburn, 3 July 1899

46 Originally to be called *Solemn Rhapsody* but changed to *Solemn Prelude* at Novello's suggestion.
47 Coleridge–Taylor to Kilburn
48 Elgar to Jaeger, 14 September 1899
49 Elgar to Jaeger, 21 September 1899
50 Coleridge–Taylor to Kilburn, 27 September 1899
51 Joseph Bennett, in *The Daily Telegraph*, 28 October 1899
52 *The Musical Times*, December 1899
53 Jaeger to Elgar, 1 November 1899
54 *The Musical Times*, December 1899

Chapter 8, Hiawatha's Departure:

55 Coleridge–Taylor to Kilburn, 23 November 1899
56 Longfellow wrote:
   You shall enter all our wigwams
   For the heart's right hand we give you.
57 Berwick Sayers, pp. 91–92
58 Marjorie Evans, *I Remember Coleridge*, p. 36
59 Marjorie Evans, loc. cit.
60 Linette Martin to the author, 2 December 1993
61 Linette Martin to the author, 26 October 1993
62 Jessie Coleridge–Taylor, *Coleridge–Taylor: Genius and Musician*
63 Linette Martin to the author, 26 October 1993
64 Berwick Sayers, p. 93
65 Coleridge–Taylor to Kilburn, 14 March 1900
66 *The Times*, 23 March 1900
67 B.B.C. Home Service, 29 August 1954
68 Dan Godfrey, *Memories and Music* (Hutchinson, 1924), p. 285
69 *Choral Music*, ed. Arthur Jacobs (Pelican, 1963)
70 B.B.C. North American Transmission, 5 October 1941
71 Herbert Thompson, writing of the rehearsal in the *Yorkshire Post*, 1 October 1900
72 E. A. Baughan: *The Musical Standard*, 13 October 1900

Chapter 9, A first faltering?:

73 Berwick Sayers, p. 94
74 Marjorie Evans, *I Remember Coleridge*, p. 40
75 Berwick Sayers, p. 91
76 Berwick Sayers, p. 116
77 Marjorie Evans, loc. cit.

78 Jessie Coleridge–Taylor, *Coleridge–Taylor: A Memory Sketch*, pp. 44–5
79 Marjorie Evans, op. cit., p. 39
80 *African Times and Orient Review*, September 1912
81 Dan Godfrey, *Memories and Music* (Hutchinson, 1924)
82 It became the Royal Philharmonic Society in 1912.
83 *The Musical Times*, June 1900
84 *The Times*, 14 September 1900
85 Jaeger to Elgar, 12 July 1900
86 *The Musical Times* 1900, p. 593
87 Jaeger to Elgar, 12 August 1900
88 *Herbert Beerbohm Tree*, Max Beerbohm (Hutchinson, 1917) p. 146
89 Berwick Sayers, op. cit., p. 114
90 *The Musical Times* 1900, p. 818
91 ibid.
92 Coleridge–Taylor to Kilburn, 14 October 1900
93 Marjorie Evans, op. cit., p. 34
94 Marjorie Evans, op. cit., p. 35

Chapter 10, **Toiling for the Festivals:**

95 *The Musical Times*, Jan–June 1900, p. 593
96 Coleridge–Taylor to A. F. Hilyer, 12 May 1901
97 Coleridge–Taylor to Kilburn, 18 February 1904
98 *The Times*, 12 September 1901
99 *The Musical Times*, 1 September 1901, p. 606 (reviewing the music score)
100 November 1901, pp. 732–733
101 *The Times*, 10 October 1901
102 Jaeger to Herbert Thompson, 4 March 1901
103 Henry R. Clayton (Novello's), 19 October 1901
104 Coleridge–Taylor to Kilburn, 17 October 1901
105 *The Musical Times*, December 1901, p. 819
106 *The Times*, 28 October 1901
107 Coleridge–Taylor to Edith Carr, 6 February 1902
108 ibid.
109 *The Sheffield Independent*, 4 October 1902
110 ibid.

Chapter 11, **A low ebb:**

111 Jaeger to Elgar, 29 May 1903
112 W. B. Yeats to Elgar, 23 March 1903

113 Reginald Nettel, *Ordeal By Music* (O.U.P., 1945), p. 65
114 Berwick Sayers, op. cit., p. 139. Kirkby Lunn, however, does not appear among the principal performers on the overall programme for the 1903 Festival.
115 Coleridge–Taylor to Hilyer, 1 September 1903
116 Coleridge–Taylor to Littleton, 10 September 1903
117 Jaeger to Elgar, 16 September 1903. Fuller Maitland was the music critic of *The Times* and Herbert Thompson was music critic of the *Yorkshire Post.*
118 Elgar to Jaeger, 17 September 1903
119 Michael Kennedy, *Portrait of Elgar* (London, 1968), p. 64
120 St Thomas's Church Choral Society, 24 February 1904
121 Coleridge–Taylor to Hilyer, 6 March 1904
122 Coleridge–Taylor to Kilburn, 18 February 1904

Chapter 12, **An awareness of colour:**

123 Marjorie Evans, op. cit., p. 40
124 Marjorie Evans, op. cit., p. 38
125 See Richard McGrady, *Music and Musicians in Early Nineteenth Century Cornwall* (University of Exeter, 1991)
126 A. B. C. Merriman, *Britons through Negro Spectacles* (1909)
127 Marjorie Evans, op. cit., p. 34
128 Marjorie Evans, op. cit., p. 36
129 Marjorie Evans, loc. cit.
130 Jessie Coleridge–Taylor, *Genius and Musician*, p. 35
131 Linette Martin to the author, 26 October 1993
132 Linette Martin to the author, 2 December 1993
133 Coleridge–Taylor to Mrs M. Hilyer, 22 February 1901
134 Coleridge–Taylor to Hilyer, 12 May 1901
135 Coleridge–Taylor to Hilyer, 12 May 1901
136 Coleridge–Taylor, letter dated 1 September 1901, perhaps not sent
137 Coleridge–Taylor to A. F. Hilyer, 11 April 1903
138 Coleridge–Taylor to Hilyer, 2 May 1903
139 Arthur S. Gray to Coleridge–Taylor, 1 June 1903
140 Coleridge–Taylor to Arthur S. Gray (although headed 'My dear sir'), undated.
141 Booker T. Washington, Atlanta speech
142 ibid.
143 W. E. B. Du Bois, *The Souls of Black Folk*
144 Coleridge–Taylor to Hilyer, 14 September 1904
145 W. E. B. Du Bois, *The Souls of Black Folk*
146 Coleridge–Taylor to Hilyer, 14 September 1904

Chapter 13, First visit to the U.S.A:

147 Dan Godfrey, *Memories and Music* (Hutchinson, 1924), p. 97
148 Berwick Sayers, op. cit., p. 159
149 Metropolitan A. M. E. 'Church Notes': Washington, *The Record*
150 Washington correspondent of *The Georgia Baptist*
151 Berwick Sayers, op. cit., p. 162
152 Booker T. Washington, in the Preface to the *Twenty–Four Negro Melodies* (dated 24 October 1904), indicates that the five were already in existence at that date.

Chapter 14, Kubla Khan:

153 Booker T. Washington, Preface to *Twenty–Four Negro Melodies*
154 Stanford to Coleridge–Taylor, 16 May 1905
155 M. Henri Junod, *Les Chants et Les Conts des Ba–Ronga*
156 Coleridge–Taylor, Foreword to *Twenty–Four Negro Melodies*
157 Coleridge–Taylor to Kilburn, 13 September 1905
158 Coleridge–Taylor to Hilyer, 30 September 1905
159 Coleridge–Taylor to Hilyer, 7 December 1905
160 Address, November 1905
161 ibid.
162 *Birmingham Gazette and Express*, 14 March 1906
163 Stanley Athenaeum, October 1906
164 *The Norwood News*, June 1906
165 ibid.
166 6 & 7 March 1906
167 Lord Coleridge to Sidney Butterworth, 28 March 1988: 'It will of course have been my branch of the family who would have given this permission and I therefore have little doubt that my memory is correct'.
168 Avril Coleridge–Taylor's MS notes on her grandfather
169 2 September 1912
170 Molly Lefebure, *Samuel Taylor Coleridge: A Bondage of Opium* (Gollancz, 1974)
171 Avril Coleridge–Taylor, *The Heritage*, p. 86
172 *The Musical Times*, 1906, p. 628
173 ibid.
174 15 June 1906
175 Marsh and Loudin, *The Story of the Jubilee Singers* (Hodder & Stoughton, 1898), p. 207

***Chapter 15*, Second visit to the U.S.A:**

176 The other works offered to Ditson were the songs 'O mistress mine', 'Once Only', 'The Gift Rose', and 'Until'.

177 Richard Aldrich, *Concert life in New York (1906–1907)* (G. P. Putnam & Sons, 1941)

178 Quoted in Ursula Vaughan Williams, *R. V. W., A biography of Vaughan Williams* (London, 1964), pp. 142–3

179 Library of Congress to the author, 4 April 1994, from Wayne D. Shirley (Music Specialist): 'Several people (including me) have searched for its papers, but in vain'.

180 Dr Doris McGinty to the author, 14 May 1994

181 ibid.

182 Jessie Coleridge–Taylor, *Coleridge–Taylor: A Memory Sketch* (London, 1942/3), p. 42

183 Marjorie Evans, *I Remember Coleridge*, p. 36

184 Berwick Sayers, op. cit., pp. 205–206

185 Coleridge–Taylor to Spiering, 12 September 1907

186 Grieg's own *Ballade* for piano is a set of variations.

187 Florence Montgomery

188 Berwick Sayers, op. cit., p. 208

189 Delius to Bantock, March 1908

190 Even though he had been brought in to replace Bantock, who had withdrawn.

***Chapter 16*, Opera and drama:**

191 Bach, *Suite in B minor*; Handel, *Concerto Grosso in D*; and Bach, *Double Violin Concerto*

192 *The Musical Times*, April 1910, p. 240

193 Sir Henry Wood, *My Life of Music* (Gollancz, 1938), p. 54, re The Arthur Rousbey Grand English Opera Company

194 Hubert Foss, *Vaughan Williams: a study* (London, 1950), p. 176

195 Andrew Hilyer to Coleridge–Taylor, 26 April 1908

196, 197, 198 ibid.

199 October 1908. It was handwritten; 'my typewriter has been out of order for the last fortnight, and the man hasn't yet been to see it — hence my pen and ink letter, which hope you will be able to understand'. (To Andrew Hilyer)

200 9–12 December 1908

Chapter 17, Recovery:

201 *The Daily Telegraph* review (15 January 1909), however, writes of
'the production, said with slight inaccuracy to be the first....'
A confusion here may arise from the fact that the Central Croydon
Choral Society gave a performance immediately afterwards.

202 15 January 1909

203 16 January 1909

204 15 January 1909

205 Marjorie Evans, op. cit., p. 31

206 As recounted to Berwick Sayers, op. cit., p. 243

207 loc. cit.

208 Coleridge–Taylor to A. Johnson, 17 January 1909

209 4 & 5 February 1910

210 V. Safonoff to Coleridge–Taylor, 26 January 1910

211 Robert Buckley, *Birmingham Gazette and Express*, 20 February
1910

212, 213 ibid.

214 Marjorie Evans. op. cit., p. 37

215 Coleridge–Taylor to Miss Carr, undated but probably July 1910.
He intended to go to Eastbourne that month, and the letter is written
on the notepaper of the Clifton Hotel, Eastbourne.

216 Coleridge–Taylor to William Read, 13 March 1910

217 George W. Cable, *The Dance in Place Congo*, 1886

218 Translation: 'when that 'tater's cooked, don't you eat it up'

Chapter 18, Carl Stoeckel:

219 Stoeckel's reminiscences, quoted by Berwick Sayers, op. cit., p. 236

220 Berwick Sayers, op. cit., p. 238

221 Coleridge–Taylor to A. T. Johnson, 21 June 1910

222 Coleridge–Taylor to A. F. Hilyer, 26 December 1910

223 Landon Ronald, in an interview with *The Musical Herald*,
December 1910, p. 355

224 Coleridge–Taylor to Hilyer, 26 December 1910

225 'O Mariners, out of the Sunlight' and 'Loud Sang the Spanish
Cavalier'

226 Leeds, 1911

227 By Virginia Eskin; see Appendix C (Recordings)

228 *The Musical Times*, May 1912

229 Alfred Noyes, too, was a friend of the Stoeckels, and had seen
Connecticut in bloom.

230 Jessie Coleridge–Taylor, *Samuel Coleridge–Taylor, Genius and Musician*, p. 51
231 *The Morning Post*, 7 December 1911
232 ibid.
233 *The Musical Times*, 1 October 1911
234 Berwick Sayers, op. cit., p. 292

Chapter 19, The Violin Concerto:

235 Stoeckel to Coleridge–Taylor, 31 January 1912
236 Both versions are in the R. C. M. library.
237 Coleridge–Taylor to William Read, 20 May 1912
238 Coleridge–Taylor to Julien Henry, 18 August 1912.
    This date may be suspect: he apparently asked Metzler only four days before, on 14 August 1912.
239 Coleridge–Taylor to Charles Lucas (Metzler & Co.); apparently dated 14 August 1912
240 Maud Powell: interview in *New York Times*, 4 March 1912
241 Maud Powell probably noticed this, as she had given the first U.S.A. performance of the Dvorak concerto.
242 The critic of *Musician*, vol. 19, no.3, March 1914, p. 201
243 ibid.
244 Maud Powell, in an interview in *New York Times*, 4 March 1912

Chapter 20, Overwork and death:

245 Coleridge–Taylor to *Croydon Guardian*, 15 February 1912
246 A coloured man; world heavyweight boxing champion, 1908–1915
247 Coleridge–Taylor to *Croydon Guardian*, 1 March 1912
248 *African Times and Orient Review*, first issue
249 The score is missing; see Lewis Foreman, *Bax: A Composer and his Times* (Scolar Press, 1983), p. 100
250 Berwick Sayers, op. cit., p. 290
251 T. C. Fairbairn, as reported by Mrs Alec Tweedie; Hiawatha souvenir programme, City Hall, Sheffield, December 1933
252 Shortly afterwards, he changed his name to Basil Cameron; he became a distinguished conductor.
253 Coleridge–Taylor to Julien Henry, 1 March 1912
254 Coleridge–Taylor to William Read, 27 March 1912
255 Francesco Berger to Coleridge–Taylor, 31 March 1912
256 *The Musical Times*, 1912, p. 320
257 Secretary of Handel Society to Coleridge–Taylor, 23 February 1912
258 Coleridge–Taylor to Julien Henry, 17 June 1912

259 ibid.
260 Coleridge–Taylor to William Read, 15 July 1912
261 Marjorie Evans, op. cit., p. 38
262 Jessie Coleridge–Taylor, *A Memory Sketch*, p. 60
263 Marjorie Evans, op. cit., p. 38.
     Coleridge–Taylor's grave will be found near to the entrance to the
     cemetery.
264 Landon Ronald to *The Daily Telegraph*, 2 September 1912
265 *The Times*, 2 September 1912
266 *The Musical Times*, 1 October 1912, p. 638
267 *The Musical Times*, 1 October 1912, p. 637
268 *The Musical Times*, 1 October 1912, loc. cit.
269 *The Manchester Guardian*, 2 September 1912
270, 271 ibid.

Chapter 21, Aftermath:

272 28 October 1912
273 Marjorie Evans, op. cit., p. 38
     The gross value of his estate was £874.
274 *The Daily Telegraph*, 23 November 1912
275 24 March 1913
276 loc. cit.
277 Marjorie Evans, loc. cit.
278 February 1913
279 *The Musical Times*, November 1912, p. 732
280 *The Musical Times*, October 1914, p. 625
281 August 1917
282 *The Musical Times*, June 1924, p. 551
283 In later years the New Symphony Orchestra was used.
284 In the first year the *Three Dream Dances* were used.
285 In conversation with the author
286 Programme, 19–24 May 1924

Appendix A: LIST OF WORKS

Since no diaries nor any manuscript catalogues have been found, the dates given here are generally those of assignment to a publisher. There was, as a rule, very little time between the completion of a work and its assignment. For manuscript compositions, the year of their composition is given, as far as it can be ascertained. For posthumous publications, their assignment date is shown, together with a date of composition if this is either known or can be inferred. While this list is as complete as possible with regard to actual titles, there may well be arrangements for forces other than those shown.

OPERAS

1898 *Dream Lovers*, op. 25. Operatic Romance for two male and two female characters; libretto by P. L. Dunbar. (Boosey)

1898 *The Gitanos*, op. 26. Cantata–operetta for female voices and piano; libretto by Edward E. Oxenford. (Augener)

1907–9 *Thelma*, op. 72. Opera in three acts; libretto thought to be by the composer. Manuscript of the opera missing; MS orchestral material of the Prelude in hire library of Boosey & Hawkes.

1910 *Endymion's Dream*. One–act opera; libretto by C. R. B. Barrett. (Novello) Described as a 'Cantata' on the published score.

INCIDENTAL MUSIC

1900 *Herod*, op. 47. Play by Stephen Phillips.
Processional; Breeze Scene; Dance; Finale (Augener, 1901)
Song, 'Sleep, Sleep, O King' (Enoch, 1900)

1902 *Ulysses*, op. 49. Play by Stephen Phillips.
'Great is he who fused the might'; 'O set the sails';
'From the green heart of the waters'; 'Nymph's Song' (Novello)

1906 *Nero*, op. 62. Play by Stephen Phillips.
Prelude; two Entractes; Intermezzo; Eastern Dance; Processional March. The published *Suite* omits the two entractes. (Novello, 1909)

1908 *Faust*, op. 70. Play by Stephen Phillips and J. Comyns Carr, based on Goethe.
Dance of the Witches; The Four Visions (Helen, Cleopatra, Messalina, Margaret); Dance and Chant (Devil's kitchen scene); Song, 'A King there Lived in Thule' (Boosey)

1911 *Forest of Wild Thyme*, op. 74. Play by Alfred Noyes.
   1 Scenes from an Imaginary Ballet (Schirmer, 1911)
   2 Three Dream Dances (Ascherberg, 1911)
   3 Intermezzo (Ascherberg, 1911)
   4a Song, 'Your Heart's Desire' (Boosey, 1920)
   4b Unison song (female voice) 'Little Boy Blue' (Boosey, 1923)
   4c Song, 'Come In' (Boosey, 1920)
   4d Unison song (children's voices) 'Dreams, Dreams' (Boosey, 1923)
   5 Christmas Overture (Boosey, 1925)
1911 *Othello*, op. 79. Play by William Shakespeare.
   Dance; Children's Intermezzo; Funeral March; Willow Song;
   Military March (Metzler)
1912 *St Agnes Eve*, [no opus number]. Poem by John Keats. Tableaux:
   1 'That ancient beadsman heard the prelude soft'
   2 'Her maiden eyes divine'
   3 'Now tell where is Madeline' (Hawkes, 1922)

BALLET

1912 *Hiawatha Ballet*, op. 82. Two suites published posthumously:
   1 *Hiawatha Ballet Suite*, in five scenes, arranged & orchestrated by
   Percy Fletcher:
       a. The Wooing; b. The Marriage Feast; c. Bird Scene and Conjurer's
       Dance; d. The Departure; e. Reunion (Hawkes, 1919)
   2. *Minnehaha Suite*, arranged & orchestrated by Percy Fletcher:
       a. Laughing Water; b. The Pursuit; c. Love Song
       d. The Homecoming (Hawkes, 1925)

MELODRAMA

Date unknown. *The Clown and the Columbine* (after Hans Andersen) for
reciter, violin, 'cello and piano. (MS.)

ORCHESTRAL WORKS

N.B. Much of Coleridge–Taylor's published orchestral work was also issued
in reductions or arrangements for other forces, from piano solo upwards.

1895 *Ballade in D minor* for violin and orchestra, op. 4 (Novello)
1896 *Symphony in A minor*, op. 8 (MS. in R.C.M. library)
1897 *Legend* (concertstück) for violin and orchestra, op. 14 (Augener)
1899 *Four Characteristic Waltzes*, op. 22, written 1898: (Novello)
   1 Valse Bohèmienne; 2 Valse Rustique; 3 Valse de la Reine;
   4 Valse Mauresque

1898   *Ballade in A minor*, op. 33, dedicated 'To my friend A. J. J.'
        [Jaeger] (Novello)
1899   Overture: *The Song of Hiawatha*, op. 30, no. 3, composed for the
        Norfolk Music Festival, 1899. (Novello)
1899   *Solemn Prelude*, op. 40, dedicated to N. Kilburn, Esq.
        Composed for the Worcester Musical Festival, 1899. (Novello)
1900   *Romance in G* for violin and orchestra, op. 39 (Novello)
1900   *Scenes from an Everyday Romance*, op. 41, no.1 (Novello)
1901   *Idyll*, op. 44 (Novello)
1901   Concert Overture: *Toussaint L'Ouverture*, op. 46 (Novello)
1902   *Hemo Dance*: Scherzo for orchestra, op. 47, no. 2 (Novello)
1902   Concert March: *Ethiopia Saluting the Colours*, op. 51, dedicated to
        The Treble Clef Club, Washington, D.C., U.S.A. (Augener)
1903   *Four Novelletten*, for string orchestra, tambourine and triangle,
        op. 52 (Novello)
1906   *Symphonic Variations on an African Air*, op. 63 (Novello)
        Fantasiestücke in A for 'cello and orchestra (MS., missing)
1910   Rhapsodic Dance: *The Bamboula*, op. 75 (Hawkes)
1911   *Petite Suite de Concert*, op. 77 (Hawkes)
        a. La Caprice de Nannette; b. Demande et Réponse
        c. Un Sonnet d'Amour; d. La Tarantelle Frétillante
1912   *Concerto in G minor for Violin and Orchestra*, op. 80,
        dedicated to Maud Powell. (Metzler)
[date unknown] Rhapsody: *From the Prairie* (MS. in Boosey &
        Hawkes' hire library)

CHORUS AND ORCHESTRA

1898–1900 *Scenes from The Song of Hiawatha*, op. 30 (Longfellow)
        (all published by Novello)
        1 1898 *Hiawatha's Wedding Feast*, for tenor solo, chorus and
        orchestra
        2 1899 *The Death of Minnehaha*, for soprano and baritone solo,
        chorus and orchestra
        3 1900 *Hiawatha's Departure*, for soprano, tenor and baritone
        solo, chorus and orchestra
1901   Cantata: *The Blind Girl of Castel–Cuille*, op. 43, for soprano and
        baritone solo, chorus and orchestra; translated by Longfellow from the
        Gascon (Novello)
1902   *Meg Blane*: A Rhapsody of the Sea, op. 48, dedicated to Miss
        Wakefield, for mezzo–soprano solo, chorus and orchestra;
        (R. Buchanan) (Novello)

1903   *The Atonement*, op. 53; Sacred Cantata, for soprano, mezzo–soprano, contralto, tenor and baritone solo, chorus and orchestra. (Alice Parsons) Composed for the Three Choirs Festival, Hereford, 1903. (Novello)

1904–5 *Five Choral Ballads*, op. 54, dedicated to the Samuel Coleridge–Taylor Choral Society. (Longfellow) (Breitkopf und Härtel)
  1 Beside the ungathered rice he lay
  2 She dwells by great Kenhawa's side
  3 Loud he sang the psalm of David
  4 The Quadroon girl (S.S.A., with baritone solo)
  5 In dark fens of dismal swamp

1905   Rhapsody: *Kubla Khan*, op. 61, for solo contralto, chorus and orchestra. (Samuel Taylor Coleridge) (Novello)

1908   *'Bon–Bon' Suite*, op. 68, for baritone solo, chorus and orchestra. (Thomas Moore) Dedicated to Doris, 'Miss Sunshine'. (Novello)
  a. The Magic Mirror; b. The Fairy Boat; c. To Rosa;
  d. Love and Hymen; e. The Watchman; f. Say, what shall we dance?

1911   *A Tale of Old Japan*, op. 76, for soprano, contralto, tenor and baritone solo, chorus and orchestra (Alfred Noyes)
  Dedicated to Mr and Mrs Carl Stoeckel (Novello)

CHORUS AND PIANO

1 Soprano and Alto:

1906   *Drake's Drum*; Henry Newbolt. (Curwen; see also T.T.B.B.)
1911   *Beauty and Truth* (Curwen)
1911   *Fall on me Like a Silent Dew* (Curwen)
1911   *Oh the Summer* (Curwen)
1911   *Viking Song* (Curwen; see also T.T.B.B.)
  (The *Viking Song* was also available in a solo voice and piano version.)

2 Two Sopranos and Alto:

1898   *Two Songs*, op. 21 (Augener)
  1 'We Strew these Opiate Flowers', Shelley
  2 'How they so Softly Rest', Longfellow, after Klopstock
1906   *A June Rose Bloomed*; L. A. Burleigh (Augener)
1908   *Encinctured with a Twine of Leaves*; Samuel Taylor Coleridge (Novello)
  The Pixies; Samuel Taylor Coleridge (Novello)
1908   *What can Lambkins Do?*; Christina Rossetti (Novello)

3 Four Parts, S.A.T.B:

1897   *Land of the Sun*, op. 15; Byron (Augener)
1901   *By the Lone Sea–shore*; Charles Mackay (Novello)
1905   *Three Part–songs*, op. 67 (Augener)
      1 'All My Stars Forsake Me', Alice Meynell
      2 'Dead in the Sierras', J. Miller
      3 'The Fair of Almachara', R. H. Horne
1910   *Whispers of Summer*; Kathleen Easmon (Novello)
1911   *The Evening Star*; Thomas Campbell (Novello)
1911   *The Sea Shell*; Tennyson (Curwen)
1911   *Summer is Gone*; Christina Rossetti (Curwen)
1911   *The Leeshore*; Thomas Hood (Novello)
1912   *Song of Proserpine*; Shelley (Novello)
Posthumous:
1920   *Isle of Beauty*; T. H. Bayly (Augener)

4 Eight Parts, S.S.A.A.T.T.B.B:

1908   *Sea Drift*, op. 69; T. B. Aldrich (Novello)

5 Male Chorus, T.T.B.B:

1910   *All are Sleeping, Weary Heart*; Longfellow (Curwen)
1910   *Loud Sang the Spanish Cavalier*; Longfellow (Curwen)
1910   *O Mariners, Out of the Sunlight*; R. Buchanan (Curwen)
1910   *O, Who will Worship the Great God Pan?*; R. Buchanan (Curwen)
Posthumous:
      Drake's Drum and *Viking Song* (arranged Percy Fletcher; Curwen)

6 Unison:

1911   *Prayer for Peace*; Alfred Noyes (Curwen)

SONGS (WITH ORCHESTRA)

1895   *Zara's Ear–rings*, Rhapsody for voice and orchestra, op. 7;
      J. G. Lockhart (MS in R.C.M. library)

SONGS (WITH PIANO)

1896   *Five Southern Love Songs*, op. 12, dedicated to Mamie Fraser.
      1 'My Love', Longfellow; 2 'Tears: A Lament', J. G. Lockhart
      3 'Minguillo', J. G. Lockhart; 4 'If thou art Sleeping, Maiden',
      Longfellow; 5 'Oh, my Lonely Pillow', Byron (Augener)

1897   *Seven African Romances*, op. 17, dedicated to Helen Jaxon;
        Paul Laurence Dunbar (Augener)
        1 An African Love Song; 2 A Prayer; 3 A Starry Night;
        4 Dawn; 5 Ballad; 6 Over the Hills; 7 How shall I woo thee?
1898   *Little Songs for Little Folks*, op. 6 [numbered thus in the first edition
        of Berwick Sayers's biography, 1915; numbered op. 19 no. 2 in the
        second edition, 1927] (Boosey)
        1 Sea–Shells; 2 A Rest by the Way; 3 A Battle in the Snow;
        4 A Parting Wish; 5 A Sweet Little Doll;   6 Baby Land
1898   *In Memoriam* (three Rhapsodies), op. 24, dedicated 'To a Friend'
        1 'Earth Fades, Heaven breaks on me', Robert Browning
        2 'Substitution', Elizabeth Barrett Browning
        3 'Weep not, beloved friends', Chiabrera (Augener)
1898   *Three Songs*, op. 29 (Augener)
        1 'Lucy', William Wordsworth
        2 'Mary', William Wordsworth
        3 'Jessy', Robert Burns
1899   *Six Songs*, op. 37 (Novello)
        1 'You'll Love me yet', Robert Browning
        2 Canoe Song, Isabella Crawford
        3 'A blood–red ring hung round the moon', Barry Dane
        4 'Sweet evenings come and go, love', George Eliot
        5 'As the moon's soft splendour', Percy Bysshe Shelley
        6 'Eleanore', Eric Mackay
1900   *The Soul's Expression*, op. 42; four sonnets by Elizabeth Barrett
        Browning, for contralto and piano; also for contralto and orchestra.
        1 The Soul's Expression; 2 Tears; 3 Grief; 4 Comfort (Novello)
1903   *Six American Lyrics*, op. 45 (Novello)
        1 'O thou, mine other, stronger part', Ella Wheeler Wilcox
        2 'O, praise me not', Ella Wheeler Wilcox
        3 'Her love', Ella Wheeler Wilcox
        4 'The dark eye has left us', J. G. Whittier
        5 'O, ship that saileth slowly on', Ella Wheeler Wilcox
        6 'Beat, beat drums', Walt Whitman
1904   *Three Song Poems*, op. 50; Thomas Moore (Enoch)
        1 Dreaming for ever; 2 The young Indian maid; 3 Beauty and song
1904/6 *Six Sorrow Songs*, op. 57; Christina Rossetti
        (Dedicated 'To my Wife')
        1 'Oh, what comes over the sea'; 2 'When I am dead, my dearest'
        3 'Oh, roses for the flush of youth'; 4 'She sat and sang alway'
        5 'Unmindful of the roses'; 6 'Too late for love'
1913   Scena: *Waiting*, op. 81, no. 1; Alfred Noyes (Boosey)
        (Also with orchestral accompaniment.)

Songs without opus numbers:

1897   *The Three Ravens*; N. G. Dohrn (Boosey)

1897   *A Corn Song*; Paul Laurence Dunbar (Boosey)

1900   *My Doll*; Charles Kingsley (Boosey)

1904   *Ah, Sweet, Thou Little Knowest*; Thomas Hood (Ricordi)

1904   *The Easter Morn*; A. Chapman (Boosey)

1904   *Eulalie*; A. Parsons (Boosey)

1904   *The Shoshone's adieu*; B. Fennell (Boosey)

1904   *Love's Questionings*; A. Parsons (Keith Prowse)

1905   *Song of the Nubian Girl*; Thomas Moore (Augener)

1905   *A Vision*; L. A. Burleigh (Maxwell Music, New York)

1905   *Genevieve*; Samuel Taylor Coleridge (Maxwell Music)

1905   *If I could love thee*; L. A. Burleigh (Maxwell Music)

1905   *Love's Passing*; L. A. Burleigh (Maxwell Music)

1905   *The Violet Bank*; E. Darling (Maxwell Music)

1906   *A Summer Idyll*; H. Hammond–Spencer (Enoch)

1906   *O, Mistress Mine*; William Shakespeare (Ditson)

1906   Rhapsody: *Once Only*; Robert Louis Stevenson (Ditson)

1906   *She Rested by the Broken Brook*; Robert Louis Stevenson (Ditson)

1907   *The Gift–Rose*; Dr F. Petersen (Ditson)

1908   *Until*; F. D. Sherman (Ditson)

1909   *A Birthday*; Christina Rossetti (Metzler)

1909   *A lovely little dream*; Sarojini Naidu (Metzler)

1909   *Five Fairy Ballads*; Kathleen Easmon (Boosey)

      1 Sweet baby butterfly; 2 Alone with mother;

      3 Big lady moon; 4 The stars; 5 Fairy roses

1909   *A Lament*; Christina Rossetti (Ricordi)

1910   *Sons of the Sea*; Sarojini Naidu (Novello)

1910   *The Links o' love*; G. E. Matheson (John Church)

1911   *Candle Lighting Time*; Paul Laurence Dunbar (John Church)

1911   *Five and Twenty Sailormen*; G. E. Matheson (John Church)

1911   *Thou Art*; M. Tulloch (Presser, Philadelphia)

1909/11 *My Algonquin*; Longfellow (Presser, Philadelphia)

1911   *Songs of sun and shade*; Marguerite Radclyffe–Hall (Boosey)

      1 'You lay so still in the sunshine'

      2 'Thou hast bewitched me, beloved'

      3 'The rainbow–child'

      4 'Thou art risen, my beloved'

      5 'This is the island of gardens'

Songs published posthumously:

1914   *The Guest*; Robert Herrick (Augener; also published with orchestral accompaniment)

1914   *Low–breathing winds*; Berwick Sayers (Augener)

1914   *An Explanation*; W. Learned (Augener)

1914   *Life and Death*; J. A. Middleton (Augener; also published in piano transcription by Alex Roloff)

1914   *Tell, O Tell Me*; E. C. Stedman (Augener)

1916   *Two Songs*:
    1 My Lady; E. R. Stephenson (Augener)
    2 Love's Mirror; F. Hart (Augener)

1918   *Solitude*; Byron (Augener)
     (Probably written in 1893)

1918   *Three Songs of Heine*; translated by E. M. Lockwood (Augener)
    1 'My pretty fishermaiden'
    2 'Thy sapphire eyes'
    3 'I hear the flutes and fiddles'

1920   Scena: *Red o' the Dawn*; Alfred Noyes (Boosey)

Songs in manuscript:

1896?   *The Three Ravens*; 'The music of the sixteenth century, arranged by S. Coleridge–Taylor.'
    1 Voice and piano (MS., R.C.M. library)
    2 Voice and piano quintet (MS., R.C.M. library)

Songs in manuscript, assigned to Augener but unpublished:

They are undated, but *The Arrow and the Song* was performed as early as October 1893. The MS. is in poor condition.

    Ah, Tell Me, Gentle Zephyrs; [poet's name illegible]
    Keep Those Eyes; Thomas Moore (See also **Duets**, below)
    We Watched her Breathing Through the Night; Thomas Hood
    She Dwelt Amidst the Untrodden Ways; William Wordsworth
    The Arrow and the Song; Longfellow
    Why does the Azure Deck the Skies? [poet's name illegible]

Songs in manuscript, whereabouts unknown:

    The Broken Oar (performed in Croydon in 1893)
    The Vengeance (listed as in MS by Berwick Sayers)
    Dimple Chin (mentioned by Berwick Sayers, p. 196)

Duets:

1903   *Keep those eyes*; Thomas Moore, for soprano and tenor (Novello)

CHURCH MUSIC

1 Anthems:

1891   *In Thee, O Lord, Have I put My Trust* (Novello)
1892   *Break Forth into Joy*; dedicated to Herbert A. Walters (Novello)
1892   *Lift Up Your Heads* (Novello)
1892   *The Lord is My Strength* (Novello)
1892   *O Ye that Love the Lord* (Novello)
1899   *By the Waters of Babylon*; Psalm CXXXVIII (Novello)
1901   *Now Late on the Sabbath Day*; for Easter (Novello)
1905   *What hast Thou Given Me* (Weekes)

2 Music for services:

1899   *Morning and Evening Service in F*, op. 18: Te Deum, Jubilate, Benedictus, Magnificat & Nunc Dimittis (Novello)
Posthumous:
1921   *Te Deum*; a simple service for parish choirs (Augener)

3 Hymn Tune:

'*Luconor*', for the hymn 'Jesu, the very thought of Thee' (Methodist Sunday School Hymnal)

INSTRUMENTAL MUSIC

1 Chamber Music:

c1893   *Sonata for Clarinet and Piano in F minor* (MS., missing)
1893   *Piano Quintet in G minor* (2 vln, vla, vc & piano), op. 1. (MS., R.C.M. library)
1893   *Nonet* (2 vln, vla, vc, bass, clt, bn, horn, piano), op. 2. (MS., R.C.M. library)
1893   *Trio in E minor for Violin, Cello and Piano*, (MS., R.C.M. library; possibly intended to be op. 6)
1893   *Suite de Pièces* (violin and piano or organ), op. 3 (Schott) Pastorale, Cavatina, Barcarolle, Contemplation

1895   *Quintet in F sharp minor* (clt, 2 vln, vla and vc), op. 10
        (Musica Rara, 1974)
1896   *Fantasiestücke for String Quartet*, op. 5, dedicated to Sir Charles
        Stanford. (Augener)
        Prelude, Serenade, Humoresque, Minuet, Dance.
        (The minuet was subsequently arranged for piano solo by Alex
        Roloff; it was published separately.)
1896   *Two Romantic Pieces for Violin and Piano*, op. 9 (Augener)
        Lament, Merrymaking
1896   *String Quartet in D minor,* op. 13 (MS., missing)
1897   *Hiawathan Sketches,* for violin and piano, op. 16 (Augener)
        A Tale, A Song, A Dance
*c*1898   *Gypsy Suite*, for violin and piano, op. 20 (Augener)
        Lament and Tambourine, A Gipsy Song, A Gipsy Dance,   Waltz
1898   *Valse Caprice,* for violin and piano, op. 23 (Augener)
*c*1898   *Sonata in D minor,* for violin and piano, op. 28 (Hawkes;
        posthumously published in 1917, edited by Albert Sammons.)
1904   *Four African Dances*, for violin and piano, op. 58, dedicated to
        John Saunders. (Augener)
1904   *Romance*, for violin and piano, op. 59, dedicated to Goldie Baker.
        (Augener)
1907   *Variations on an Original Theme*, for 'cello and piano
        (Augener; published posthumously in 1918)
1909   *Ballade in C minor,* for violin and piano, op. 73; dedicated to
        Zacharewitsch. (Augener)

KEYBOARD MUSIC

1 Piano:

*c*1893   *Piano Sonata* in C minor (MS., missing)
1897   *Two Moorish Tone Pictures*, op. 19 (Augener)
        Andalla, Zarifa (In 1915, Augener published a simplified edition of
        Zarifa, made by Alex Roloff.)
1897   *Three Humoresques, op.* 31 (Augener)
        In D, in G minor, in A.
        (Also available in versions orchestrated by Avril Coleridge–
        Taylor: Boosey and Hawkes Hire Library.)
1899   *African Suite*, op. 35 (Augener)
        1 Introduction; 2 A negro love song; 3 Valse; 4 Danse Nègre
        (The Danse Nègre was originally written for the Piano Quintet; it
        exists also in versions for string quintet and for orchestra.)

1900	*Nourmahal's Song and Dance*, op. 41 (Augener)

1900   *Nourmahal's Song and Dance*, op. 41 (Augener)

1904   *Moorish Dance*, op. 55 (Augener)

1904   *Three Silhouettes*, op. 38 (Ashdown)
       Tambourine, Lament, Valse

1904   *Three Cameos*, op. 56 (Augener)

1905   *Two Oriental Valses*, op. 19 no. 1 (Forsyth)
       Zuleika, Haidee

1905   *Twenty–Four Negro Melodies*, op. 59 (Ditson)
       At the Dawn of Day; The Stones are Very Hard; Take Nabandji;
       They will not Lend me a Child; Song of Conquest; Warrior's Song;
       Oloba; The Bamboula; The Angels Changed my Name;
       Deep River; Didn't my Lord deliver Daniel?; Don't be Weary,
       Traveller; Going up; I'm Troubled in Mind; I was Way Down
       A–Yonder; Let us Cheer the Weary Traveller; Many Thousand Gone;
       My Lord Delivered Daniel; Oh, He Raise a Poor Lazarus;
       Pilgrim's Song; Run, Mary, Run; Sometimes I Feel like a
       Motherless Child; Steal Away; Wade in the Water

1906   *Scènes de Ballet*, op. 64 (Augener)
       In C, A, A flat and B flat (Orchestrated by Avril Coleridge–
       Taylor: Boosey and Hawkes Hire Library.)

1907   *Forest Scenes* (Five Characteristic Pieces), op. 66, dedicated to
       Frances Taylor. (Augener)
       The Lone Forest Maiden; The Phantom Lover Arrives;
       The Phantom Tells his Tale of Longing; Erstwhile they ride;
       The Forest Maiden Acknowledges her Love, Now Proudly they
       Journey Together Towards the Great City

1908   *Papillon* (Augener)

1909   *Valse Suite: Three Fours*, op. 71, dedicated to Myrtle Meggy.
       In A minor, A flat, G minor, D and E flat (Augener)

1911   *Two Impromptus* (Augener)
       In A, in B minor

2 Organ:

1898   *Melody, Elegy and Arietta* (Novello, 'The Village Organist')
       (The Elegy is a re–working of the principal idea of the first
       movement of the *Nonet*; see Example 11.)

1911   *Three Impromptus*, op. 78 (Weekes)
       In F, C and A minor
       (Also posthumously arranged and published for piano)

Undated, but published 1913: *Interlude*
       (Larway, 'The Modern Organist', no. 3)

TRANSCRIPTIONS AND ARRANGEMENTS

Deep River; arranged for violin and piano (MS; N.B. It is possible that this
   may be Maud Powell's arrangement.) It was also arranged for Salon
   Orchestra by Frank Walker (1939, Hawkes & Son, London, Ltd)
Keep Me from Sinking Down; violin arrangement made for Maud Powell
   (Autograph in Yale University Library)
Many Thousand Gone (The original slow movement of the *Violin
   Concerto*; autograph in Royal College of Music.)
1896 Dvorak: Allegretto Grazioso from *Symphony in G*, op. 88,
   arranged for violin and piano (Novello)
1896 Ernst, H. W. Allegro from *Violin Concerto* in F sharp minor,
   op. 23 (orchestration; MS., whereabouts unknown)

Appendix B: BIBLIOGRAPHY

COLERIDGE–TAYLOR, Avril, *The Heritage of Samuel Coleridge–Taylor* (Dennis Dobson, London, 1979)

COLERIDGE–TAYLOR, Avril, 'The Music of Coleridge–Taylor' (*Sound*, April 1947)

COLERIDGE–TAYLOR, Avril, 'My Father and his Music' (*Fanfare*, Birmingham, 1948)

COLERIDGE–TAYLOR, Jessie, *Coleridge–Taylor: Genius and Musician. A Memory Sketch* (John Crowther Ltd., Bognor Regis and London, 1942–43)

COLLES, H. C., Article in the *Dictionary of National Biography*

EVANS, MARJORIE, 'I Remember Coleridge', *Under the Imperial Carpet: Essays in Black History 1780–1950*, ed. Rainer Lotz and Ian Pegg (Rabbit Press, Crawley, 1986), pp. 32–41

GREEN, Jeffrey P., 'Perceptions of Samuel Coleridge–Taylor on his death, September 1912' (*New Community*, vol. 12. no. 2, [1985,] pp. 321–5)

McGILCHRIST, Paul and GREEN, Jeffrey P., 'Some recent research findings on Samuel Coleridge–Taylor' (*Black Perspectives in Music*, vol. 13, no. 2, Fall 1985, pp. 151–78)

MONTHLY MUSICAL RECORD, 1912, p. 253: obituary

MUSICAL QUARTERLY, 1922, p. 180: H. Antcliffe, 'Some notes on Samuel Coleridge–Taylor'

MUSICAL TIMES, 1912, p. 637: Hubert Parry, 'Samuel Coleridge–Taylor: A Tribute'

MUSICAL TIMES, 1909, p. 153: 'Mr Coleridge–Taylor'

(BERWICK) SAYERS, W. C., *Samuel Coleridge–Taylor — Musician* (London, 1915; revised edition, 1927)

TORTOLANO, WILLIAM, *Samuel Coleridge–Taylor: Anglo–black composer 1875–1912* (Scarecrow, 1977)

YOUNG, Percy M., 'Anglo–Black'; review of *Samuel Coleridge–Taylor: Anglo–black composer 1875–1912* (Scarecrow, 1977) in *The Musical Times*, 1977, p. 821

YOUNG, Percy M., 'Samuel Coleridge–Taylor 1875–1912' (*The Musical Times*, 1975, pp. 703–705)

Extensive References:

FIFIELD, Christopher, *True Artist and True Friend. A Biography of Hans Richter* (Clarendon/O.U.P., 1993)
KENNEDY, Michael, *Portrait of Elgar* (O.U.P., London, 1968)
LOTZ, Rainer and PEGG, Ian (ed.), *Under the Imperial Carpet*, Essays in Black History 1780–1950 (Rabbit Press, Crawley, 1986)
NETTEL, Reginald, *Music in the Five Towns* (O.U.P., London, 1944)
REDWOOD, Christopher (ed.), *An Elgar Companion* (Sequoia Publishing, in association with Moorland Publishing Co., Ashbourne, Derby, 1982)
REID, Charles, *Malcolm Sargent* (Hamish Hamilton, London, 1968)
SHAFFER, Karen A., *Maud Powell, Pioneer American Violinist* (The Maud Powell Foundation, Iowa State University, 1988)

Occasional References:

BREWER, Herbert, *Memories of Choirs and Cloisters* (John Lane, The Bodley Head, 1931)
CARLEY, Lionel, *Delius: A Life in Letters, 1862–1908* (Scolar, London, 1983)
FOREMAN, Lewis (ed.), *From Parry to Britten* (British Music in Letters, 1900–45) (Batsford, London, 1987)
GOOSSENS, Eugène, *Overture and Beginners* (Methuen, 1951)
MOORE, Jerrold Northrop, *Elgar and his Publishers* (O.U.P., 1987)

Background:

BODEN, Anthony, *Three Choirs: A History of the Festival* (Alan Sutton, 1992)
DUNBAR, Paul Laurence, *Lyrics of Lowly Life* (Chapman and Hall, 1897)
FYFE, Christopher, *A History of Sierra Leone* (O.U.P., 1962)
FYLE, C. Magbaily, *The History of Sierra Leone* (Evans Bros., 1981)
GEISS, Imanuel, *The Pan-African Movement* (Methuen, 1974)
HURLSTONE, K. (ed.), *William Hurlstone, Musician. Memories and Records by his Friends* (London, 1947)
LORIMER, Douglas, *Colour, Class and the Victorians* (Leicester University Press, 1978)
MARSH, J. B. T., *The Story of the Jubilee Singers* (Hodder and Stoughton, London, 1898)
NEWELL, H.G., *William Yeats Hurlstone. Musician and Man*, (London, 1936)

NOYES, Alfred, *Two Worlds for Memory* (Shead and Ward, 1953)

GREENE, H. Plunket, *Sir C. V. Stanford* (Edward Arnold, 1935)

SOUTHERN, Eileen, *Biographical Dictionary of Afro–American and African Musicians* (Greenwood Press, 1982)

STANFORD, Sir Charles Villiers, *Pages from an Unwritten Diary* (Edward Arnold, 1914)

WEBB, Patrick, *Algernon Ashton, 1859–1937* (British Music Society, vol. 14, 1992)

YOUNG, Kenneth, *Music's Great Days in the Spas and Watering–Places* (Macmillan, 1968)

YOUNG, Percy M., *George Grove, 1820–1900* (Macmillan, 1980)

Appendix C: RECORDINGS
(Compiled by Stuart Upton)

This list, alphabetically arranged, is selective and not complete.

Items marked * are private recordings held by the National Sound Archive.
Pearl and Rare Recorded Edition (RRE) are obtainable from
    Michael G. Thomas, 5A Norfolk Place, London W2 1QN.
Pearl CDs are obtainable from Pavilion Records Ltd,
    Sparrows Green, Wadhurst, Sussex, TN5 6SJ.

78 rpm/LP/CD/tape:

African Dances, op. 58
    No. 2 in F; Peggy Cochrane (violin with piano acc.)
        ACO GI5662 (78 rpm)
    No. 4 in D minor; Arthur Beckwith (violin with piano acc.)
        HMV C974 (78 rpm)
African Romances, op. 17
    No. 4. 'Dawn'; Alma Gluck (soprano)
        HMV 2–3391 (78 rpm); Rococo 5291 (LP)
African Suite, Op. 35
    No. 4. Danse Nègre; London Symphony Orchestra (Freeman)
        Col. M32782 (78 rpm)
Ballade in D minor, op. 4
    Michael Ludwig (violin), Virginia Eskin (piano)
        Koch 3–7056 2H1 (CD)
Ballade in G minor, op. 73
    A. Saltmarsh (violin), Avril Coleridge–Taylor (piano)
        Tape 1363*
Ballade in A minor, op. 33
    Royal Liverpool Philharmonic Orchestra (Grant Llewellyn)
        Argo 436 401–2 (CD)
Bamboula: Rhapsodic Dance, op. 75
    1 Band of H. M. Coldstream Guards (Lt. R. G. Evans)
        HMV C1022 (78 rpm); RRE185 (LP)
    2 Bournemouth Symphony Orchestra (Kenneth Alwyn)
        VESD7161 (LP) EL2701454 (cassette tape)
    3 B. B. C. Concert Orchestra (Avril Coleridge–Taylor)
        Tape T1393*

Characteristic Waltzes, op. 22
    1 New Light Symphony Orchestra (Ainslie Murray)
       HMVB8378/9 (78 rpm); Pearl Gemm 9965 (CD)
    2 (I & III only) Victor Olof Sextet
       HMV2346 (78 rpm); RRE185 (LP)
A Christmas Overture (from *Forest of Wild Thyme*), op. 74, no. 5
    1 Symphony Orchestra (Dr Malcolm Sargent)
       HMVC2485 (78 rpm); Pearl Gemm 9965 (CD)
    2 B. B. C. Wireless Symphony Orchestra (Percy Pitt)
       Col.9137 (78 rpm); RRE185 (LP)
Concerto in G minor for Violin and Orchestra, op. 80
    [extract:] A. Saltmarsh (violin), Avril Coleridge–Taylor (piano)
    Tape M5995*
Dream Dances (*Forest of Wild Thyme*), op. 74, no. 2.
    1 London Palladium Orchestra (Clifford Greenwood)
       HMVB8876/7 (78 rpm); Pearl Gemm 9965 (CD)
    2 The Mayfair Orchestra (George W. Byng)
       HMVC1120 (78 rpm); RRE185 (LP)
    3 Hastings Municipal Orchestra (Basil Cameron)
       Decca M11&16 (78 rpm)
Eleanore, op. 37, no. 6 (song; Eric Mackay)
    1 Tudor Davies (tenor, with orchestral accompaniment)
       HMVD1273 (78 rpm)
    2 Webster Booth (tenor, with piano accompaniment)
       HMVB9451 (78 rpm); EMIGX2547 (LP)
    3 Henry Wendon (tenor)
       Col.DB2083 (78 rpm): HMVHQM 1228 (LP)
    4 Stuart Burrows (tenor)
       Oiseau–Lyre Sol 324 (LP)
    5 Roy Henderson (baritone)
       Decca F1699 (78 rpm)
'Faust' Incidental Music, op. 70; 'Dance of the Witches'
    Regent Concert Orchestra (William Hodgson)
    B&H BH1922 (78 rpm)
Five Fairy Ballads, no. 3, 'Big Lady Moon'
    Violet Openshaw (contralto) with piano accompaniment
    HMVB688 (78 rpm)
Forest of Wild Thyme, op. 74: see *A Christmas Overture, Dream
Dances, Intermezzo, Scenes from an Imaginary Ballet*
Hiawatha: see *Song of Hiawatha*
'Hiawatha' Ballet Music, op. 82, no. 1
    1 New Queen's Hall Orchestra (Alick Maclean)
       Col.L1450/1 (78 rpm); RRE185 (LP)

2 Band of H. M. Coldstream Guards (Lt. R. G. Evans)
   HMVC1057 (78 rpm)

3 [extracts:] Lutetia Wagram Orchestra (Fernand Heurteur)
   Col.D11067 (French) (78 rpm)

4 [extracts:] The Regent Concert Orchestra (William Hodgson)
   B&H BH1922 (78 rpm)

Impromptus, op. 71.

No. 1 in A: R. Arnold Grier (Organ)
Zonophone 5229

Intermezzo (*Forest of Wild Thyme*), op. 74, no. 3

1 Symphony Orchestra (Dr Malcolm Sargent)
   HMVB8113 (78 rpm); Pearl Gemm 9965 (CD)

2 Cedric Sharp Sextet
   HMVC1894

3 W. Steff–Langston (organ of the Elite Cinema, Wimbledon)
   Col. 4319 (78 rpm)

A Lament (Christina Rossetti)

Avril Coleridge–Taylor (voice) with N. Turner (piano)
Tape 1393*

Life and Death (J. A. Middleton)

1. Webster Booth (tenor, with piano)
    HMVB9451 (78 rpm)

2 Peter Dawson (baritone, with piano)
   HMVB8325 (78 rpm)

'Minnehaha' Suite, op. 82, no. 2

1 The Grosvenor Orchestra
   ACO G16046/47 (78 rpm)

2 [extracts:] The Regent Concert Orchestra (William Hodgson)
   B&H BH1916 (78 rpm)

'Othello': Suite from the incidental music, op. 79

1 New Symphony Orchestra (Dr Malcolm Sargent)
   HMVB4273/4 (78 rpm); Pearl Gemm 9965 (CD)

2 Band of H. M. Coldstream Guards (Lt. R. G. Evans)
   HMVC1099 (78 rpm); RRE185 (LP)

3 B. B. C. Concert Orchestra (Avril Coleridge–Taylor)
   Tape T1393*

4 (No. 4, 'Military March', only) Frederick Bayco (organ)
   HMVCLP1777 (LP)

5 ('Willow Song' only)
   a. Mavis Bennett (soprano)   HMVB2929
   b. Lorely Dyer (soprano)   Tape M4330*

Petite Suite de Concert, op. 77
1　Philharmonic Orchestra (George Weldon)
　　HMVSXLP 30123 (LP)
2　Philharmonic Orchestra (George Weldon)
　　MFP4510 (LP)
3　Bournemouth Municipal Orchestra (Dan Godfrey)
　　Col. DX651/2 (78 rpm); Pearl Gemm 9965 (CD)
4　The Piccadilly Orchestra (De Groot)
　　HMVC1218 & 1233 (78 rpm); RRE185 (LP)
5　London Symphony Orchestra (Dr Malcolm Sargent)
　　HMV2372/3 (78 rpm)
6　(No. 2, 'Demande et Réponse' only) B.B.C. Concert
　　Orchestra (Avril Coleridge–Taylor)
　　Tape 1393*
7　Queen's Hall Light Orchestra (Sydney Torch)
　　Col.DB2479/80 (78 rpm)
8　(Piano solo) Virginia Eskin (Piano)
　　Koch 3–7056 (CD)
9　(Arranged for two pianos) Rawicz and Landauer
　　Col.DB2205/6 (78 rpm)

Quintet for Clarinet and Strings, op. 10
1　Georgina Dobreé and Amici Quartet
　　Discourses ABM23 (LP)
2　Harold Wright and Hawthorne Quartet
　　Koch 3–7056 2H1 (CD)

Scenes from an Imaginary Ballet (from *Forest of Wild Thyme*), no. 3
　　Alec Rowley (piano)
　　Anglo–French 2053 (78 rpm); Pearl Gemm 9965 (CD)

She Rested by the Broken Brook (Stevenson)
1　John McCormack (tenor) and Gerald Moore (piano)
　　HMVDa1778 (78 rpm)
2　John McCormack (tenor) and Edwin Schneider (piano)
　　HMV (Victor USA) HLM 1176 (LP)

Sonata for Violin and Piano, op. 28
　　Albert Sammons (violin) and William Murdoch (piano)
　　Col.L1396/7 (78 rpm)

St Agnes Eve: tableaux music
　　Nos. 1 and 2: Regent Concert Orchestra (William Hodgson)
　　B&H BH1909 (78 rpm)

The Song of Hiawatha, op. 30: a. 'Hiawatha's Wedding Feast',
      b. 'The Death of Minnehaha', c. 'Hiawatha's Departure'
1 **Cantatas a, b and c complete**: Welsh National Opera (cond.
    Kenneth Alwyn), with Helen Field (soprano), Arthur Davies (tenor),
    Bryn Terfel (baritone)
    Argo CD430356–2 (CD); MC430356–4 (cassette tape)
2a. *Hiawatha's Wedding Feast*
    i. Walter Glynn (tenor), Royal Choral Society, Royal Albert Hall
      Orchestra (Dr Malcolm Sargent)
      HMV C1931/4 (78 rpm)
    ii. Richard Lewis (tenor), Royal Choral Society, Philharmonia
      Orchestra (Sir Malcolm Sargent)
      HMV ALP1899 (LP); ESD7161 (LP)
    iii. Anthony Rolfe–Johnson (tenor), Bournemouth Symphony
      Orchestra and Chorus (Kenneth Alwyn)
      HMV EL2701451 (LP)
    iv. [excerpts:] Alexandra Choir, Sinfonia of London (Charles
      Proctor) Gramo 7EP
    v. 'Onaway, Awake, Beloved' (tenor solo) only:
     1 Tudor Davies (tenor) with orchestra
     HMVD1142 (78 rpm); Pearl Gemm 9965 (CD)
     2 Webster Booth (tenor) with orchestra
     HMVC3407 (78 rpm); HMV7009 (LP)
     (and many other recordings ...)
2b. *The Death of Minnehaha,* Elsie Suddaby (soprano), George Baker
    (baritone), Howard Fry (bass), Royal Choral Society and Royal
    Albert Hall Orchestra (Dr Malcolm Sargent)
      HMVC2210/3 (78 rpm)
2c. *Hiawatha's Departure*, excerpt: 'Spring had come' (Elsie Suddaby,
    soprano) with orchestra
      HMVB3476 (78 rpm)
Sons of the Sea; Sarojini Naidu. Peter Dawson (baritone) with orchestra
      HMVC2728 (78 rpm); Pearl Gemm 9965 (CD)
Sorrow Songs, op. 57; Christina Rossetti
    1 'Oh, What comes over the Sea?'
      Avril Coleridge–Taylor, with piano accompaniment
      Tape T1393*
    2 'When I am Dead, My Dearest'
      Violet Openshaw (contralto), with piano accompaniment
      HMVB572 (78 rpm)
    3 'Unmindful of the Roses'
      Arthur Reckless (baritone) with orchestra
      HMVB8285 (78 rpm); Pearl Gemm 9965 (CD)

Summer is Gone, part–song; Glasgow Orpheus Choir
    (Sir Hugh Roberton)
    HMVE407 (78 rpm); EMI Starline MRS 5175 (LP)
Songs of Sun and Shade, Marguerite Radclyffe–Hall;
    no. 2 'Thou Hast Bewitched Me, Beloved'
    Arthur Reckless (baritone) with orchestra
    HMVB8285 (78 rpm); Pearl Gemm 9965 (CD)
    no. 4 'Thou Hast Risen, My Beloved'
      i. Tudor Davies (tenor) with piano accompaniment
         HMVE414 (78 rpm)
      ii. John Thorne (baritone) with piano accompaniment
         ACOG16064 (78 rpm)
     iii. Turner Layton (tenor) with piano accompaniment
         Col.FB3031 (78 rpm)
     iv. Arthur Reckless (baritone) with orchestra
         HMVB8285 (78 rpm); Pearl Gemm 9965 (CD)
    no. 5 'This is the Island of Gardens'
      i. Arthur Reckless (baritone) with orchestra
         HMVB8285 (78 rpm); Pearl Gemm 9965 (CD)
      ii. Avril Coleridge–Taylor, with piano accompaniment
         Tape T1393*
Sweet Evenings come and go, Love, from *Six Songs*; George Eliot
    Walter Hyde (tenor) with piano accompaniment
    HMVE22 (78 rpm); Rubini GV5 (LP)
Symphonic Variations on an African Air, op. 63
    Royal Liverpool Philharmonic Orchestra (Grant Llewellyn)
         Argo 436401–2 (CDs)
Three Fours suite, op. 71
    Nos. 2 and 6 only: Albert Sandler and his Palm Court Orchestra
         Col.DB2212 (78 rpm)
Twenty–Four Negro Melodies, op. 59
    1 Complete: Frances Walker (piano)
         Orion OR78305/306 (LP) [U.S.A.]
    2 Virginia Eskin (piano):
    'Take Nababji', 'Going Up', 'Deep River', 'Run, Mary, Run',
    'Sometimes I Feel Like a Motherless Child', 'The Bamboula'
         Koch 3–7056–H1 (CD)
Viking Song
    1 Stuart Bardner (baritone)   HMVE193 (78 rpm)
    2 E. De Gorgoza   HMV5–2105 (78 rpm)
    3 Choir of the Covent
         of Jesus and Mary   Decca 9426 (78 rpm)

INDEX OF WORKS MENTIONED IN TEXT

GENERAL INDEX